# Divers Guide To Michigan

## By Steve Harrington

Foreword by Ken Vrana

## Maritime Press

Copyright 1990
Maritime Press
PO Box 275
Mason, MI 48854

ISBN 0-9624629-9-3

Cover Design By: Michael DeFoe

Cover Photo: Luke Pavlovich investigates the broken mast
            on the bow of the CONGDON off Isle Royale.
            By Lewis J. Pavlovich.

Diving books are always dedicated to authors' parents and this book is no exception. Parents, after all, endure much apprehension as they watch their children strap a metal tank on their backs and 10 pounds of lead on their waists and jump into the water. This book is dedicated to Mom and Dad for holding their breaths while their teenager explored local mudholes.

This book is also dedicated to the young people who remind me that nothing in life is **that** serious.

# Acknowledgment

At the risk of omitting someone, I must thank Jed Jaworski, "Ranger" Bietau, Jim and Pat Stayer, Ken Pott, Mark Rowe, Bill Beck, Pete Lindquist, Lew Pavlovich, Sleeping Bear Dunes National Lakeshore, Isle Royale National Park, Michigan Sea Grant, Dennis Dougherty, Bill Kenner, Nate Morgan, Steve DenBoer, Janene Sonnega and especially Ken Vrana for their help in making this project a reality.

-- Steve Harrington

Some information for this book was obtained from "Michigan Bottomland Preserves Inventory," a Michigan Sea Grant College Program publication.

# Foreword

As divers, we maintain a close, special relationship with water; working and playing within its confines. Its quality, and the health of its organisms are important to us.

During the 1960s, we believed our lakes were dying -- victims of pollution and toxic contaminants. Since the early 1970s, substantial progress has been made in Great Lakes cleanup. Water visibility in the upper Great Lakes can consistently reach 50 feet. Visibility in the lower lakes ranges from five to 30 feet.

The use of our shipwreck resources in Michigan has also changed. Divers guided by a "treasure" ethic, who espoused a rule of "finders, keepers," initially took souvenirs from any shipwrecks they could find. During the 1970s, the increasing acceptance of a "conservation" ethic by sport divers spurred passage of protective laws.

Within Michigan's Great Lakes boundaries rest an estimated 6,000 shipwrecks, most of expectional appearance due to the preservative qualities of cold, fresh water. These sunken vessels are now recognized as non-renewable public resources. Removal of artifacts is restricted. This gives you an excellent opportunity to explore, photograph and videotape shipwrecks in pristine condition.

An important feature of Michigan law is a provision for designation of Great Lakes bottomland or underwater preserves. Currently, nine underwater preserves have been authorized, totaling 1,920 square miles -- an area the size of Delaware.

Increasingly, Great Lakes underwater preserves are viewed as national scuba diving destinations and attract many out-of-state visitors. Expenditures from sport divers and accompanying non-divers are very important to small, northern Michigan coastal communities that are trying to broaden their economic bases.

To complement the Great Lakes, more than 12,500 inland lakes and 36,000 miles of rivers and streams are available for skin and scuba diving, fishing, boating, canoeing and quiet contemplation. Almost 40 percent of Michigan's land area is underwater and available for your exploration!

Local businesses and community organizations are developing additional services and facilities for sport divers. Their objective is to make your recreational experiences enjoyable and satisfying.

Michigan offers much more than shipwrecks and sport diving. You will be surrounded by almost 3,300 miles of coastal shoreline, more than any state except Alaska. This means that you can find a place nearby to relax in an atmosphere of freshwater tranquility. It's a subtle environment of abundant and varied shorelands. Colorful, striated rocks of Lake Superior contrast with beautiful white sand dunes of Lake Michigan, and soft limestone bluffs and beaches of Lake Huron.

Deer, small mammals, wading and diving ducks, wild geese and countless shore birds grace these incredible water resources. Seemingly endless forests of mixed hardwoods and conifers provide excellent opportunities for camping, hiking and sightseeing. Three national parks, four national forests and scores of wonderful state parks and state forests have a wide range of outdoor attractions, services and facilities. Michigan businesses are eager to show their friendliness and hospitality.

These are a few reasons to "dive Michigan."

The rest is up to you, and therein lies a challenge. The only way that our unique freshwater resources will be wisely used is through the understanding and involvement of people. This is a critical stewardship responsibility that will shape the behavior of future users.

Sport divers can and should be active participants in this process. It begins with curiosity, which leads to exploration and learning. The understanding and appreciation that develops can provide a spark -- a spark that can influence others and grow into a flame of involvement.

I wish all of you satisfying recreational experiences and stimulating challenges. Michigan has an underwater world of opportunity for both.

Ken Vrana
Bottomland Preserves Specialist
Michigan Sea Grant Extension

# Contents

# Introduction

Planning a dive in Michigan? You're in for a treat.

If you think Michigan's sand dunes, forests, hunting, fishing and camping are outstanding, wait until you explore the state's underwater wonderland.

Michigan water is among the clearest and cleanest in the world. Large schools of game fish are not uncommon and shipwreck reefs and unusual geologic features offer divers a unique underwater experience.

And there are plenty of people ready to help you enjoy your diving experience. Dive shops and charter operators are scattered throughout the state and eagerly share their knowledge of Michigan's underwater world. An abundance of motels, hotels and campgrounds leave little excuse for making dive trips short.

Michigan's bottomland preserve program makes it a leader in shipwreck conservation. But there are plenty of Great Lakes dive sites outside of the preserves and inland lakes and rivers to keep sport divers exploring for a lifetime. And more and more are doing just that.

There is plenty of fun for skin and scuba divers. A mask, fin, and snorkel are all that is required for exploring old docks, reefs and shallow shipwrecks, especially in areas like the Manitou Passage. Scuba divers can enjoy deeper sites where Michigan's cool, fresh water has suspended in time our maritime heritage.

This book is designed to help plan dive trips. It offers information on where to go, how to get there and tips for divers visiting an area for the first time. Lists of dive shops, recompression chambers, charter operators and sources of travel information make planning easy and enjoyable.

So, enjoy Michigan's underwater wonderland. You're in for a treat!

-- Steve Harrington

# Using This Guide

This guide is intended to be an aid to planning skin and scuba diving experiences. Divers should understand that conditions of shipwrecks change occasionally so information in this guide may become outdated.

It is also important to note that many new shipwrecks are being discovered each year in the Great Lakes as technology improves and becomes more widely used.

Maps in this book are not intended for navigation purposes. They are included for illustrative purposes only. Most Great Lakes dive sites in this book are buoyed in the summer and fall months, the Loran coordinates are provided to help find buoys or the sites themselves if buoys are missing.

Visibility varies at dive sites and the range stated for each site does not account for divers stirring up sediments. Visibility ranges include those areas where lights are required, thus, deep visibility assumes divers are using lights.

The depths of dive sites are generally expressed as ranges to account for the amount of shipwreck "rise" from the bottom. Also, some dive sites are located on sharply angled bottoms and parts are found at varying depths.

The level of expertise required for dive sites accounts for factors other than depth. Visibility, current and entanglements were considered for each dive site. Generally, however, sites of depths between 0 and 35 feet are considered basic. Depths of 35 to 110 feet are considered intermediate and greater depths, and those involving penetration, are advanced.

Sites that involve penetration diving are sometimes ranked "intermediate to advanced," which means that divers with intermediate skills can safely explore the exterior of a shipwreck.

Remember that there is no substitute for common sense and objective evaluation of each diver's abilities. This guide is intended to provide general information and should not be relied upon to evaluate diving ability.

# Michigan Diving

There are about 36,000 miles of streams, 11,000 inland lakes and 38,575 square miles of Great Lakes water in Michigan. That makes it a diver's paradise.

But Michigan diving is not entirely like warm ocean diving. There are differences that must be considered to have the most enjoyable dive experience.

Perhaps the most important aspect to consider for Michigan diving is water temperature. It is often cold. But technology has provided sport divers with wet and dry suits to overcome this difficulty.

How cold is cold? In most of Lake Superior, the water temperature rarely exceeds 55°F even in the hottest summers. In shallow water in Lakes Huron, Michigan and Erie, on the other hand, the water temperature can near 80°F in late summer. The temperatures of inland lakes and streams can vary greatly.

Because of this variability, it is best to plan on cold water. That means wearing wet or dry suits, watching air consumption closely and keeping an eye out for hypothermia -- the cooling of the core body temperature. The cold water also means that it is especially important to be in good physical condition.

Michigan diving can be exciting because of the variety of aquatic environments available for exploration. Although there are few, if any, lakes and streams that have not been visited by sport divers, many portions of those lakes and streams are unexplored.

The cold, fresh water of the region is an ideal preservation medium. Unlike salt water, oxidation is relatively slow and there are few organism that attack wooden hulls, especially in deep water. Divers are likely to discover tools from Michigan's lumbering era, fishing equipment -- including boats and motors -- from careless fishermen and other artifacts from the past.

Divers must be careful when collecting artifacts, especially in the Great Lakes. Michigan has adopted a system of bottomland preserves where unauthorized removal of artifacts can mean stiff fines, imprisonment and confiscation of dive equipment, boats and vehicles. Most Michigan divers have adopted a strong preservation ethic so that artifacts are left in place for others to discover and enjoy.

The temptation to explore can be overwhelming. Remember to play it safe. Don't exceed your skill level. We want you to enjoy diving for a long time.

# Inland Lakes

Inland lakes often provide Michigan divers with their first open water diving experiences. Most lakes were formed by "gouging" of receding glaciers and range in depth from less than 10 feet to more than 150.

These lakes provide divers with an opportunity to observe unusual aquatic vegetation and fishlife. At times, especially during spawning season, large schools of colorful gamefish can be seen in shallow water.

Inland lakes also contain a record of human activity. That record may be nothing more than golf balls littering the bottom, or it could be artifacts from Michigan's busy lumbering days more than a century ago. Some divers have even discovered rare Native American pottery.

Some lake bottoms sport abandoned cars or small pleasure craft. Most contain interesting natural features that make Michigan's inland lakes popular dive sites.

The bottom of Michigan's inland lakes is variable. It may consist of fine sediments -- "muck" -- or the bottom may be gravel or sand. Generally, the finer the particles making up the bottom, the poorer the visibility.

That means lakes in northern Michigan, where sand and gravel bottoms prevail, often offer the greatest visibility. No matter what the bottom, divers can expect a wide range of visibility, even in a single dive.

Although the visibility of many inland lakes is 15 feet or more, there is always the threat of a "muck out" -- visibility of less than one inch because another diver kicked up fine bottom sediments. Unlike tropical diving, Michigan can test divers' ability to remain calm in a rapidly changing underwater environment. Be prepared.

Water temperature is another change that can occur rapidly and unexpectedly. In warm weather, the water of inland lakes does not always mix. That creates a layer of warm water near the surface and a layer of cold water near the bottom. The point where this temperature change occurs -- often very distinctly -- is called the "thermocline."

The layer of warm water may be 30 or 40 feet thick, or it may be only inches. Either way it is best to be prepared by keeping close track of air and wearing wet or dry suits.

# Rivers

Rivers offer a special diving experience. Some Michigan rivers are very deep -- 80 or more feet near impoundments. But most are relatively shallow, about 15 feet or less.

Visibility can be a problem. Sediments washed into rivers by rains and through erosion are a major environmental concern and can reduce visibility drastically. Visibility is often only

Divers enjoy even the coldest water with the use of wet and dry suits.

a few feet at best. But in mid-summer, the water is frequently more comfortable than deep lake diving.

Obviously divers must be prepared for currents. The strength of those currents can vary greatly and for the careful diver they rarely pose a risk. But one diver lost his life in a relatively small stream when he ventured too close to an impoundment spillway and was trapped by the force of the rushing water.

River bottoms frequently change from year to year. That provides divers with an opportunity for annual exploration. Virtually all Michigan rivers were used to transport logs during the lumbering era. As a result, underwater "logjams" are not uncommon and provide an ideal opportunity for observing fish. Tools discarded more than a century ago are not uncommon "treasures."

Rivers, especially near bridges, can yield many surprises. Frequently rivers are a favorite dumping area for stolen items such as bicycles, motorcyles -- even cars! Guns, knives and jewelry have also been found in some rivers.

Diving in impoundment areas is much like inland lake diving, but visibility is frequently reduced and bottoms of fine sediments are common.

# Great Lakes

Diving in the Great Lakes offers special attractions -- and challenges.

The temptation to exceed one's ability is great when deep-water shipwrecks are involved. In the last few years, there has been an increase in the number of diving accidents in the Great Lakes. Before making a Great Lakes dive, plan well and evaluate everyone's diving skills before hitting the water.

The Great Lakes can offer a combination of inland lake and river conditions. A thermocline is not unusual and underwater currents can surprise unsuspecting divers. In some cases, currents can be an advantage. Skin diving in shallow water can be exhilirating when floating divers travel quietly then surface dive to investigate artifacts or surprise a school of fish.

Currents can cover and uncover shallow water dive sites with sand in a matter of days. Deeper dive sites -- those in 30 feet of water or more -- are generally less susceptible to Mother Nature's whims.

For Great Lakes diving, there is little that can beat a dive charter service. Local dive shops often offer this service or can provide divers with information.

Dive charters give sport divers the opportunity to visit new areas with no guesswork about dive site location, depth and conditions. Charters also give divers the opportunity to share their experiences with new friends. Michigan divers have a reputation for friendliness and enthusiasm.

Two-tank dives are standard for most half-day dive charters. Sport divers with their own equipment can expect to pay about $50 for half-day dive charter services.

Charter boat operators are required to be licensed by the state and their boats are inspected regularly for sea worthiness and safety equipment. Many dive charters offer discounts for dive instructors or divemasters. And some have on-board compressors for extended excursions.

Not all Great Lakes diving requires a boat. Some of the most enjoyable diving can be had off abandoned docks that once served booming lumber communities. Piers also offer good diving opportunities. Some shipwrecks, such as those in the Manitou Passage area, are readily accessible from shore.

Diver down flags are required and although boats must stay at least 200 feet away, it is best to have someone watching for trouble topside.

## Diving Dangers

Eels, barracudas, sharp coral and sharks are no threat to Michigan divers.

Michigan's cold weather is tough on venomous animals. The most frequent problem sport divers encounter is poison ivy growing on the shore.

But Michigan waters are not without dangers that can surprise even experienced divers.

Divers are not the only ones to enjoy lakes and streams. Fishermen and water skiers have also discovered this resource. For divers, that means keeping a watchful eye on topside activity.

Although boaters are required to keep at least 200 feet from dive flags, not all boaters know that. And some are too inattentive to notice the warnings. If diving from a boat, it is best to keep one person topside to warn boaters and be sure the anchor remains secure.

A high-pitched whine is often the only clue divers have that a motorboat is in the area. If that occurs, remain deep until the sound fades, then ascend up an anchor line if possible to check out the situation.

To avoid problems, many divers, especially those visiting inland lakes and streams, dive early in the morning or at night to avoid heavy boat traffic. Divers in the Great Lakes rarely have such worries, but occasionally, curious boaters wander too close for safety.

It is a good idea to keep a sharp diving knife handy. More than one diver has been entangled in discarded fishing line. This danger is especially prevalent around piers and log jams where fish -- and fishermen -- congregate. Lines and cable on shipwrecks can present dangers that can best be handled by careful diving practices.

Another danger is hypothermia, the cooling of the core body temperature. Because much of Michigan's water is cold for most of the year, divers must dress properly. More and more divers are turning in their wetsuits for the comfort of dry suits. In some areas, such as Isle Royale in Lake Superior, wet suits are rarely seen because of the comfort and safety offered by dry suits.

Decompression sickness is always a concern for scuba divers. Fortunately, Michigan has an effective emergency medical evacuation system. There are recompression chambers in some of the most popular diving areas and as sport diving increases in popularity, it is likely that even more chambers will be available.

One of the most sophisticated recompression chambers and dive medicine treatment centers is located at Bronson Methodist Hospital in Kalamazoo. Information and tours of the facility are available.

Perhaps the best way to avoid trouble underwater is through preparedness. Be ready for virtually any condition so that the risk of panic is less. Rapid temperature changes, currents, muck outs and other factors can increase the chances of encountering the unexpected.

Knowledge of first aid, including cardio-pulmonary resuscitation, is important. Sport divers always appreciate a partner who has such specialized knowledge.

# Environmental Quality

The quality of the water environment is an emerging issue for Great Lakes divers. There are the obvious health hazards with water pollution but there are other threats to sport diving.

Recently, the zebra mussel has been reported in Lake Michigan. This or-ganism is believed to have reached the Great Lakes by "hitching" a ride in the ballast of an ocean-going ship. If this mussel reproduces as biologists expect, it may obscure shipwrecks and natural underwater features sport divers enjoy.

Michigan has a tough environmental

The Michigan Department of Natural Resources has an extensive system of public access sites on lakes and rivers throughout the state.

enforcement policy but they must be aware of the problem in order to act. That means if sport divers want to continue to enjoy some of the clearest, cleanest water in the country, they must protect it. If divers spot a potential source of pollution they should report it to the Michigan Department of Natural Resources.

# Great Lakes

The Great Lakes comprise the largest collection of freshwater in the world. Lakes Michigan, Huron, Superior, Ontario and Erie are valuable resources but they are also environmentally fragile.

The Great Lakes collect water from throughout the Midwest and portions of Canada. Contaminated water from those areas too frequently finds its way to the Great Lakes. That is important to divers because water quality affects visibility, health risks and plant and animal life found in and near the water. It is little wonder that Great Lakes divers are emerging as strong advocates of water quality.

Besides the introduction of exotic species, such as the zebra mussel, divers are concerned about toxic chemicals, increased salinity, diversion, turbidity and sedimentation. Environmental issues are complex, but divers are making their voices heard through the political process.

The Great Lakes offer a variety of underwater environments. Generally, the water is colder than inland lakes and streams and a dry suit maximizes comfort, although wetsuits are often adequate. Divers should also be aware of underwater currents, unpredictable weather patterns and boat traffic.

Underwater currents are variable. One day may be still and the next could bring a current not unlike that found in a river. Although generally not a problem even for the novice diver, currents should be considered to avoid drifting away from a boat or shore.

Unpredictable weather and boat traffic warrant a topside observer. Some divers get careless and fail to leave someone topside to watch for trouble. This can be a fatal mistake.

Topside observers can warn boaters to maintain their distance and watch weather conditions. If a boat drifts on its anchorage, a topside observer can account for that situation and prevent an unwelcome surprise for divers in the form of a derelict.

Not all Great Lakes diving requires a boat. Some very interesting dives can be had at old dock sites accessible from shore. More and more skin and scuba divers are finding that dock ruins provide a tremendous exploration opportunity.

When venturing into open water, however, it is best to know the area. Some divers first use a dive charter before exploring on their own. This gives them a chance to learn unusual features of the area and become familiar with local diving conditions. Most charter operators welcome questions and offer advice for later visits.

Smart divers use boats large enough to handle the Great Lakes. Small fishing boats may be great for inland lakes, but waves can build quickly on the Great Lakes. Inflatables are becoming increasingly popular on the Great Lakes because of their economy, stability and convenience for divers. And don't overlook the value of having a vhf radio on board in the event help is needed.

The best advice is to err on the side of safety. If divers question weather conditions and the capability of their boats, it is best to try an inland dive site and save the Great Lakes for another day.

Michigan has a unique set of laws that prohibit most "souvenir collecting" in the Great Lakes. Those laws are covered in the chapter devoted to diving laws. Divers should be aware that those laws are often enforced by other divers. If you bring up a "souvenir" don't be surprised if another diver -- perhaps someone in your own party -- notifies authorities.

While Canada has a strict set of no-collecting regulations similar to Michigan's, other Great Lakes states are still considering such laws. Some believe it won't be long before other states become aware of the value of keeping shipwrecks intact where they rest.

Whenever enjoying Great Lakes diving, remember that the Great Lakes are environmentally fragile. Divers, as direct observers of the underwater environment, can have tremendous impact on the policies that affect water quality.

# ROCKAWAY

The ROCKAWAY was a scow-schooner, a workhorse of the Great Lakes, that was lost about 2 1/2 miles northwest of South Haven in Lake Michigan on Nov. 19, 1891.

The wreck of the ROCKAWAY was discovered by accident when a perch fishing charter boat's anchor became tangled in the anchor chain of the ship. Since that time, it has been the focus of extensive archeological work by Kenneth R. Pott, curator of the Lake Michigan Maritime Museum in South Haven.

As a result of Pott's work, much is known about the history of the ship and the condition of the site. The availability of this information is likely to make the ROCKAWAY a popular dive site.

The ROCKAWAY was lost in a fierce autumn storm while transporting a load of lumber from Ludington to Benton Harbor. The crew of five stayed with the stricken vessel until it became waterlogged. They were all rescued.

The ship was 106 feet long, 24 feet wide and had a depth of seven feet. It was rigged as a schooner and rated at 164 gross tons.

The ROCKAWAY was built in 1866 at Oswego, N.Y.

Today, the ROCKAWAY is broken into three major pieces on a level plain in 65 to 70 feet of water. The stem structure and centerboard trunk remain upright. The upper decks are gone and there are no cabins at the site.

The keelson and centerboard with immediate port and starboard sides are still attached. The starboard section is broken at the chine and lies parallel and immediately adjacent to the inner starboard section. The outer port section has pivoted away from the central port structure at the bow and lies about 30 feet out.

The ROCKAWAY's windlass lies about 35 feet forward of the bow. The length of the wreckage is about 110 feet.

There is much sand in the area and as much as half of the wreckage is covered but many interesting artifacts remain to attract divers interested in exploration.

Initial dives on the ROCKAWAY should concentrate on following the wreck's centerline or keelson structure. Divers may want to fan out from there to the starboard sides. The centerboard trunk stands about six feet off the bottom.

There is an interesting chain pile lying in the starboard bow quarter. A hand lever for operating the ship's windlass projects from under the keelson on the starboard side. Mast steps can be seen in the keelson.

There are no penetration diving opportunities at the site but divers may find this wreck especially interesting after visiting the Lake Michigan Maritime Museum. Interpretive displays of certain artifacts illustrate the wreck and the lives of those who sailed such ships. Information about the wreck and dive site are available by contacting the museum at (616) 637-8078.

| | |
|---|---|
| **Location:** | About 2 1/2 miles northwest of the South Haven pier heads, about 1 7/8 miles from shore. |
| **Loran:** | 42264.4/86184.5 |
| **Depth:** | 65 - 70 feet. |
| **Visibility:** | 2 - 12 feet. |
| **Level:** | Intermediate. |

# IRONSIDES

The IRONSIDES was a 231-foot, twin-screw steamer that hauled passengers and freight until it foundered four miles west of Grand Haven in Lake Michigan.

The IRONSIDES was carrying a cargo of general merchandise when it was lost on Sept. 15, 1873. It was built in 1864 in Cleveland, Ohio.

The IRONSIDES is a popular West Michigan dive site. Although there is no penetration diving at this site, divers can find many interesting shipbuilding features. Arches used to strengthen the hull are well preserved at this site.

Although the IRONSIDES is visited frequently throughout the summer, weather is usually most cooperative and visibility the best in October. Mornings, before autumn breezes build waves, are best to explore this wreck, which lies on a sandy bottom.

Charters to this site can be arranged through the Spring Lake Divers Den, (616) 842-4300.

| | |
|---|---|
| **Location:** | Four miles west of Grand Haven. |
| **Loran:** | 32525.1/49494.5 |
| **Depth:** | 110 - 120 feet. |
| **Visibility:** | 5 - 15 feet. |
| **Level:** | Intermediate to advanced. |

# IDA

The wreck of the IDA is accessible from the Lake Michigan shore for skin and scuba divers.

The IDA was a three-masted schooner that capsized in an autumn, northwest gale in 1908. The ship, which was built in 1867, had seen a long life as a Great Lakes freighter.

The crew of the IDA abandoned ship about 12 miles north of Frankfort and the remains, including its cargo of lumber, drifted to within two miles of the city where it was declared a total loss.

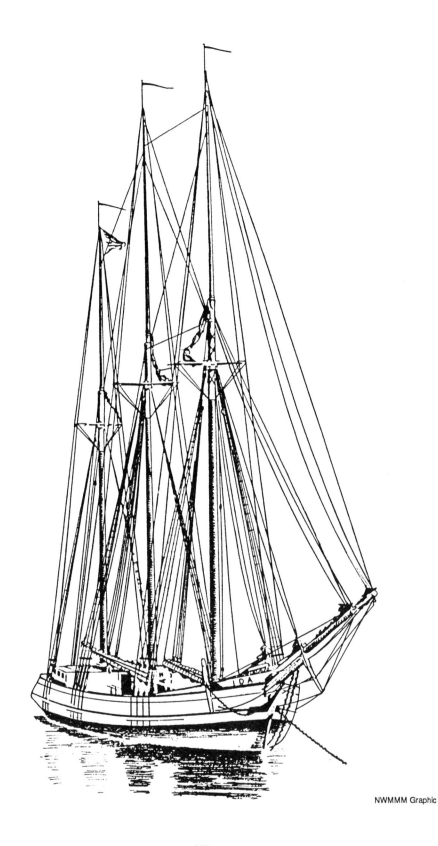

IDA

Today, divers can find a mass of timbers in shallow water. A massive anchor chain and other large artifacts remain at the site, although parts of the wreckage may be obscured by shifting sand.

Divers can gain access to the IDA from shore from the Congregational Church Assembly located in the tiny community of Pilgrim off Pilgrim Highway (M-22), north of Frankfort. It is best to obtain permission from the Assembly office before using their walkway to the beach.

The IDA lies in about 12 feet of water about 75 yards from shore directly out from the Assembly walkway. It is believed that some of the Assembly cabins were constructed from lumber salvaged from the wreck of the IDA.

| | |
|---|---|
| **Location:** | Two miles north of Frankfort, 75 yards from shore out from Congrega – tional Church Assembly beach access. |
| **Depth:** | 10 - 15 feet. |
| **Visibility:** | 10 - 20 feet unless visibility is reduced because of wave action. |
| **Tips:** | Do not attempt to dive when heavy seas are running because of turbulence at this shallow site. |
| **Level:** | Basic. |

# Traverse Bay

Clear water and attractions at Traverse City make Grand Traverse Bay a popular destination for skin and scuba divers.

July and August are the best months to visit Traverse Bay because water is the warmest. But those are also busy months for boaters, so caution must be used to prevent accidents. Watch boat traffic and be sure to disply a diver down flag prominently.

Information about Traverse Bay diving, including charters, is available from Scuba North, (616) 947-2520.

The area around the Traverse City power plant offers divers a chance to see many fish, driftwood and old bottles on a gravel bottom. Divers can access this site by parking on the west side of the power plant which is prominent on Bay Shore Drive. Divers should look to the northeast of the parking area to the intake pipe.

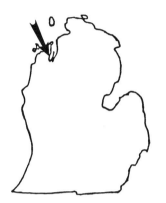

| | |
|---|---|
| **Location:** | Northeast of the Traverse City power plant off Bay Shore Drive. |
| **Depth:** | 0 - 40 feet. |
| **Visibility:** | 10 - 25 feet. |
| **Tips:** | There is a gradual drop off, most divers can explore to 40 feet safely with an 80 cubic-foot tank. |
| **Level:** | Basic. |

The rock jetty is a feature of Traverse Bay that offers excellent shore-accessible diving.

The jetty is located at Elmwood Township Park off Bay Shore Drive (M-22) about two miles north of Traverse City. There is a steep drop off with a 50-foot wooden tugboat in about 40 feet of water. Many fish can be seen when exploring this structure.

This is a popular night-diving site and is located just two blocks from Scuba North dive shop.

| | |
|---|---|
| **Location:** | Elmwood Township Park, two miles north of Traverse City off M-22. |
| **Depth:** | 5 - 50 feet. |
| **Visibility:** | 15 - 30 feet. |
| **Tips:** | Air and assistance is avail- able at nearby Scuba North dive shop. |
| **Level:** | Basic to intermediate. |

Clinch Park is located at the base of the west arm of Traverse Bay off Bay Shore Drive. Here, divers can find a huge lumber pile, aquatic life and antique bottles.

Access is obtained easily by proceeding out from the boat ramp. But divers must be aware of boat traffic in the area. This area is most commonly visited by divers in the spring and fall and during the evening to avoid boat traffic.

| | |
|---|---|
| **Location:** | Clinch Park behind zoo. |
| **Depth:** | 10 - 40 feet. |
| **Visibility:** | 10 - 25 feet. |
| **Tips:** | Wade out from the boat ramp and go north for about 100 yards. |
| **Level:** | Basic. |

# F.T. BARNEY

The F.T. BARNEY was a two-masted schooner headed through the Straits of Mackinac with a load of coal in 1868 when it collided with another ship.

The remains of the 354-gross ton F.T. BARNEY were discovered relatively recently north of Rogers City in Lake Huron. How the ship that was involved in an accident so many miles away came to rest upright and intact where it did is a mystery.

Although the F.T. BARNEY has been visited by relatively few sport divers, it is considered an important archeological study site because of the condition of the wreck. The masts and cabin are still intact suggesting that the ship sank slowly despite a hefty cargo.

There are many small artifacts, including personal items, still at this site. This is proof that Michigan sport divers are committed to preserving the integrity of shipwrecks they visit. In 1989, the F.T. BARNEY was explored with the use of a remote-operated vehicle (ROV). The ROV was used to obtain high-resolution video images of the wreck for archeological study and education programs.

The rope rigging of the F.T. BARNEY has disintegrated so there is no significant danger of entanglement associated with this wreck. But the cabin area of the ship can be dangerous because of narrow passages. Most hatches of the ship are clogged with the load of coal. Experienced divers prefer to explore the wreck site from the outside and penetration diving is not encouraged.

Divers may be surprised to find a crows nest still intact on one mast of the ship, which was built in Vermilion, Ohio in 1856.

The F.T. BARNEY was granted special preserve status to ensure conservation of artifacts at the site. The Rogers City community is concerned about the removal of artifacts and the site is watched closely.

Divers can usually find sport fishing charter operators willing to take them out to the site.

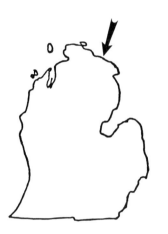

| | |
|---|---|
| **Location:** | Four miles north of Rogers City in Lake Huron. This site is usually buoyed. |
| **Depth:** | 150 - 160 feet. |
| **Visibility:** | 5 - 20 feet. |
| **Tips:** | Do not disturb artifacts. Narrow passages make penetration of cabin area treacherous. At least one other shipwreck has been discovered in this area. |
| **Level:** | Advanced. |

# SAGAMORE

The SAGAMORE is an excellent example of the whaleback steamer-barges that were once common bulk freighters on the Great Lakes.

The 308-foot SAGAMORE was at anchor on a foggy day in the shipping channel near the entrance of the St. Marys River in Lake Superior on July 29, 1901. The SAGAMORE was loaded with a cargo of iron ore when it was struck on her starboard side by the NORTHERN QUEEN.

The SAGAMORE sank almost immediately, taking the captain and two crew members with her. When the ship sank, the pilot house was separated from the steel hull. Otherwise, the ship is intact and is a popular dive destination.

The hatches of the SAGAMORE are open and provide easy

The whaleback SAGAMORE sank in 1901 after being rammed by another ship. Two men died in the mishap.

penetration diving. A ladder is located in the bow. The wreck is located in 70 feet of water and rises about 25 feet from the gravel bottom.

Divers also find large schools of perch around the SAGAMORE and burbots are not uncommon. This site is not buoyed because it is located in the shipping channel. Before visiting the SAGA-MORE, it is a good idea to contact the U.S. Coast Guard Station at Sault Ste. Marie to let them know that a boat will be anchored at the site. They will advise ships entering the shipping channel of your presence.

Charters can be arranged by contacting Lake Superior Charters at (906) 632-6490.

| | |
|---|---|
| **Location:** | Near the entrance to the St. Marys River in Lake Superior off Gras Cap Reef. |
| **Loran:** | 31072.9/47771.9 |
| **Depth:** | 45 - 75 feet. |
| **Visibility:** | 15 - 30 feet. |
| **Tips:** | Be sure to keep U.S. Coast Guard informed of activity at the site and keep someone topside to avoid problems with large ships. |
| **Level:** | Intermediate to advanced. |

# Miscellaneous Dive Sites

The following information is provided in outline form to provide a quick reference to many interesting dive sites outside of the Great Lakes bottomland preserve system.

### ALBEMARLE

This was a schooner built in 1867 in Buffalo, N.Y. and wrecked in the same year it was constructed. It was carrying iron ore and lies in about 12 feet of water in the Straits of Mackinac. Loran: 31188.7/48183.1.

### ANGLO SAXON

This was a 134-foot schooner that was built in 1864 at Port Dalhancie, Ontario. It wrecked in 1887 at the Straits of Mackinac and lies in about 13 feet of water. Loran: 31309.6/48102.8.

## ANNA C. MINCH

The ANNA C. MINCH was a steel steamer that collided with another ship on Nov. 11, 1940. The 387-foot ship was built in 1903 in Cleveland, Ohio and was carrying a load of lumber. It lies about 1 1/2 mile south of Pentwater in 35 to 40 feet of water in Lake Michigan. Loran: 32326.3/49029.9 (bow); 32327.1/49030.7 (stern).

## JACOB BERTSCHY

This steamer sank after striking the Port Austin Reef in Lake Huron in 1879. The 139-foot ship was carrying a cargo of lumber at the time it wrecked 900 feet southeast of the Grindstone City pier. Remains are broken up and scattered in about 10 feet of water. Loran: 30861.7/49181.4.

## CARL D. BRADLEY

The CARL D. BRADLEY was a 623-foot steel freighter that foundered in a storm on Nov. 18, 1958 about 12 miles southwest of Gull Island in northern Lake Michigan. It was not carrying a cargo at the time of the disaster. The ship was built in 1927 in Lorain, Ohio and lies in about 80 feet of water. Loran: 32427.2/49190.4.

## C.H. JOHNSON

This 137-foot schooner stranded in the Straits of Mackinac at Gross Cap on Sept. 26, 1895. It was built in 1870 at Marine City. The remains are broken up and scattered in about 13 feet of water. Loran: 31247.7/48061.7.

## FRED McBRIER

The FRED McBRIER collided with another ship in October 1890. The 161-foot steamer was built at West Bay City, Ind. in 1881. Its remains lie in 92 feet of water seven miles east of

Waugochance Point in northern Lake Michigan. Loran: 31287.8/ 48085.3.

## HAVANA

The HAVANA was a 136-foot canal schooner that was built in 1871 in Oswega, N.Y. It foundered on Oct. 3, 1887 carrying a load of iron ore. The wreck occurred about six miles north of St. Joseph, about one mile from shore in Lake Michigan. Remains lie in 55 feet of water. Loran: 32888.1/50021.9.

## WILLIAM HOME

The 141-foot schooner WILLIAM HOME foundered on Sept. 25, 1894 near Point Seul Choix in Lake Michigan with a cargo of iron. The ship was built in 1871 in Clayton, N.Y. Loran: 32482.5/ 48732.4.

## J.H. OUTHWAITE

This ship was a 224-foot steamer that burned at the Straits of Mackinac in 1905. It was built in 1886 in Cleveland, Ohio and its remains lie in 30 feet of water. Loran: 31187.3/48184.3.

## KATE WINSLOW

The KATE WINSLOW was a 202-foot schooner that stranded off Point Seul Choix in Lake Michigan in October 1897. It was hauling a cargo of iron. The ship was built at East Saginaw, Mich. in 1872. Its remains lie in 84 feet of water. Loran: 31356.4/ 48026.4.

## ALBERT MILLER

The ALBERT MILLER was a 141-foot steam-barge that burned on Aug. 30, 1882. The ship was loaded with a cargo of lumber and sank one mile off Au Sable Point in Lake Superior. It was built in 1889 in Algoma, Mich. Loran: 32242.9/48166.7.

Travel Bureau Photo

Some Great Lakes dive sites, especially old docks, are accessible to skin and scuba divers from shore.

## NOVADOC

The NOVADOC was a 248-foot steel freighter that stranded on March 17, 1947 off Jupiter Beach near Pentwater. It was carrying a cargo of furnace coke. Its remains are found in 12 to 15 feet of water. Loran: 32365.4/49063.5.

## ST. ANDREWS

The ST. ANDREWS was a 143-foot schooner that was built in 1857 in Milan, Ohio. The ship foundered in 1878 at the Straits of Mackinac. Loran: 31180.7/48195.3.

## SALVOR

The SALVOR was a 253-foot steel barge that stranded on Sept. 26, 1930, 2 3/4 miles north of the Muskegon lighthouse. Its remains and cargo of stone lie in 25 feet of water in Lake Michigan. Loran: 32467.0/49355.8.

## STATE OF MICHIGAN

The STATE OF MICHIGAN was a 165-foot packet freighter that was built in 1873 in Manitowoc, Wis. The steamer foundered on Oct. 18, 1901 off White Lake, Mich. in Lake Michigan. Its remains lie in 75 to 80 feet of water. Loran: 32453.8/49263.3.

## THOMAS KINGSFORD

The THOMAS KINGSFORD stranded at the Straits of Mackinac on March 9, 1935. The 86-foot dredge was built in 1895 in Buffalo, N.Y. Its remains lie in 14 feet of water. Loran: 31341.0/48069.0.

## UGANDA

The UGANDA was a 291-foot steamer that sank after it was cut by ice on April 19, 1913. It went down in about 210 feet of water near White Shoals in Lake Michigan. The freighter was built in 1892 in West Bay City, Mich. Loran: 31321.7/48047.2.

# Isle Royale

Diving at Isle Royale National Park is unique. Visibility ranges from 30 to 100 feet and 10 major shipwrecks offer a variety of diving opportunities.

But water clarity and attractive shipwrecks come with a price -- cold water.

Lake Superior water is cold at all times. The temperature at the surface hovers around 50°F even in late summer. Below 50 feet, divers can expect temperatures of 34°F to 37°F. That means a good wetsuit is required at a minimum for virtually all diving. Dry suits are standard for divers who regularly visit Isle Royale.

Each year, about 500 divers visit the island and make an average of six dives each. That shows that Isle Royale is a popular place for extended visits.

Because Isle Royale is located in the middle of Lake Superior, it "attracted" ships -- those that simply failed to navigate properly and others that sought refuge in rough weather.

Although visibility outside of shipwrecks is excellent, visibility within those wrecks quickly deteriorates when fine silt is disturbed. Entanglement in cables and lines is a real danger. A diving line and redundant lights are recommended for interior exploration.

Because Isle Royale is a national park, there is an unusual set of regulations intended to protect fragile underwater sites of particular archeological value. Do not succumb to the temptation of disturbing or "collecting" artifacts. There are also regulations regarding camping and boating.

Charter operators must be licensed by the National Park Service so unless divers have their own boats capable of handling the Great Lakes, the selection of commerical dive charters is limited. Because air tanks cannot be refilled on the island, many dive charter operators have on-board compressors.

Divers without a compressor can often make arrangements to fill have their tanks filled by charter operators. Those arrangements should be made before leaving for the island.

Besides shipwrecks, Isle Royale offers interesting underwater natural features. Large, untouched copper veins are popular attractions. Divers also enjoy collecting greenstones -- Michigan's official gem.

# Rules

Some of the rules at Isle Royale that may affect divers include:

- Visiting and diving is permitted only between April 16 and Oct. 31.
- All divers must register at a ranger station and obtain a free permit before diving. Before leaving, the permit must be returned. This system is used to gain important information about diving activities in the area.
- Do not remove or disturb any artifacts. Collecting **any** "souvenirs," no matter how small, may mean fines and imprisonment.
- No spear guns are permitted.
- Use mooring buoys whenever available. If no such buoys are provided, tie off to a **stable** piece of wreckage. Do not anchor in a wreck area. Note: the most popular dive sites have mooring buoys available. If not, anchor near the wreck site, send a diver down to secure a line on stable piece of wreckage or rock, and then retrieve the anchor line. Avoid disturbing any shipwreck debris with an anchor.
- The following areas are closed to sport diving: Passage Island small boat cove, inland lakes, land-associated underwater cultural and archeological sites -- "known or unknown."
- Compressors may be used at the Scuba Cache in Rock Harbor, Windigo Information Center, public docks and on board private vessels. Compressors must not violate the island's noise regulations.
- Divers are subject to all other regulations on Isle Royale. Copies of those regulations are available in advance by writing to the National Park Service.

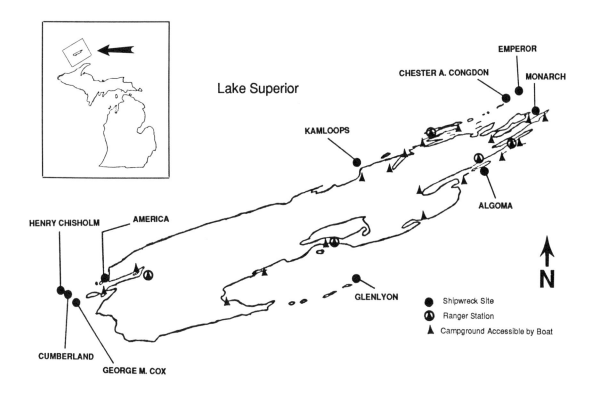

Lake Superior

EMPEROR

CHESTER A. CONGDON

MONARCH

KAMLOOPS

HENRY CHISHOLM

AMERICA

ALGOMA

GLENLYON

CUMBERLAND

GEORGE M. COX

● Shipwreck Site

Ⓐ Ranger Station

▲ Campground Accessible by Boat

N

## Isle Royale National Park

# Boating

All boats visiting the island must register at one of the ranger stations.

Overnight docking is permitted only at certain designated campgrounds and docks. A map of those facilities and a brochure detailing boating regulations is available from the National Park Service.

Fuel is available from mid-May to late September at Windigo and Rock Harbor, although diesel fuel is not available at Windigo. Pre- and post-season service is available at Windigo and Mott Island. Pump out facilities are available at Rock Harbor and Windigo.

The Mott Island and Windigo ranger stations monitor vhf channel 16. The Windigo station monitors the channel from 8 a.m. to 5 p.m. each day and the Mott Island station monitors the channel from 8 a.m. to 4:30 p.m. on weekdays. Marine weather forecasts are available from all ranger stations.

Great Lakes Chart No. 14976 is recommended for all boaters cruising waters around the Isle Royale. The chart is available at Windigo, Rock Harbor and Houghton. The chart can also be ordered from the Isle Royale Natural History Association.

Be aware that the bottom is rocky and it is often difficult to secure an anchor. Whenever divers are below, it is a good idea to have at least one person topside to monitor weather and lake conditions, watch for other boats and to be sure the boat does not drift.

# AMERICA

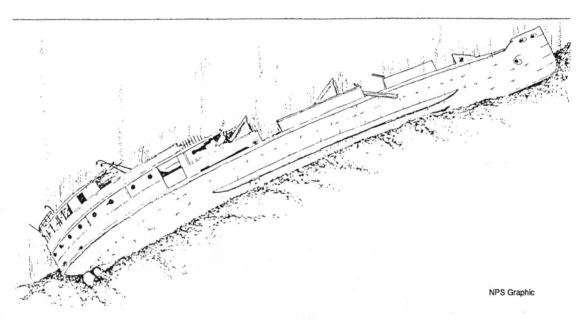

NPS Graphic

An artist's view of the AMERICA shows the stern intact.

The AMERICA was a 183-foot passenger and package freighter that sank in 1928. The steel-hulled steamer was built in 1898 and was a familiar sight in the region because it served many Lake Superior communities. It is one of the most popular dive sites at Isle Royale.

The ship sank after it struck a reef in Washington Harbor. No lives were lost in the accident. An unsuccessful salvage effort was mounted in 1965.

The bow of the ship has been damaged by ice and waves. The midship and stern are intact, including the engine room, galley, social hall and some cabins. A silt-laden storeroom near the galley has been dubbed the "forbidden" room after a 1976 diving fatality occurred there.

As a result of that death, the door to the room was removed to increase the size of the opening. But the area is still dangerous and it is not a place to push one's air supply.

NPS Graphic

This overhead view of the AMERICA shows damage to some of the superstructure of the ship.

| | |
|---|---|
| **Location:** | North Gap of Washington Harbor |
| **Loran:** | 46082.3/31909.2 |
| **Depth:** | 2 - 80 feet |
| **Visibility:** | 30+ feet |
| **Tips:** | Watch for cables and interior visibility problems. The bow is marked with a buoy from May 15 to Oct. 1. |
| **Level:** | Basic to advanced. |

# CUMBERLAND
# HENRY CHISHOLM

Although these shipwrecks occurred 21 years apart, they are so closely associated that they can be considered a single dive site.

Divers describe the site as a "mass of confusion" or a "jumble of timbers" because wreckage from both ships is scattered and overlaps. The site provides a fascinating glimpse into the nature of wooden ship construction of the late 1800s.

Divers cannot see all of the wreckage from one point so this site requires some "exploring" to see all that is there.

The CUMBERLAND was a 214-foot side-wheeler built in 1871 to carry passengers for a rapidly developing excursion trade. It had a number of close calls before it struck Rock of Ages reef on July 25, 1877 with enough force to push half the ship onto the reef.

After several weeks of attempting to pull it free, the ship-wreck was abandoned and autumn storms eventually sent it to the bottom.

At 270 feet, the CHISHOLM was the largest steambarge on the Great Lakes at the time of its construction in 1880. The CHISHOLM also had a history of close calls -- running aground and collisions.

On Oct. 21, 1898, the CHISHOLM struck the Rock of Ages reef at full speed -- about 9 knots. Crewmen quickly realized that the ship was a total loss and three days later, the ship broke up and sank during a gale.

No lives were lost in either shipwreck.

Divers visiting the site can expect to find a mass of timbers, boilers, an engine, other machinery, rudders and propellers. Careful inspection of the remains reveals that the CUMBER-LAND is broken into distinctly smaller pieces than the CHISHOLM.

The CHISHOLM engine should be considered a single dive site and is buoyed separately. The maximum depth of this dive is 140 feet. The buoy is tied off on the top of the engine,

Parts of the paddle wheel from the CUMBERLAND provide a glimpse into marine architecture of the 1880s.

about 110 feet deep. The CHISHOLM engine should be visited only by advanced divers.

This site provides no opportunity for penetration diving.

| | |
|---|---|
| **Location:** | Near Rock of Ages Lighthouse |
| **Loran:** | 46068.9/31935.9 |
| | 46068.0/31936.0 (CHISHOLM EN- |
| | GINE) |
| **Depth:** | 20-140+ feet |
| **Visibility:** | 30+ feet |
| **Tips:** | This is a good area for exploration as some machinery from the CUMBER-LAND is still unaccounted. The remains of the 30-foot CUMBERLAND paddlewheels, which lie in about 80 feet of water in the north-northeast section of the wreck site, are especially interesting. |
| **Level:** | Basic to advanced. |

# GEORGE M. COX

NPS Photo

The GEORGE M. COX hard aground at the Rock of Ages in 1933.

The 259-foot steel passenger steamer was originally named the PURITAN when it was constructed in 1901. The ship made many trips between Chicago and other Lake Michigan cities before it was recruited for service in WWI. After the war, it returned to Great Lakes passenger service.

Early in 1933, the ship was renamed after the owner of the transportation company that purchased it. The COX was elegantly refitted and the subject of much attention when it began its maiden voyage under the new name. But that trip was the first and last for the COX.

In a heavy fog on May 27, 1933, the ship struck a portion of the Rock of Ages Reef about one mile from the lighthouse. The ship was traveling at 17 knots at the time of the collision and four people were injured. No lives were lost.

The COX remained on the reef for a month until it broke up and sank stern first. When the ship came to rest on the bottom, much of the superstructure was flattened and there is little opportunity for penetration diving except for a small portion of the stern.

The COX is a popular dive site but small artifacts were

removed long ago. Divers can expect to find scattered wreckage of all sorts and much machinery. A large rip in the ship's
hull is believed to have resulted when it dropped off the ree

| | |
|---|---|
| **Location:** | Southwest of Rock of Ages Light-house. |
| **Loran:** | 46069.8/31934.9 |
| **Depth:** | 10-100 feet |
| **Visibility:** | 30+ feet |
| **Tips:** | Some debris has migrated, including some remains of the CHISHOLM and CUMBERLAND into the COX wreck site. There may be some unaccounted for remains between the two wreck sites. |
| **Level:** | Basic to advanced. |

# GLENLYON

The 328-foot GLENLYON was built as the WILLIAM H.
GRATWICK in 1893.    The GLENLYON was a steel-hulled
package freighter but also served passengers and hauled bulk
grain. Few Great Lakes ships saw such diversity of duties.

On Nov. 1, 1924, the GLENLYON was loaded with
145,000 bushels of wheat when it sought refuge from a fierce
storm in Siskiwit Bay. But upon entering the bay, the steamer
ran hard aground on a submerged reef off Menagerie Island.

The captain ordered the ship scuttled to secure it to the reef
to wait out the storm and for salvage later. No lives were lost
in the accident.

But the GLENLYON could not be salvaged and it disappeared from the reef that winter.

The GLENLYON is one of the shallowest of the "metal
wrecks" at Isle Royale, and it is completely broken up from

This late view of the package freighter GLENLYON shows freight elevators and gangway hatch cranes.

ice. Except for a small forward deck cabin, there are no opportunities for penetration diving. Divers can find much machinery, including the ship's triple-expansion engine, exposed for easy inspection.

| | |
|---|---|
| **Location:** | Glenlyon Shoal north of Menangerie Island. |
| **Loran:** | 46188.5/31808.3 |
| **Depth:** | 15-100+ feet |
| **Visibility:** | 30+ feet |
| **Tips:** | Wreckage is strewn about an area 900 feet long. Easy exploring with some large sections intact. The area is protected from north and northwest winds. |
| **Level:** | Basic to intermediate. |

# ALGOMA

The ALGOMA was a 263-foot steamer capable of transporting more than 800 passengers. The steel-hulled ship was built in England in 1883. It was one of the first ships on the Great Lakes with electric lights.

The ALGOMA was one of fleet of ships known for their swiftness. But on Nov. 7, 1885, the ALGOMA became lost in a fierce storm and ran aground on Isle Royale. About 45 lives were lost in the wreck and there were 14 survivors.

During salvage efforts, only a few bodies were discovered. It was believed by some that island residents robbed the dead and sunk the bodies. This was proven false.

Machinery from the ALGOMA was recovered. The bow of the ALGOMA has yet to be found and sport divers frequently search for it, hoping it will be intact. But archeologists believe it broke up in the wreck and fragments lie to the west of the wreck site.

The ALGOMA is completely broken up. There are no opportunities for penetration diving. But archeologists are anxious to learn of discoveries of new fragments, especially west of the wreck site.

| | |
|---|---|
| **Location:** | South of Mott Island. |
| **Loran:** | 46177.8/31738.3 |
| **Depth:** | 10-100+ feet |
| **Visibility:** | 30+ feet |
| **Tips:** | Wreckage is widely scattered with few large pieces intact. |
| **Level:** | Basic to intermediate. |

# MONARCH

The wreck of the wooden-hulled steamer MONARCH is shrouded in mystery. It is unknown why the 240-foot ship crashed at cruising speed into The Palisades, a rocky cliff at Blake Point on Dec. 6, 1906. Some speculate that weather of

The MONARCH after alterations that included the addition of cabins aft of the pilot house. The vessel had this configuration when lost.

-20°F and blowing snow contributed to the accident. Others suggest a faulty compass.

The MONARCH was a passenger and package freight vessel loaded with grain and "general merchandise" when it crashed into the rocks. One life was lost when an 18-year-old watchman fell into the icy water. The exact number of passengers and crew is not known, but two passengers were considered heroes.

One man risked his life to make it to shore to secure a line from the stricken ship. A woman fashioned meals from canned salmon and flour salvaged from the ship to boost morale and provide much-needed nourishment. Some survivors had to hike eight miles across the island for rescue several days later.

Two years after the shipwreck, the engines and boilers were salvaged. The MONARCH sank shortly after the accident and additional remains were discovered recently north of the wreck site in about 150 feet of water.

Divers can expect to see massive sections of hull, decking and machinery. Many small artifacts have been removed, but there are still some beer bottles filled with grain and stoppered with cotton at the site.

The remains of the MONARCH are massive but there are no opportunities for penetration diving.

| | |
|---|---|
| **Location:** | Immediately offshore from The Palisades on the north side of Blake Point. |
| **Loran:** | 46171.2/31702.5 |
| **Depth:** | 10-150 feet |
| **Visibility:** | 30+ feet |
| **Tips:** | Watch for cable. Although broken up, this site provides an excellent opportunity for divers interested in marine architecture. There is a rapid dropoff. |
| **Level:** | Basic to advanced. |

# EMPEROR

The 525-foot steel bulk freighter EMPEROR was launched late in 1910. It had a history of productive seasons until it ran aground at Canoe Rocks on June 4, 1947.

A navigational error is blamed for the wreck. The ship stayed afloat for about 30 minutes after the accident but it began to take on water quickly.

The ship, loaded with 10,000 tons of iron ore, sank so quickly that some lives were lost when crew members were sucked beneath the water. At least one lifeboat was capsized by the turbulent waters stirred by the sinking. Twelve lives were lost from a crew of 33.

The EMPEROR is split but remains in a single major piece. It is one of Isle Royale's most popular dive sites. Most divers prefer to explore the EMPEROR with two dives -- one to investigate the bow and one on the stern. Although the

NPS Graphic

An artist's view of the EMPEROR shows the stern intact in deep water.

bow has been severely damaged by ice, the stern is nearly intact. The bow is in water ranging from 30 to 80 feet and gives divers a chance to explore cargo holds. The bow is a good dive for beginners and the stern section should be reserved for advanced divers.

The intact stern section starts in about 80 feet and goes to a depth of 150 feet at the propeller. The engine room is about 140 feet deep.

The buoy is attached to a pad eye near the forward edge of the stern cabin roof. Descending the buoy line is the best method of accessing the shipwreck. The stern may be entered through windows -- glass is believed to have been blown out during the sinking. The engine room may be entered by a blown-out skylight. Doors are open or missing, which provides for easy access.

The engine room is well preserved with the emergency wheel and throttle still intact. Some cabins are also intact and can be entered. On the port side, the forward cabin contains six bunks and was the quarters for the deck hands. Proceeding to the stern, divers can see the crew's dining room, kitchen and pantry areas.

The EMPEROR was not the first ship to collide with Canoe Rocks. In 1910, the steel package freighter DUNELM ran aground. It was freed a few weeks later, but evidence of the accident is still present.

The remains of the stranding of the 250-foot DUNELM are

located about 100 yards east of the EMPEROR bow in about 60 feet of water. Those remains include wreckage of a life-boat and anchors and chain.

| | |
|---|---|
| **Location:** | Northeast end of Canoe Rocks. |
| **Loran:** | 46150.0/31712.1 (stern buoy) |
| | 46150.6/31711.8 (bow buoy) |
| **Depth:** | 30-175 feet |
| **Visibility:** | 30+ feet |
| **Tips:** | Caution must be used when exploring interior because of depth and reduced visibility from silt. |
| **Level:** | Basic to advanced. |

# CHESTER A. CONGDON

NPS Photo

The CHESTER A. CONGDON rested shortly on Canoe Rocks before breaking up into two pieces and sliding off into deeper water.

The CHESTER A. CONGDON was a 532-foot steel bulk freighter. It was built in 1907 and frequently carried grain and iron ore.

The CONGDON ran aground at Canoe Rocks in a thick fog
on Nov. 6, 1918. It was loaded with about 400,000 bushels of
wheat and at first it was believed that removing the cargo
would save the ship. But a storm blew up and broke the ship
in two on the rocks two days later.

The loss, at $1.5 million, was the most costly on the Great
Lakes at the time. Extensive salvaging was accomplished on
the bow.

NPS Graphic

This artist's view of the bow of the CONGDON shows it upright. The stern section lies
in deep water.

The bow section sank upright at the base of a steep cliff. The stern section of the ship received minor damage but much of that section lies in water more than 130 feet deep. A portion of the stern section is accessible in about 70 feet of water. The stern is not buoyed.

Divers can enjoy exploring the bow section of the ship, which includes an intact pilot house. The wreck lies on a steep angle and questions remain as to how the two sections came apart. Much of the wreck can be explored in 50 to 130 feet of water on the north side of the reef.

Wreckage on the reef between the two sections offers an exploration opportunity in shallow water.

| | |
|---|---|
| **Location:** | Congdon Shoal south of Canoe Rocks. |
| **Loran:** | 46147.8/31717.4 (bow) |
| **Depth:** | 70-110 feet on bow; 50-200 feet on stern; 10 feet on reef. |
| **Visibility:** | 30+ feet. |
| **Tips:** | Because of its depth, much of the stern section is unexplored. But the most interesting features are found on the shallower bow section. |
| **Level:** | Intermediate to advanced. |

# KAMLOOPS

The 250-foot package freighter KAMLOOPS was lost without a trace in early December 1927. The ship failed to survive a fierce, early winter storm as it rushed to complete the shipping season. Twenty-two lives were lost in the shipwreck which is believed to have occurred when the ship capsized in heavy seas near shore.

The KAMLOOPS was constructed in 1924 and hauled grain to and from many Great Lakes ports.

The ship's remains were discovered by sport divers in 1977. A few artifacts have been removed and some remaining

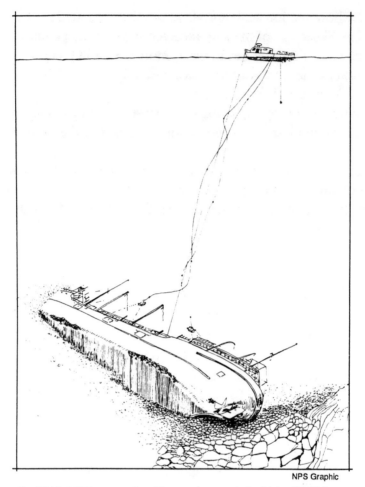

The KAMLOOPS was explored by remote-operated vehicles (ROVs).

artifacts, such as the emergency steering wheel, have been padlocked in place by sport divers.

Although the KAMLOOPS lies mostly intact with some damage to the bow, it is an extremely dangerous site for sport diving because of its depth. Much of the ship lies in more than 200 feet of water only 75 yards west of 12 O'Clock Point.

The KAMLOOPS is included in this section for information purposes only. Diving on the KAMLOOPS is **not** recommended because of the extreme depth. The National Park Service -- and accepted sport diving practices -- discourage divers from visiting this site.

| Location: | Directly offshore from Kamloops Point at the north end of Todd Harbor. |
| --- | --- |
| Loran: | 46124.4/31786.1 |
| Depth: | 175-260 feet. |
| Visibility: | 30+ feet. |
| Tips: | Avoid this shipwreck. It is too deep for sport diving. It is included in this chapter in the event technology advances to make such deep sport diving reasonably safe. |
| Level: | Very advanced only or with remote-operated vehicles. |

# Emergencies

The nearest recompression chamber is at Marquette. Assistance is available by contacting the National Park Service, which monitors vhf channel 16. The Park Service has procedures for evacuation and treatment and can activate a search and rescue operation.

The park is a wilderness area and there are no public telephones. Communication is available only through the park radio system.

Divers should prepare themselves well for accidents because of the remoteness of the area. Training in cardio-pulmonary resuscitation and first aid is recommended.

# Getting There

Statistics show that nearly twice as many divers use charters than private means to explore Isle Royale.

Visitors can get to Isle Royale by ferry from Houghton, Copper Harbor and Grand Portage, Minn. The cost ranges from $56 to $70 for roundtrip, adult tickets. Additional fees are frequently charged for boats, canoes, outboard motors and air tanks.

Seaplane service is available to Isle Royale at a cost of

about $120 for a roundtrip.

Current information about transportation to Isle Royale is available by asking for a brochure entitled "Getting There" from the National Park Service.

# Accommodations

There are many campgrounds on Isle Royale accessible from the water. Rock Harbor Lodge offers spacious rooms and cottages on Isle Royale. Lodge rooms cost about $65 per person per day based on double occupancy. Housekeeping cottages cost about $36 per person per day based on double occupancy.

More information about Rock Harbor Lodge is available by contacting the National Park Service or National Park Concessions, Inc., PO Box 405, Houghton, MI 49931, telephone (906) 337-4993.

# Important Addresses/Phone Numbers

Isle Royale National Park and
Isle Royale Natural History Association
87 N. Ripley
Houghton, Michigan 49931
(906) 482-0986

Dive Charter Operators:

Thunder Bay Marine Services
PO Box 2565
Thunder Bay, Ontario P7B 5G1
Canada

Superior Trips
2540 Buchanan St. NE
Minneapolis, Minnesota 55418

Northland Divers, Inc.
3000 White Bear Ave.
Maplewood, Minnesota 55109

Superior Diver, Inc.
PO Box 388
Grand Portage, Minnesota 55605

Scuba Adventures, Inc.
Bill Gardner
1080 Roselawn Ave.
Roseville, Minnesota 55113

# Bottomland Preserves

The Michigan Bottomland Preserve system is the result of efforts by sport divers to protect shipwrecks from "souvenir" hunters. Too many divers saw their favorite dive sites disappearing piece by piece.

Designation of an area as a bottomland preserve costs state taxpayers nothing. But it tells sport divers that a Great Lakes area has a particularly interesting collection of wrecks or natural features on the bottom.

Bottomland preserves also attract tourists -- a fact not lost on local businesses. As a result, sport divers generally receive warm welcomes to the preserves and nearby communities. Restaurants, motels and resorts may offer special prices for divers visiting their areas.

But there is a set of expectations for sport divers. They are expected to respect the resources -- natural or man-made -- that brought them to the bottomland preserve. That means **no collecting** of any type. Sport divers should keep their "goody" bags topside or risk criminal prosecution.

The chances of seeing law enforcement officers patrolling bottomland preserves is remote. But the chances of being reported by other divers is great. Some sport divers have "turned in" members of their own diving parties for pilfering even small artifacts.

Charter operators are equally strict about their enforcement of laws that prohibit the removal of artifacts. Not only do they risk stiff penalties that include confiscation of their boats and equipment, but they also realize that even the most complete wreck sites can be stripped clean in a single season. That is not good for future charter business.

Why is Michigan so conservation oriented? The reason lies with the sport diving community. Divers largely

# Michigan's Bottomland Preserves

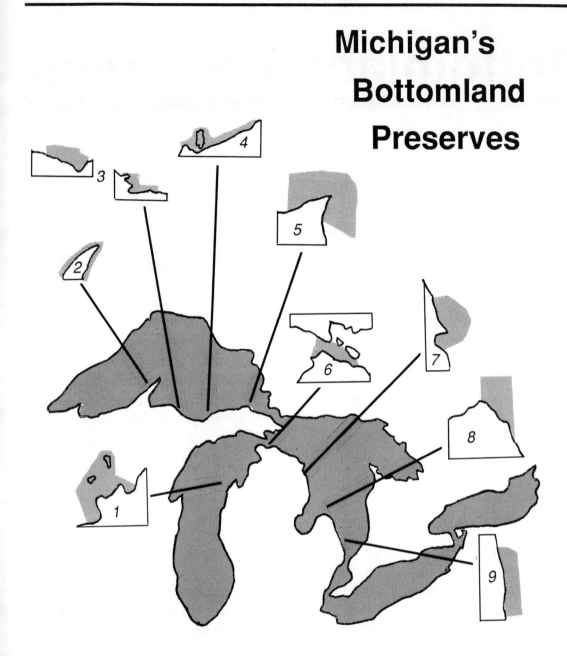

1 Manitou Passage

2 Keweenaw Preserve

3 Marquette Preserve

4 Alger Preserve

5 Whitefish Point Preserve

6 Straits of Mackinac Preserve

7 Thunder Bay Preserve

8 Thumb Area Preserve

9 Sanilac Shore Preserve

drafted Michigan's tough laws establishing and protecting bottomland preserves. They respect and enjoy sport diving so much that they wanted to preserve it for others.

They have done their job well. Michigan is recognized as a leader in shipwreck preservation. Teams of volunteer sport divers have been trained in maritime archeology and are a vital part of ongoing research that is teaching us about our maritime heritage. Divers are providing valuable data, including video and still photos, that help archeologists interpret our past.

Other states are watching Michigan. Although sport divers in those states have yet to take the lead in passing preservation laws, many are also concerned about the future of sport diving in the Great Lakes. The future may see a system of underwater parks where divers and non-divers can enjoy shipwrecks, fish and geologic structures that were once only read about.

Two representatives from each bottomland preserve are voting members on the Michigan Underwater Preserves Council, Inc. (MUPC), a non-profit corporation. The MUPC promotes diving in the bottomland preserves. The group has developed a system of uniform mooring buoys so that visiting boats do not drag their anchors through wreck sites and damage artifacts.

The MUPC also offers advice to state officials charged with supervising the bottomland preserves. This unusual cooperation between the MUPC, sport divers, businesses and state officials has made Michigan one of the premier dive destinations in the U.S.

More information about the bottomland preserves, including ongoing archeological research, is available by writing to the agencies listed below:

**Michigan Travel Bureau**
PO Box 30226
Lansing, MI 48909

**Michigan Underwater Preserves Council**
C/O Peter Lindquist
410 Mill St.
Munising, MI 49862

**Alger Underwater Preserve**
PO Box 272
Munising, MI 49862

**Keweenaw Underwater Preserve**
Keweenaw Tourism Council
PO Box 336
Houghton, MI 49931

**Manitou Passage Bottomland Preserve**
Northwest Michigan Maritime Museum
PO Box 389
Frankfort, MI 49635

**Sanilac Shores Underwater Preserve**
PO Box 47
Port Sanilac, MI 48469

**Straits of Mackinac Underwater Preserve**
C/O St. Ignace Chamber of Commerce
11 S. State St.
St. Ignace, MI 49781

**Thumb Area Bottomland Preserve**
Lighthouse County Park
7320 Lighthouse Road
Port Hope, MI 49468

**Thunder Bay Underwater Preserve**
PO Box 65
Alpena, MI 49707

**Whitefish Point Underwater Preserve**
C/O Paradise Area Chamber of Commerce
PO Box 82
Paradise, MI 49768

**Michigan Department of Natural Resources**
Land & Water Management Division
PO Box 30028
Lansing, MI 48909

**Michigan Department of State**
Bureau of History
717 W. Allegan
Lansing, MI 48918

**Michigan Sea Grant Extension Program**
Michigan State University
334 Natural Resources Building
East Lansing, MI 48824

**U.P. Extension Center**
Michigan Sea Grant
1030 Wright St.
Marquette, MI 49855

**Michigan Sea Grant**
MSU Cooperative Extension Service
Government Center
400 Boardman Ave.
Traverse City, MI 49684

**Michigan Sea Grant**
MSU Cooperative Extension Service
PO Box 599
Tawas City, MI 48764

**Michigan Sea Grant**
MSU Cooperative Extension Service
County Building, 11th Floor
Mount Clemens, MI 48043

# Alger Preserve

The Alger County Bottomland Preserve consists of 113 square miles of Lake Superior bottomlands. Within its boundaries are eight major shipwrecks.

Also in or near the bottomland preserve are underwater natural features for divers to explore.

The Alger Preserve includes the area off the City of Munising, once a major Upper Peninsula port. Ships came to this harbor to load and unload cargoes of iron ore, refined iron, wood, charcoal, lumber and limestone.

But bad weather and unseen shoals combined to cause ships to run aground, collide or founder in heavy seas. Many ships were battered by north winds against the steep cliffs that form the Pictured Rocks.

Today, the area is a popular dive site because of a variety of attractions. Divers can visit unusual rock formations -- including caves -- or many shipwrecks. One such shipwreck, the steamer SMITH MOORE, sank in the east channel of Munising Bay shortly after colliding with another ship. The SMITH MOORE is a popular dive site with the hull intact.

Other shipwrecks, such as those in Trout Bay and on Sand Point, are little more than a confusing pile of timbers. Still, such sites provide interesting diving and an opportunity to learn

much about shipbuilding in the 1800s.

Local divers have established a ritual with local fish. The divers provide food and the fish eat it.

Large schools of rock bass, whitefish, burbots and perch can be found around many shipwrecks in this area. Divers frequently bring dog food, cheese and other food, which attracts even more fish. One popular food is cheese from an aerosol can.

Visibility in the Alger Preserve is among the best found anywhere in the Great Lakes. The substrate is of resistant sandstone and limestone. There are relatively few small particles that remain suspended to cloud the water. Visibility of less than 20 feet is unusual. An unusual white sand is found in this area and creates outstanding beaches.

Divers visiting areas where wreckage is scattered should be aware that maritime archeological studies are still be conducted in this area. Moving wreckage, no matter how small and apparently insignificant, can affect studies that have been underway for years. It is better to inspect artifacts where they lie.

Locating dive sites in this area is easy. Virtually all are buoyed. Few local divers use Loran coordinates to identify locations. Be prepared to head out with just a general idea of where to find a buoy, but divers are rarely disappointed because the buoys are obvious.

The northern boundary of the Alger Preserve extends to the 150-foot depth. Part of the area is under the jurisdiction of the National Park Service.

Before or after dives, there are many natural features to entertain visitors to this region. The Pictured Rocks National Lakeshore provides many miles of trails between Munising and Grand Marais. There are several scenic waterfalls and sand dunes in the Munising area to provide a backdrop for great photographs.

# Boating

Although there is a strong temptation to attempt access from shore at some Alger Preserve dive sites, that is rarely possible or safe.

The shoreline is predominantly resistant sandstone that forms steep cliffs. Although some dive sites appear accessible from a map, be aware that the cliffs can be extremely dangerous.

Boats can be used to access all of the dive sites. And boaters may be comforted by the thought that rough weather rarely interferes with sport diving in these relatively protected waters. Boaters should keep an eye out for changing weather patterns and they should note several natural harbors in the Munising and Grand Island areas that can provide refuge.

A boat launch is available in Munising, which also hosts marina facilities. Limited support services for boaters are available outside of the Munising area.

Boat launches are also located at Sand Point in the Pictured Rocks National Lakeshore and at the mouth of Anna River one mile northeast of Munising.

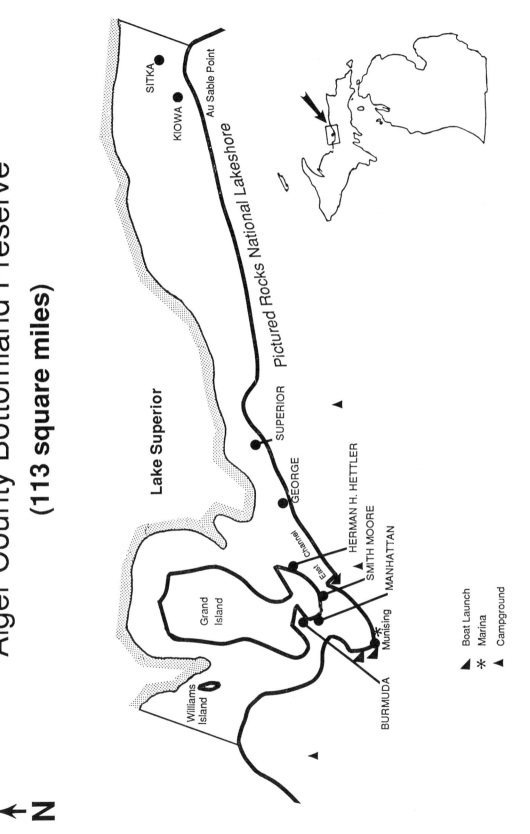

# Alger County Bottomland Preserve
## (113 square miles)

N

Lake Superior

Williams Island

Grand Island

Pictured Rocks National Lakeshore

Au Sable Point

SITKA

KIOWA

SUPERIOR

GEORGE

East Channel

HERMAN H. HETTLER

SMITH MOORE

MANHATTAN

Munising

BURMUDA

Boat Launch

* Marina

Campground

# Ferry Dock Landing

A landing west of Munising is a popular skin diving site.

This is the site of a ferry that once ran between the mainland and Grand Island. Because Grand Island was recently purchased by the U.S. Forest Service, many expect this site to again be used for ferry service to the island.

Divers can expect to find a variety of old bottles, tools and other artifacts in up to 30 feet of water. This site is accessible from shore.

| | |
|---|---|
| **Location:** | Off Ferry Dock Road west of Munising. |
| **Depth:** | Up to 30 feet. |
| **Visibility:** | 25 - 40 feet. |
| **Tips:** | Look for a variety of artifacts. Good visibility and schools of game fish can be expected. |
| **Level:** | Basic. |

# Caves/Rock Walls

The resistant sandstone common to the Alger Preserve provides sport divers with an opportunity to explore unusual features created by the force of waves.

Along the Pictured Rocks National Lakeshore and on the southeast shore of Trout Bay on Grand Island, divers will find rock ledges at about 30 feet. Between these ledges and the surface are areas eroded by the water. These "caves" rarely have cavities deeper than 20 feet, but they offer interesting sport diving opportunities.

Also associated with this resistant sandstone are rock walls. The walls have interesting patterns and provide clues to the forces of nature that formed the continent 13 million years ago.

Although some areas are especially popular for cave and rock

Travel Bureau Photo

The Pictured Rocks National Lakeshore provides divers with opportunities to explore shallow caves created by erosion.

wall diving, virtually any area along sandstone cliffs provides these features. Popular areas include Miners Caves near Miners Castle northeast of Munising and Battleship Row off Au Sable Point.

# MANHATTAN

During a storm on Oct. 25, 1903 the MANHATTAN sought refuge in the Munising Harbor. The 252-foot steamer was carrying a cargo of wheat and was headed for Buffalo, N.Y. from Duluth, Minn.

On Oct. 26, the storm subsided and the MANHATTAN headed out the East Channel of the harbor when a steering malfunction caused the crew to loose control of the wooden-hulled ship. The MANHATTAN struck a reef and a fire broke out, apparently from a fallen lantern on board.

The ship burned to the water line and sunk without a loss of life. After the sinking, some of the ship's machinery was recovered. Much of the remains were removed as a hazard to navigation.

Today, divers can find timbers from the hull of the ship and miscellaneous pieces of machinery and equipment on the north side of the East Channel. There is no penetration diving at the site.

| | |
|---|---|
| **Location:** | North side of East Channel, off south end of Grand Island. |
| **Loran:** | 31648.3/47438.1 |
| **Depth:** | 20 - 30 feet. |
| **Visibility:** | 25 - 40 feet. |
| **Level:** | Basic. |

# BURMUDA

The 394-ton schooner BURMUDA wrecked on the east side of Murray Bay at the south end of Grand Island in October 1870. Little is known about the ship except that it ran ashore near Marquette with a load of general merchandise in 1869. The ship was removed from rocks and saw further service on Lake Superior.

The BURMUDA was reported in shallow water at Grand Island and some salvage work may have occurred on the wreck.

Today, the wreck is nearly intact, upright and provides a fascinating dive site. Divers can inspect cargo holds, but cabins are no longer attached to the deck. There is some opportunity for penetration diving but the condition of the wreck makes it a good one for even novice divers.

The BURMUDA is in shallow water and provides a good opportunity for underwater photography. There are usually many fish, particularly rock bass and perch, associated with this wreck.

The BURMUDA has been incorrectly identified in the past as the DREADNAUGHT and GRENADA.

| | |
|---|---|
| **Location:** | East side of Murray Bay at south end of Grand Island. |
| **Depth:** | 12 feet to deck, 30 feet to keel. |
| **Visibility:** | 25 - 40 feet. |
| **Tips:** | Bring fish food. |
| **Level:** | Basic. |

# SMITH MOORE

The 223-foot wooden-hulled SMITH MOORE is one of the most popular dive sites at the Alger Preserve.

The SMITH MOORE was a steamer built in 1880 in Cleveland, Ohio. The steam barge, equipped with sails, was a common sight in the Munising and Marquette harbors. It primarily hauled iron ore but on at least one occasion is known to have transported passengers from Marquette to Pictured Rocks.

The SMITH MOORE was noted for being a fast ship but it sank when it collided with the steam-barge JAMES PICKANDS on July 13, 1889.

The SMITH MOORE was running in a dense fog when it was struck in the East Channel out of Munising Bay. The SMITH MOORE was loaded with soft iron ore and was declared a total loss. At the time of its sinking, the masts of the ship protruded

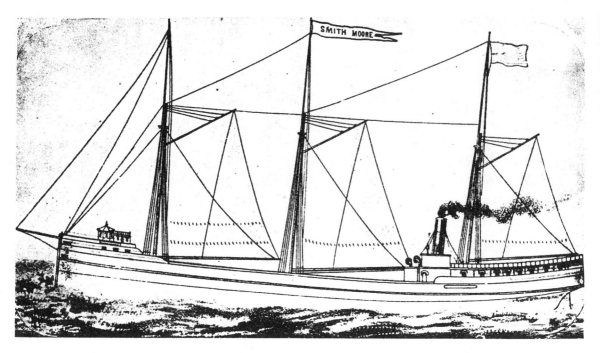

This early lithograph of the SMITH MOORE depicts the ship under full sail.

15 feet above the surface of the water.

The cabins were blown off the deck when it when down. But the deck of the vessel remains and offers divers a chance for penetration diving. Some years, sand drifts onto the deck of the SMITH MOORE and local divers "blow" it off with a variety of devices.

| | |
|---|---|
| **Location:** | East Channel between Grand Island and mainland. |
| **Loran:** | 31642.2/47442.2 |
| **Depth:** | 90 - 110 feet. |
| **Visibility:** | 25 - 40 feet. |
| **Tips:** | Bring fish food. This wreck often attracts large schools of whitefish. |
| **Level:** | Intermediate to advanced. |

# Sand Point Wrecks

Around Sand Point, northeast of Munising, there is a collection of shipwrecks in relatively shallow water. Although this collection is off a sandy beach in only 15 feet of water, it is best to investigate this site with a boat. Distances can be deceiving and it is too far to swim to this site from shore.

From a boat, divers can spot large pieces of shipwrecks that have run aground on the point. The hulls and cabins of these ships were destroyed by waves and ice.

This is a good site for skin diving. Look for three major pieces from unidentified schooners.

| | |
|---|---|
| **Location:** | Sand Point northeast of Munising. |
| **Depth:** | 15 feet. |
| **Visibility:** | 25 - 40 feet. |
| **Tips:** | Do not attempt to swim to this dive site. |
| **Level:** | Basic. |

# HERMAN H. HETTLER

On Nov. 23, 1926, the wooden steamer HERMAN H. HETTLER was headed for Munising Harbor seeking shelter from a gale when a reported compass variation caused the 210-foot ship to hit a reef off Trout Point.

The ship was carrying a cargo of table salt from Ludington to Duluth, Minn. when it struck the reef in heavy snow. The HERMAN H. HETTLER struck the reef hard and the heavy seas pounded the ship until it was a total loss.

The ship was built in 1890 and primarily carried lumber. Several years after the wreck, the HERMAN H. HETTLER was dynamited as a hazard to navigation. Wreckage is scattered and there is no penetration diving at this site.

| | |
|---|---|
| **Location:** | Off the east end of Trout Point on Grand Island. |
| **Loran:** | 31632.2/47431.4 |
| **Depth:** | 33 feet. |
| **Visibility:** | 25 - 40 feet. |
| **Level:** | Basic. |

# GEORGE

The GEORGE was once a beautiful sailing vessel. The 203-foot schooner ran into a storm on Oct. 24, 1893 along the Pictured Rocks area.

The GEORGE attempted to make it to the shelter of Grand Island and nearly made it until the rigging gave way. The ship eventually drifted in the heavy seas and ran aground near the Pictured Rocks.

Much of the equipment on the GEORGE was recovered soon after the wreck. Today, all that remains is a pile of timbers. There is no penetration diving at this site. This is a good skin diving site.

| | |
|---|---|
| **Location:** | Off Pictured Rocks National Lakeshore north of Miners Castle. |
| **Loran:** | 31604.5/47430.6 |
| **Depth:** | 15 feet. |
| **Visibility:** | 25 - 40 feet. |
| **Tips:** | This wreck can be spotted from the surface. Although close to shore, do not attempt to access it from steep cliffs. |
| **Level:** | Basic. |

# SUPERIOR

The SUPERIOR was a sidewheel steamer that was built in 1845 in Perrysburg, Ohio.

The ship was carrying freight, cattle and a few passengers when it ran into rough weather on Oct. 30, 1856. The SUPERIOR was unable to handle the heavy seas ran aground against Pictured Rocks.

The SUPERIOR was crushed by waves and little remains but wreckage in shallow water. The engine was removed from the wreck and later used in a sawmill.

Travel Bureau Photo

Many ships were battered against the rock walls of Pictured Rocks.

| | |
|---|---|
| **Location:** | Off Pictured Rocks National Lakeshore. [46 Deg. 33' 45''; 86 Deg. 24' 91''] |
| **Depth:** | 12 feet. |
| **Visibility:** | 25 - 40 feet. |
| **Tips:** | This wreck can be spotted from a boat or from nearby cliffs. |
| **Level:** | Basic. |

# KIOWA

The KIOWA was a 251-foot steel steamer that wrecked in a blizzard on Nov. 30, 1929.

The ship was headed from Duluth, Minn. to Chicago, Ill. with a load of flax when the cargo shifted. The KIOWA was unable to steer and ran aground on a reef south of Au Sable Point.

Although much of the ship was salvaged for scrap metal during World War II, there is enough machinery and other ship parts to attract divers. The wreck lies in three main pieces. Limited penetration diving is possible at this dive site.

| | |
|---|---|
| **Location:** | On a reef south of Au Sable Point. |
| **Loran:** | 31499.8/47425.1 |
| **Depth:** | 30 - 40 feet. |
| **Visibility:** | 25 - 40 feet. |
| **Tips:** | There is much machinery left to inspect. This is a good place for underwater photography. |
| **Level:** | Basic. |

# SITKA

The SITKA ran aground at the Au Sable Reef, off Au Sable Point, on Oct. 4, 1904. The wooden steamer was headed to Toledo, Ohio from Marquette with a cargo of iron ore when it ran aground on the reef for no apparent reason.

A storm came up a day after the wreck and pounded it to pieces on the rock. The crew of the SITKA managed to salvage personal items and navigational equipment before abandonment.

Today, the SITKA is a mass of timbers on the reef. There is no penetration diving at this site. This site, accessible only by boat, is a good place for skin diving.

| | |
|---|---|
| **Location:** | On Au Sable Reef, about one mile off Au Sable Point. |
| **Loran:** | 31474.0/47421.1 |
| **Depth:** | 15 feet. |
| **Visibility:** | 25 - 40 feet. |
| **Tips:** | The Au Sable Reef has claimed other ships. Look for other wreckage in the area. |
| **Level:** | Basic. |

# Emergencies

The nearest recompression chamber is located in Marquette, about 45 miles west of Munising. Search and rescue is handled by the Alger County Sheriff's Department. Most sheriff's deputies are scuba divers and have emergency medical training. An ambulance, operated out of Munising, is staffed by deputies.

The Alger County Sheriff's Department monitors vhf channel 16. The department has a diver emergency medical treatment program.

A U.S. Coast Guard Auxiliary station at Munising has a few small boats available for search and rescue on a limited basis. The National Park Service has a small boat available for search and rescue upon request during the summer.

A U.S. Coast Guard Station at Marquette can provide search and rescue operations if required.

# Accommodations

The Munising area attracts many visitors because of the Pictured Rocks National Lakeshore. Many cabins, campgrounds and motel rooms are available. During July and August, it is best to make reservations to avoid lodging disappointments. More information is available from the Alger Chamber of Commerce in Munising.

# Important Addresses/Phone Numbers

Alger County Sheriff's Department
Munising, MI 49862
(906) 387-4444

U.S. Coast Guard Station Marquette
400 Coast Guard Road
Marquette, MI 49855
(906) 226-3312

Munising Memorial Hospital
Munising, MI 49862
(906) 387-4110

Sea & Ski Scuba, Inc.
PO Box 634
Munising, MI 49862
(906) 387-2927 or
(906) 387-2670

Pictured Rocks National Lakeshore
PO Box 40
Munising, MI 49862
(906) 387-2607
(906) 387-3700 (General information)

Alger County Chamber of Commerce
PO Box 139
Munising, MI 49862
(906) 387-2138

**Charter Operators:**

Grand Island Venture
410 Mill St.
Munising, MI 49862
(906) 387-4477

Three Devils Dive Charters
PO Box 617
Munising, MI 49862
(906) 387-3165

Tomasi Tours, Inc.
455 East Ridge St.
Marquette, MI 49855
(906) 225-0410

Pictured Rocks Cruises, Inc. (sightseeing)
PO Box 355
Munising, MI 49862
(906) 387-2379

# Keweenaw Preserve

The Keweenaw Peninsula offers the most striking geologic formations in Michigan. As a result, divers can find unusual diving opportunities in this 103-square mile preserve.

The Keweenaw Underwater Preserve follows 65 miles of shoreline. Most of that preserve area is less than 200 feet deep and there are 12 major shipwrecks within its boundaries. The preserve includes an area around Manitou Island, which is found at the tip of the Keweenaw Peninsula.

The Keweenaw Preserve offers much more than shipwreck diving. Mineral formations can be explored in relatively shallow water -- 20 feet or less -- and are accessible from virtually anywhere along the shore. That makes the Keweenaw an ideal skin and scuba diving destination.

The combination of pre-historic volcano action and glaciers created a geological and mineral wonderland. Divers can expect to find virgin copper and silver veins extruding from conglomerate rocks. Occasionally, other minerals such as silver, greenstones, agate and datolite, can be found in shallow water.

Because the bottom is resistant rock (primarily a conglomerate), there are relatively few sediments to cloud the water in this region. That means exceptional clarity -- and visibility. Diving in this area provides an opportunity for outstanding underwater photography.

Clear water comes with a price -- temperature. Like most Lake Superior sites, divers can expect frigid water, even in the hottest summers. A drysuit is standard for diving in this area although good wetsuits in shallow, protected areas are often adequate.

Because it has only been relatively recently that technology has made extensive sport diving possible in such cold water, many of the shipwrecks in this region have retained many artifacts. Divers can find many brass fittings, equipment, bottles and other items scattered with debris. With Michigan's stiff penalties for removing such artifacts, future generations are assured quality sport diving in the Keweenaw Preserve.

Many of the shipwrecks of this region are within 150 feet of shore, which makes it convenient for skin and scuba divers to visit these sites.

Winters are especially long and cold in this region. As a result, ice builds up in great quantities. The force of large "icebergs" moving in relatively shallow water has crushed abandoned ships and scattered debris.

That means fewer penetration diving opportunities, but greater exploration opportunities for basic and intermediate divers. Whenever diving in the Keweenaw Preserve, it is a good idea to be alert for discoveries of shipwreck debris. And divers should not be surprised to find large schools of gamefish, especially salmon and lake trout, sharing the pure Lake Superior water.

The Keweenaw Peninsula, jutting out into Lake Superior, was a logical place for ships to seek refuge from fierce storms that often arose suddenly on the largest body of freshwater in the world. But even with modern navigational aids, the rocky reefs pose a formidable hazard. The 1989 wreck of the 180-foot U.S. Coast Guard cutter MESQUITE is an example of the dangers presented by the geologic formations of this region.

The Keweenaw Peninsula was once busy with shipping activity. During the logging era, ships carried millions of board feet from its harbors. During the mining era, ships carried millions of tons of rich copper.

Although the region was never densely populated, the lack of agriculture required frequent shipments of food -- another reason for ships to visit the Keweenaw Peninsula's harbors.

The maritime heritage of this region is preserved by several organizations that strive to remind residents and visitors of the sacrifices others made to settle this area.

In addition to outstanding underwater geologic formations, there are many terrestrial sites worth visiting. There are remnants of once-productive mining operations. Six lighthouses in the region offer tours and a glimpse of the dangers that threatened the shipping industry.

Copper Harbor and Houghton offer easy access to Isle Royale, another popular sport diving destination. Isle Royale divers may want to consider adding the Keweenaw Preserve to their itinerary.

# Boating

Boaters in this region should have a good navigational chart that shows reefs and shoals. The resistent conglomerate rock commonly found in this area is unforgiving and can be very destructive to hulls of any material.

Boaters in the Copper Harbor and Portage Lake Ship Canal should be aware of the regular ferry service to Isle Royale in addition to large ship traffic. Divers should avoid exploring in these busy shipping channels.

Marinas with fuel and transient accommodations can be found in the Houghton-Hancock area, Eagle and Copper Harbors. Boat launches can be found near Hancock, Eagle and Copper Harbors and at Little Traverse and Bete Grise Bays.

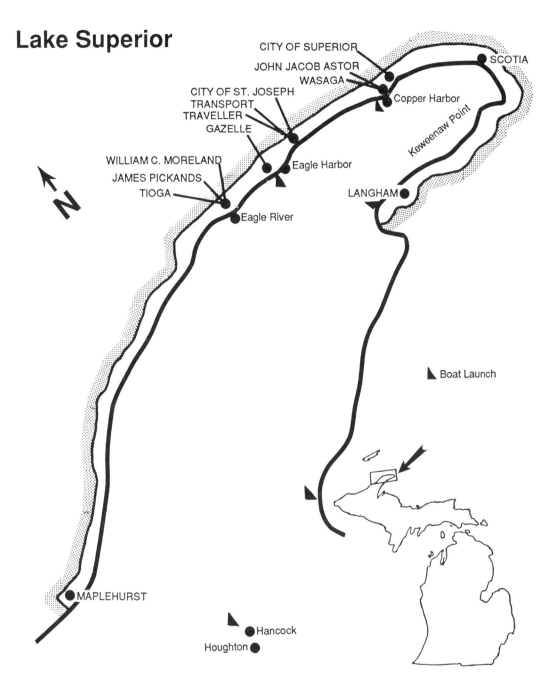

# Keweenaw Bottomland Preserve
## (103 square miles)

Although sport fishing is popular, it is best not to rely on others for assistance. Lake Superior is a vast body of water and if trouble arises, other boaters may not be able to hear distress calls.

The best bet is prevention. Be sure to keep track of weather developments. Reliable boats are motors are essential; do not venture into Lake Superior without confidence in the condition of equipment.

If on-water assistance is needed, there is a U.S. Coast Guard Station at   Hancock , which monitors vhf channel 16.

# MAPLEHURST

The MAPLEHURST was a 230-foot steel steamer that got caught in a fierce storm on Dec. 1, 1922.

The ship was hauling a load of coal to a western Lake Superior community when the storm struck. The captain decided to try to make it to the shelter of the canal when the MAPLEHURST showed signs of breaking up near the upper entry.

Because they feared the force of the waves, only nine of the ship's crew dared jump from the ship to a lifeboat. Eleven men perished in the disaster.

The MAPLEHURST was extensively damaged during the storm and no salvage was attempted. The wreck was dynamited as a hazard to navigation.

Much of the MAPLEHURST is covered with sand. Visible remains are scattered.

| | |
|---|---|
| **Location:** | Houghton side of upper entry, 75 yards west of the 1,350 mark of the southwest pier. |
| **Depth:** | 15 - 20 feet. |
| **Visibility:** | 20 - 40 feet. |
| **Tips:** | This is a good skin diving site but should be avoided by all divers in heavy seas because of turbulent action of waves. |
| **Level:** | Basic. |

# JAMES PICKANDS

Divers inspect the remains of a boiler from the COLORADO or JAMES PICKANDS.

Mark Rowe Photo

The JAMES PICKANDS headed for Chicago with a load of Duluth iron ore when the 232-foot wooden steamer ran into dense smoke from a forest fire on Sept. 22, 1894.

The crew was blinded by the thick smoke and ran aground hard on Sawtooth Reef (sometimes called Eagle River Reef) off Eagle River. Shortly after the JAMES PICKANDS ran aground, a storm came up and broke the ship in two. It was abandoned as a total loss.

Five years before this accident, the JAMES PICKANDS collided

with the SMITH MOORE near Munising Harbor. The collision
was the end of the SMITH MOORE.

Today, divers can find a variety of broken wreckage high on
Sawtooth Reef. The boilers and rudder are interesting dive attractions. The wreckage of two other ships, the COLORADO, which
wrecked in 1898, and the FERN, which wrecked in 1901, is also
scattered at this site.

| | |
|---|---|
| **Location:** | Sawtooth Reef at the mouth of Eagle River. |
| **Loran:** | 47257.1/88179.3 |
| **Depth:** | 10 - 30 feet. |
| **Visibility:** | 20 - 40 feet unless reduced by sediments from Eagle River. |
| **Level:** | Basic. |

# WILLIAM C. MORELAND

The 580-foot steel steamer WILLIAM C. MORELAND was
only two months old when it ran aground at Sawtooth Reef on Oct.
8, 1910.

The weather was calm and visibility was good when the accident
occurred, but the captain claimed smoke from a forest fire obscured the shore making it difficult to determine how far off the
ship was.

The WILLIAM C. MORELAND was loaded with iron ore when
it ran aground. Before salvage attempts could be made, a storm
moved the ship further onto the reef. Later that season, storms
interrupted salvage attempts and the ship was declared a total loss.

Late that fall, after the WILLIAM C. MORELAND had attracted
hundreds of tourists, a 278-foot section of the ship's stern was
salvaged. The section was towed to Superior and was joined with a
new bow in 1916 to create the 580-foot SIR TREVOR DAWSON.
That ship sailed until it was scrapped in Spain in 1970.

Today, the bow of the WILLIAM C. MORELAND is flattened
from the pressure of ice. Wreckage is scattered over a wide area
but it is a popular dive site because the ship's remains are fascinating.

This photo shows the WILLIAM C. MORELAND at Ashtabula Harbor, Ohio.

| | |
|---|---|
| **Location:** | On Sawtooth Reef across from the mouth of Eagle River. |
| **Loran:** | 31832.9/46551.1 |
| **Depth:** | 35 - 45 feet. |
| **Visibility:** | 20 - 40 feet unless reduced by sediments from Eagle River. |
| **Level:** | Basic to Intermediate. |

# TIOGA

The TIOGA was a 285-foot steel package freighter that grounded on Sawtooth Reef on Nov. 26, 1919.

The TIOGA was built in Buffalo, N.Y. in 1885 and was considered a state-of-the-art vessel at the time of her construction. The ship apparently wandered off course in a blinding snow storm.

A few days after the ship grounded, a gale came up and by the time the storm subsided, nothing could be seen of the TIOGA on the reef. It was abandoned as a total loss.

The pilot house of the TIOGA was removed and the rest of the ship has been crushed and scattered on the reef. The boilers and engine are interesting to inspect.

Canal Park Museum Photo

The TIOGA was a package freighter than ran aground on Nov. 26, 1919.

| Location: | Sawtooth Reef. |
|---|---|
| Loran: | 47257.1/88179.3 |
| Depth: | 30 - 35 feet. |
| Visibility: | 20 - 40 feet. |
| Level: | Basic. |

# GAZELLE

The 158-foot GAZELLE was a sidewheeler that struck rocks on Sept. 8, 1860 while attempting to enter Eagle Harbor in a storm. The ship was constructed two years earlier in Newport, Mich.

and many of the remains of the ship were removed in 1864.

The remains of the GAZELLE make an interesting "orientation" dive -- a chance for divers to become acquainted with diving in this area.

| | |
|---|---|
| **Location:** | Entrance to Eagle Harbor. |
| **Depth:** | 20 - 30 feet. |
| **Visibility:** | 20 - 40 feet. |
| **Level:** | Basic. |

A diver explores wreckage from the TIOGA.

Mark Rowe Photo

# TRAVELLER

The TRAVELLER was a 199-foot sidewheeler that burned and sank in Eagle Harbor on Aug. 17, 1865.

The ship was a frequent visitor to Eagle Harbor, hauling passengers and freight, including an occasional cargo of copper ore. The TRAVELLER had just arrived at a wharf when it was discovered to be on fire. Passengers and crew managed to remove most baggage before the ship sank in about 20 feet of water.

The TRAVELLER was built in 1852 at Newport, Mich. It was rated at 603 gross tons.

Today, the TRAVELLER is among the most visited dive sites in the area. The hull and keel are torn apart but are visible on the sandy bottom.

| | |
|---|---|
| **Location:** | Northwest of life boat house in Eagle Harbor. |
| **Depth:** | 20 feet. |
| **Visibility:** | 20 - 40 feet. |
| **Level:** | Basic. |

# CITY OF ST. JOSEPH TRANSPORT

The CITY OF ST. JOSEPH was a 254-steel barge that was lost while under tow by the JOHN ROEN on Sept. 21, 1942. The ship broke free and struck a reef during a gale. The TRANSPORT, another steel barge, broke free from the JOHN ROEN about a half-hour later.

The ships were enroute to Port Huron from Grand Marais, Minn. with loads of pulpwood. The CITY OF ST. JOSEPH, originally constructed as a passenger vessel, sank quickly after it struck the reef with the loss of the cook.

The TRANSPORT originally served as a car ferry between Detroit and Windsor. In 1934, it was converted to haul bulk freight. Its remains lie about 110 yards inshore from the wreck of the CITY OF ST. JOSEPH on a small reef about 1/4 mile from the mouth of Little Grand Marais Harbor.

Divers will find both wrecks flattened from the pressure of years

Mark Rowe Photo

A diver examines bits on the wreck of the CITY OF ST. JOSEPH.

Mark Rowe Photo

A diver explores machinery from the wreck of the CITY OF ST. JOSEPH.

of wave and ice action. At the site of the CITY OF ST. JOSEPH, divers can find the bow windlass and chain, rudder and stern towing machinery. Some equipment from the TRANSPORT was salvaged.

| | |
|---|---|
| **Location:** | About 1/4 mile off the mouth of Little Grand Marais Harbor. |
| **Loran:** | 31777.6/46581.4 |
| **Depth:** | 10 - 35 feet. |
| **Visibility:** | 20 - 40 feet. |
| **Tips:** | Divers frequently visit both sites during the same dive because of their close proximity. |
| **Level:** | Basic. |

# JOHN JACOB ASTOR

The JOHN JACOB ASTOR is one of the oldest shipwrecks of the Keweenaw Peninsula.

The 78-foot brig was used extensively in the fur trade of the region. Missionaries and explorers also relied on the ship, which was owned by the American Fur Company.

The JOHN JACOB ASTOR was blown into a Copper Harbor reef during a storm on Sept. 21, 1844. Although the ship was in one piece after the storm, efforts to free it before winter storms took their toll were unsuccessful.

Much of the rigging and equipment were saved before the ship broke up that winter. The JOHN JACOB ASTOR was built in 1835. Her main anchor was recovered in 1976.

Divers can expect to find many small pieces of hull and timbers at this site.

| | |
|---|---|
| **Location:** | Fort Wilkins Dock. |
| **Depth:** | 20 - 35 feet. |
| **Visibility:** | 20 - 40 feet. |
| **Level:** | Basic. |

# CITY OF SUPERIOR

The CITY OF SUPERIOR was only three months old when it wrecked at the Lighthouse at Copper Harbor on Nov. 10, 1857.

The 190-foot steamer hauled passengers and freight in the region but was caught in a blinding snow storm while attempting to make Copper Harbor. The CITY OF SUPERIOR wandered off course and ran aground about 100 feet from the lighthouse.

The ship was pounded by waves from a rising storm and eventually broke in two. Although much of the cargo was salvaged and passengers and crew were rescued, the CITY OF SUPERIOR was a total loss.

The ship's rudder was recovered in the 1970s, but little remains of the ship except small pieces of the hull.

| | |
|---|---|
| **Location:** | Near Copper Harbor Lighthouse. |
| **Depth:** | 15 - 35 feet. |
| **Visibility:** | 20 - 40 feet. |
| **Level:** | Basic. |

# WASAGA

The WASAGA was a 238-foot Canadian steamer that burned and sank in Copper Harbor on Nov. 6, 1910.

The ship was carrying a cargo of farm equipment and general freight when it sought refuge in Copper Harbor from a rising northwest storm. Without explanation, the forward section was discovered engulfed in flames.

The crew managed to escape and the WASAGA burned to the waterline. Most of the cargo and the ships' engines and machinery was salvaged.

Divers can find portions of the WASAGA's keel at this site.

| | |
|---|---|
| **Location:** | 150 yards northeast of the Harbour Haus Restaurant in Copper Harbor. |
| **Depth:** | 25 - 35 feet. |
| **Visibility:** | 20 - 40 feet. |
| **Level:** | Basic. |

# SCOTIA

The SCOTIA was built in Buffalo, N.Y. in 1873 and was considered a fast steamer of the era. The ship was bound for Duluth, Minn. when it ran into an autumn snow storm on Oct. 24, 1888. Before tugboats could arrive to pull the ship off the rocks, it broke in two.

The SCOTIA's boilers, engine and machinery were recovered and part of the hull was salvaged for scrap.

The remains of the SCOTIA are widely scattered.

| | |
|---|---|
| **Location:** | Off the old rocket launch pad at Keweenaw Point, about 100 feet from shore. |
| **Depth:** | 15 feet. |
| **Visibility:** | 20 - 40 feet. |
| **Level:** | Basic. |

# LANGHAM

The LANGHAM was heavily laden with coal bound for Port Arthur when it sought refuge from a storm in Bete Grise Bay on Oct. 23, 1910.

While the crew of 17 was waiting for the storm to subside, the LANGHAM caught fire and burned to the waterline. It sank in about 105 feet of water.

Divers will find the ship's boilers, engines and machinery intact. The decks were burned off, but much of the hull is still visible.

| | |
|---|---|
| **Location:** | Bete Grise Bay. |
| **Depth:** | 90 - 105 feet. |
| **Visibility:** | 20 - 40 feet. |
| **Level:** | Intermediate to advanced. |

Canal Park Museum Photo

The TOM ADAMS was later named the LANGHAM.

# CITY OF BANGOR
# ALTADOC

The 444-foot CITY OF BANGOR ran aground on Keweenaw
Point during a storm on Nov. 30, 1926. A little more than a year
later, on Dec. 7, 1927, the ALTADOC ran aground near the same
place.

The CITY OF BANGOR was loaded with general freight, including 230 new Chrysler cars. The ship ran into trouble when ice
built up on the decks and water eventually put out the ship's fires.
The CITY OF BANGOR blew ashore and her hull was punctured
by sharp rocks.

A few weeks after the wreck, after the water around the ship was
frozen, a road was constructed through eight miles of forest to the
point. A ramp was constructed and the cars were driven off the
ship and taken back to Detroit by train for refurbishing.

The ALTADOC was light and headed for Fort William when it
ran into a fierce, early winter storm. During the storm, the ship's
rudder broke and the ALTADOC was driven onto the rocks of

Keweenaw Point, about 1,000 feet from the wreck of the CITY OF BANGOR.

The 365-foot ALTADOC caught fire and smoldered for a month. The crews of both ships were rescued.

Although the wrecks of these ships is still fresh in the memories of many elder Keweenaw residents who treasure aging photographs of the disasters, divers are likely to be disappointed at the sites. Both ships were extensively salvaged and little remains of the wrecks.

Wreckage from the ships can be found in about 15 feet of water about four miles west of Keweenaw Point.

# Emergencies

The only U.S. Coast Guard Station on the Keweenaw Peninsula is located at Hancock. Because some dive sites are remote, vhf radio signals may not reach this station if help is sought. For that reason, it is best to use extreme boating caution, especially because reefs that claimed large ship can also damage dive boats.

The U.S. Coast Guard monitors vhf channel 16 and is responsible for search, rescue and handling on-water emergencies. Arrangements for medical care can be made by the Coast Guard.

The Keweenaw County Sheriff's Department is a small department, often with a single officer on duty. The department does not monitor vhf channels but the dispatcher can arrange for emergency transportation.

The nearest recompression chamber is located at Marquette General Hospital in Marquette.

The telephone number for the Coast Guard Station at Hancock is: (906) 482-1520. The telephone number for the Keweenaw County Sheriff's Department is (906) 337-0528.

# Accommodations

Because the Keweenaw Peninsula is sparsely populated, overnight accommodations are limited. Major cities, primarily Houghton, Hancock and Calumet offer hotel and motel accommodations.

Campgrounds are also uncommon. But the Copper Country State Forest provides many trails and quiet areas where campers willing to "rough it" can spend several nights undisturbed. Good campsites for rustic camping can also be found in many areas along the Lake Superior shore.

Information about campsites, hotels and motels can be obtained from the Keweenaw Tourism Council, (906) 482-2388.

# Important Addresses/Phone Numbers

U.S. Coast Guard Station
Hancock, MI
(906) 482-1520

Keweenaw County Sheriff's
Department
Eagle River, MI 49924
(906) 337-0528

Keweenaw Tourism Council
PO Box 336
Houghton, MI 49931
(906) 482-2388
(800) 338-7982 (outside MI)

Keweenaw Peninsula Chamber
of Commerce
PO Box 336
Houghton, MI 49931
(906) 482-5240
(906) 337-4579

Keweenaw County Historical Society
Eagle Harbor, MI 49951

# Manitou Passage

*When French explorers first came to this region, they learned of how the Manitou islands and Sleeping Bear Dune were created according to Chippewa Indian legend.*

*The Indians told the explorers that a mother bear and her two cubs fled a Wisconsin forest fire by swimming across Lake Michigan. When the mother bear reached the Michigan shore, she climbed a steep bluff to watch for her young.*

*Within sight of shore, the cubs tired and drowned. The mother waited and waited, but her young never arrived. Eventually, the mother bear died of sorrow atop the bluff.*

*The Great Manitou, a spirit Indians believed governed the natural world, was touched by the mother bear's devotion. As a tribute, he created a great mound of sand, Sleeping Bear Dune, where the mother died in her sleep. The Manitou islands mark the spots where the cubs drowned.*

The Manitou Bottomland Preserve hosts a variety of shallow shipwrecks and natural features. It is also believed to contain the remains of many shipwrecks yet to be found.

The most striking aspect of the Manitou Preserve is sand. The Sleeping Bear Dunes National Lakeshore virtually surrounds the preserve and it is the volume of sand that makes this area unique for visiting divers.

The sand is always in motion. As a result, shipwrecks and reefs are periodically covered and exposed. That makes the Manitou Passage especially attractive for divers looking for exploration opportunities. Each year, "new" shipwrecks are discovered and "old" ones are covered. That means that any dive can yield new discoveries -- even

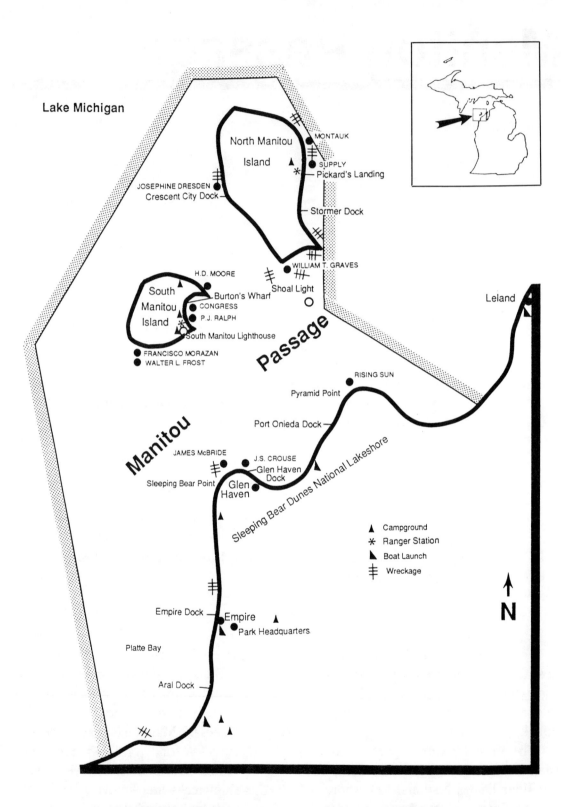

Lake Michigan

North Manitou
Island

MONTAUK
SUPPLY
Pickard's Landing

JOSEPHINE DRESDEN
Crescent City Dock

Stormer Dock

WILLIAM T. GRAVES

H.D. MOORE

South
Manitou
Island

Burton's Wharf
CONGRESS
P.J. RALPH

Shoal Light

South Manitou Lighthouse

FRANCISCO MORAZAN
WALTER L. FROST

Leland

RISING SUN

Pyramid Point

Port Onieda Dock

Manitou

JAMES McBRIDE

J.S. CROUSE
Glen Haven
Dock

Sleeping Bear Point

Glen
Haven

Sleeping Bear Dunes National Lakeshore

Passage

▲  Campground
✳  Ranger Station
◣  Boat Launch
╪  Wreckage

↑
N

Empire Dock

Empire
Park Headquarters

Platte Bay

Aral Dock

# The Manitou Passage
(282 square miles)

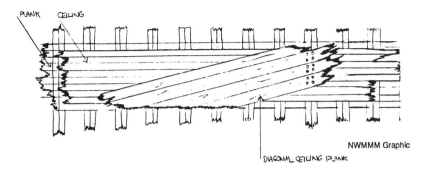

PLANK  CEILING

NWMMM Graphic

DIAGONAL CEILING PLANK

Maritime archeologists are researching searching several wreck sites in the Manitou Passage Preserve. Drawings of wreckage document the forces that sank ships.

in shallow water.

Recently, one of the most active dive sites for exploration in the preserve has been areas south and east of North Manitou Island. Maritime archeologists, with the help of many volunteer sport divers, are documenting shipwreck remains and searching for wrecks known to be in those areas. One recent discovery is the wreckage of the WILLIAM T. GRAVES, the first bulk freighter on the Great Lakes, which foundered on North Manitou Shoal in 1885.

Because most of the shipwrecks in the Manitou Passage are in shallow water, there is little opportunity for penetration diving. Waves and ice have broken up the wrecks, except for those in deep water and the FRANCISCO MORAZAN, a steel-hulled freighter that sank in shallow water off South Manitou Island in 1960.

Besides shipwrecks, the Manitou Passage hosts many shoals of rock and sand that attract large schools of fish around massive boulders.

The Manitou Passage has a long and colorful history. Much of that history is tied to the docks that once lined the coast to service schooners and steamers that transported goods throughout the Great Lakes.

Today, those docks are little more than pilings. But they are home to schools of fish and unusual artifacts. They are easily accessible from shore and skin and scuba divers find dock ruins a fun attraction.

Because many shipwrecks are in shallow water in the Manitou Passage, it is an area popular with skin divers. This is a preserve where a minimum of equipment is required. Even non-divers can marvel at wrecks in 25 feet of water.

Another feature of the Manitou Preserve is its association with the Sleeping Bear Dunes National Lakeshore. The National Park Service offers a variety of interpretative programs for all visitors.

Some charter operators make arrangements with the Park Service for group tours of the lighthouse on South Manitou Island. The tour explains how shoals

Although the Manitou Passage had warning devices such as this lighthouse on South Manitou Island built in 1840, ships still ran aground on unseen shoals. Tours of this lighthouse are offered daily by the National Park Service.

and bad weather combined to make the Manitou Passage an especially treacherous area for ships. The tour includes a visit to the top of the lighthouse tower, which offers a splendid view of the passage.

The Park Service has jurisdition over much of the mainland associated with the Manitou Preserve and a portion of the surface water. Park Service rang-

ers monitor diving activity and are available to assist in emergencies.

Free registration is required before camping on the Manitou islands. Be sure to obtain brochures about those islands before planning trips. Park Service rules are designed to protect natural and cultural features as well as ensure visitor safety.

# Boating

Although boats are not required to visit some of the most interesting dive sites in the Manitou Preserve, boats can provide quick and easy access to others.

Boaters should be prepared for rapid weather changes. There are currents of cold water in the Manitou Passage that can cause dense fog without warning. A good compass -- and ability to use it properly -- are vital. Detailed nautical charts are also important.

The depth of the Manitou Passage fluctuates greatly and quickly. Small boats drafting less than four feet rarely have any problem navigating. But nearly every year small boats run into problems through inattention.

Gull Point at South Manitou Island, North Manitou Shoals and reefs in Platte Bay are potential problem areas. Boaters should use caution when exploring the southwest shore of North Manitou Island and any area around dock ruins.

A shipping channel runs through the passage and is used frequently by ocean-going ships of all types. The channel follows very deep water, however, and should pose no threat to sport divers.

Many boaters "beach" their vessels on the sandy shores that are commonly found throughout the preserve area. Be aware that open fires on beaches are forbidden by the National Park Service, which patrols the Sleeping Bear Dunes National Lakeshore. Before camping, check Park Service regulations.

U.S. Coast Guard stations at Traverse City, Charlevoix and Frankfort monitor vhf channel 16 for distress calls. On occasion, direct radio communication with the Coast Guard in some areas of the preserve is limited. In that circumstance, other boaters can assist by relaying emergency messages.

A permanent, concrete boat ramp is available at the municipally-operated marine in Leland. There is a small fee for using the ramp, but the facility can handle even very large boats. Boaters should note that the ramp is steep and water makes it slippery. Removing a large boat can mean traction problems, but assistance is usually available.

Boaters must also be aware that sand periodically fills large portions of the Leland harbor, which is protected by a limestone breakwall. Early in the season (April and May), it is a good idea to proceed cautiously. Dredging, if done at all, is usually accomplished late in the season.

July is generally the peak month for this marina, so reservations should be made for slip space.

The marina offers a variety of services for boaters and nearby Fishtown offers tourists other attractions. Grocery stores, a gas station with mechanics, restaurants and lodging are available in the city -- a short walk from the marina.

Leland offers direct access to the Manitou Preserve. But it is also a popular fishing area. Be watchful of other boat traffic.

Small boats can use the launch at Empire. It is a seasonal facility not suitable for very large boats. There is no charge for using the launch, which is located at the village park on Lake Michigan.

Empire is a small, friendly community. There are several "homey" restaurants, an art gallery, historical museum with maritime artifacts, and an extensive play area for children. Empire also hosts the headquarters for the Sleeping Bear Dunes National Lakeshore. The headquarters features an interpretive center that focuses on maritime heritage.

A paved boat ramp is located at the mouth of Platte River at the southern end of Platte Bay. This no-cost ramp, located at the end of Lake Michigan Road, should be used only by small boats because of shallow water at the mouth of the river. Once in Platte Bay, look for rocky reefs extending from the southern shore of the bay.

For a small fee, boaters can launch even large boats from the municipal boat launch in Frankfort. This paved facility is located considerably south of the Manitou Preserve but Frankfort offers many amenities, including a full-service marina.

The Frankfort boat launch is located south of Main Street on Betsie Bay. Frankfort is a popular sport fishing area so boaters should be watchful of boat traffic.

# Dock Ruins

Dock ruins are among the most popular -- and accessible -- dive sites in the Manitou Preserve.

The Manitou Passage was one of the first areas settled west of the Straits of Mackinac. As a result, many docks and wharves were constructed to serve schooners and steamships using the

Although the distance between Sleeping Bear Point, foreground, and South Manitou Island is seven miles, there are many shoals and coves that make navigation difficult.

passage and to transport goods to and from fledgling communities.

Many of those communities disappeared early in the 1900s as the lumbering industry moved north. Left behind were massive pilings that are the remains of once-busy docks. Today, those docks provide shallow dive sites that are especially attractive to skin divers.

Dock ruins are often considered a "junk yard" of sorts. It was a common practice for ships' crewmen to dispose of unwanted items, such as bottles, by simply tossing them into the water. Old machinery and carts used to transport goods on docks were often cast into the water when they outlived their usefulness. That makes dock diving especially appealing. The shifting sands of the Manitou Passage constantly cover and uncover such artifacts.

Some dock ruins offer a glimpse into the lives of those who used the structures more than a century ago. Be aware, however, that the same rules regarding souvenir collecting apply to dock ruins as shipwrecks.

Year after year, docks were rebuilt. Often, docks were rebuilt atop old pilings. That may give some dock ruins a "calico" appearance where some features are relatively new while others are decades old.

Dock ruins are also popular with fish. They often gather around protective pilings. Divers can expect to see yellow perch, carp, trout and salmon.

Major dock ruins in the Manitou Preserve are buoyed for the convenience of divers and for the safety of boaters.

# Aral Dock

Aral was once a thriving lumber town. It boasted a sawmill and other facilities that made it a frequent stop for freighters around the turn of the century.

As lumbering faded, so did Aral. It ceased to exist around 1907. A historical marker at the sign tells of the boom town that once bloomed at the now-remote site.

Topside, the only evidence of a once-extensive dock is three pilings near shore. Underwater, however, are remains of pilings extending about 200 yards from shore. Most pilings appear to have been cut near the bottom.

| | |
|---|---|
| **Location:** | At the end of Esch Road (610) in Benzie County. [44 Deg. 45' 50"; 86 Deg. 03' 35"] |
| **Depth:** | 4 - 20 feet |
| **Visibility:** | 2 - 30 feet (Visibility reduced when waves create turbulent conditions in shallow water. Occurs when there is a strong westerly wind.) |
| **Tips:** | This site is easily accessible with ample parking. It is also a popular swimming beach. For security reasons, divers may not want to leave equipment on the beach unattended. |
| **Level:** | Basic. |

At the end of the pilings, divers may find anchor chain and an anchor from an unidentified ship. A large propeller from a steamer is also in the area. Divers may wish to explore south of the dock to find miscellaneous wreckage from many ships that unsuccessfully sought refuge from storms in Platte Bay.

Maritime historians note that it is near this site, at the mouth of Otter Creek, where survivors of the famed steamer WESTMORELAND spent three chilly days and nights in December 1854.

# Empire Dock

The Empire Dock was used extensively for the lumber trade. It was used somewhat for the shipping of produce. Except for concrete structures on shore, there is little evidence of the ruins topside.

Divers can use remains on shore to guide their exploration of the area. Shifting sand in this area may uncover machinery.

Information about the history of the village is available at the historical museum in Empire.

| | |
|---|---|
| **Location:** | At the municipal park at the west end of the village. [44 Deg. 46' 25"; 86 Deg. 04' 00"] |
| **Depth:** | 4 - 15 feet |
| **Visibility:** | 2 - 30 feet (Visibility reduced when waves create turbulent conditions in shallow water. Occurs when there is a strong westerly wind.) |
| **Tips:** | This is a popular swimming beach. It is easily accessible and there is plenty of parking. The beach is the rock-laden but a sandy bottom is found offshore. |
| **Level:** | Basic. |

# Glen Haven Dock

The Glen Haven Dock was used extensively for lumber and produce trade. Small freighters frequently used this harbor because it offered some protection from west and southwest winds.

Groups of pilings make these ruins easy to locate.

Divers will find the wreck of the J.S. CROUSE, and wreckage of perhaps two other ships, at the base of pilings in about 12 feet of water. A horse-drawn cart that once ran on rails to transport goods on the dock is located in seven feet of water. Machinery may also be found by curious divers.

| | |
|---|---|
| **Location:** | Off 209 just east of the U.S. Life Saving Service Station in Leelanau County. Look for an old fruit storage building. The dock ruins are directly offshore. [44 Deg. 55' 30"; 86 Deg. 01' 30"]. |
| **Depth:** | 5 - 15 feet |
| **Visibility:** | 10 - 30 feet |
| **Tips:** | Roadside parking available. |
| **Level:** | Basic. |

# Port Oneida Dock

An unknown shipwreck can be found by divers exploring the Port Oneida dock ruins. There is a record of a small schooner running around on rocks in about 14 feet of water.

This was once a thriving port that serviced small freighters. Today, there is little evidence of the dock ruins remaining topside. Shifting sands in this area make discoveries possible each diving season.

| Location: | At the end of Kilderhouse Road north of Glen Arbor in Leelanau County. [44 Deg. 57' 10"; 85 Deg. 56' 45"]. |
|---|---|
| Depth: | 5 - 15 feet |
| Visibility: | 2 - 30 feet (Visibility reduced when waves create turbulent conditions in shallow water. Oc – curs when there is a strong west– erly wind.) |
| Tips: | Many Petoskey stones, the fossil ized remains of ancient coral, can be found in this area. |
| Level: | Basic. |

# Burton's Wharf

Burton's Wharf was the main dock for South Manitou Island. And because virtually all goods arriving or leaving the island were transported by freighters, it was a busy facility.

Through the years, the wharf underwent several major re-buildings. As a result, it is a massive underwater structure -- one of the most popular for sport divers.

Since Burton's Wharf was used so extensively, there is a significant collection of artifacts associated with it. Divers can find

| Location: | In the middle of the crescent that forms South Manitou Harbor, at the end of an old roadway. [45 Deg. 01' 32"; 86 Deg. 05' 00"]. |
|---|---|
| Depth: | 5 - 45 feet. |
| Visibility: | 5 - 30 feet (depending upon depth). |
| Tips: | The bottom slopes steeply in this area. Divers must watch depth closely when exploring. |
| Level: | Basic to intermediate. |

these artifacts with relative ease because the wharf's position in South Manitou Harbor makes it somewhat stable.

Burton's Wharf served many large vessels through the years so its remains lie in water as deep as 45 feet.

# Crescent City Dock

NWMMM Photo

The JOSEPHINE DRESDEN was blown ashore at Crescent City. Wreckage still litters the west side of North Manitou Island.

Although only the tops of a few pilings can be seen protruding from the water, the Crescent City Dock was a substantial structure.

The dock served a lumbering boom town that had its heyday from 1907 to 1917. Beachcombers frequently discover new wreckage from several ships known to have foundered in the area. Perhaps the best-known ships to have wrecked at the dock is the JOSEPHINE DRESDEN.

Divers can explore an extensive system of underwater pilings that extend several hundred yards. The remains attract a variety of fish.

Divers can expect to find almost anything at the Crescent City Dock ruins. An anchor off the JOSEPHINE DRESDEN was once found in shallow water, but it was quickly covered by shifting sand before its exact location could noted by maritime archeologists.

Timbers of the JOSEPHINE DRESDEN and other ships litter the shoreline.

| | |
|---|---|
| **Location:** | On the west side of North Manitou Island where the remains of Crescent City can be found. [45 Deg. 06' 57''; 86 Deg. 03' 35'']. |
| **Depth:** | 3 - 20 feet. |
| **Visibility:** | 2 - 30 feet (Visibility reduced when waves create turbulent conditions in shallow water. Occurs when there is a strong westerly wind.) |
| **Tips:** | If arriving by boat, proceed into the area slowly because of many large boulders several hundred yards from shore. Once the dock ruins are located, come straight in, from west to east. |
| **Level:** | Basic. |

# Stormer Dock

Little evidence of this unbuoyed dock remains. It was one of two main docks that served North Manitou Island after 1920. The Stormer Dock was preferred by some ships because it offered slight protection from northern winds and the bottom was relatively stable.

Divers can expect to find old pilings and machinery at this site. Exploration may yield significant discoveries because many shipwrecks known to have been lost on the east side of North Manitou Island have yet to be found.

| Location: | Almost directly across from the old cemetery on North Manitou Island. [45 Deg. o5' 00"; 85 Deg. 58' 59"]. |
|---|---|
| **Depth:** | 5 - 12 feet. |
| **Visibility:** | 20 feet |
| **Tips:** | Look for evidence of pilings top–side. Bottom is relatively stable so visibility is generally very good. A slight current may carry divers northward. |
| **Level:** | Basic. |

# Pickard's Landing

Pickard's Landing includes several dock ruins that served North Manitou Island for more than 100 years.

This site was chosen for a dock because sand bars do not build

| Location: | About 200 yards north of the National Park Service dock on the east side of North Manitou Island. [45 Deg. 07' 15"; 85 Deg. 58' 30"]. |
|---|---|
| **Depth:** | 5 - 15 feet. |
| **Visibility:** | 10 - 20 feet. |
| **Tips:** | This is a popular skin diving site. If using the National Park Service dock, use caution because of shallow water surrounding that dock. |
| **Level:** | Basic. |

up directly east of it. Less than 100 yards either way, sand bars create shoals that must be avoided by those arriving by boat.

Pickard's Landing consists of an extensive matrix of pilings, many are visible from the surface. The site attracts many game fish and the sandy bottom may yield exciting discoveries.

# JAMES McBRIDE

The JAMES McBRIDE was a 121-foot brig built in New York in 1848. The JAMES McBRIDE carried many loads of grain between Chicago to Buffalo, but it's most notable cargo was of salt from the British West Indies. This load was delivered to Chicago late in 1848 and was touted as the first shipment direct from the Atlantic Ocean.

The ship collided with another and sank near Milwaukee, Wis. in 1855. It was raised and rebuilt and continued service for two more years.

On Oct. 19, 1857, while returning from a trip from Chicago to the Manitou islands, the JAMES McBRIDE was driven ashore at Sleeping Bear Bay by a gale.

Today, the JAMES McBRIDE can be seen from the top of dunes at Sleeping Bear point. Its hull, stern-first, protrudes from the base of a sand dune in about 15 feet of water. The sternpost is about five feet below the water's surface.

This shipwreck has been studied extensively by maritime archeologists. It is well-preserved by a layer of sand that sometimes obscures virtually all of the wreck.

This is a good wreck for skin divers to explore, especially if access is from the mainland. It is a long walk to the site from the nearest roadway. Visitors can walk from the U.S. Life Saving Service interpretive center at Glen Haven or the dune climb a few miles south.

To avoid a long walk, a boat is required. But it is worth a climb to the top of the nearest sand dune to look for other wreckage in the area. The JAMES McBRIDE is not the only ship lost at Sleeping Bear Point.

There is no opportunity for penetration diving.

| | |
|---|---|
| **Location:** | Off Sleeping Bear Point. [45 Deg. 02' 30"; 86 Deg. 00' 00"]. |
| **Depth:** | 5 - 15 feet. |
| **Visibility:** | 2 - 30 feet (Visibility reduced when waves create turbulent conditions in shallow water. Occurs when there is a strong westerly wind.) |
| **Tips:** | If this wreck is not visible on one trip, try it again. The sand shifts rapidly in this area and can uncover yet-undiscovered artifacts. |
| **Level:** | Basic. |

# J.S. CROUSE

The J.S. CROUSE was a small steam freighter of 90 feet. It was built in 1898 in Saugatuck, Mich. for the coarse freight and lumber trades.

The wooden-hulled J.S. CROUSE was purchased by Charles Anderson in 1907 and was used extensively in the Manitou Passage. In later years, he operated the small ship out of South Manitou Island, where he owned a farmed.

This boat was called a "rabbit" boat -- one that had a covered hold, exposed freight deck and machinery, crew quarters and pilot house at the stern. Eventually, the upper deck of the J.S. CROUSE was removed to accommodate cargoes of lumber and posts.

On Nov. 15, 1919, the J.S. CROUSE was loaded with lumber and potatoes at the Glen Haven dock. Shortly after departing for Traverse City, it caught fire and sank near the dock. Today, the remains of the J.S. CROUSE can be seen at the Glen Haven dock.

Wreckage from this ship, and perhaps two others, is strewn throughout the Glen Haven dock area. Sport divers are likely to find a variety of wreckage, including machinery, in the area.

There is no opportunity for penetration diving.

NWMMM Photo

The J.S. CROUSE was a small freighter -- 90 feet long -- that carried fruit, lumber and other cargoes before catching fire at the Glen Haven dock on Nov. 15, 1919.

| | |
|---|---|
| **Location:** | At Glen Haven dock off 209 in Leelanau County. [44 Deg. 55' 30 '' ; 86 Deg. 01' 30'']. |
| **Depth:** | 12 - 15 feet. |
| **Visibility:** | 10 - 30 feet |
| **Tips:** | Roadside parking available. Good skin diving site. |
| **Level:** | Basic. |

# RISING SUN

The RISING SUN was a 133-foot steamer used by the House of David colony on High Island to transport people and produce between the colony and the religious order's headquarters in Benton Harbor, Mich.

The wooden-hulled RISING SUN was built in Detroit in 1884

The RISING SUN aground off Pyramid Point in 1917. Today, the boilers and machinery make it an interesting dive site.

and was originally used as a passenger and freight vessel. It spent much of its time on the Great Lakes making trips between Cheboygan and Sault Ste. Marie.

In 1913, the ship was sold and served the colony until a storm blew up on Oct. 29, 1917. The ship left High Island loaded with potatoes, rutabagas and lumber and headed for a safe mainland port. But the captain became confused in a blinding fog and the RISING SUN ran aground at Pyramid Point.

The ship was abandoned with no loss of life. It was not salvaged but much of the wooden structure has broken up. A single-piston steeple tower engine lies on its side and heavy machinery and bilge framing remain. Occasionally, unusual artifacts emerge from the sandy bottom. On clear days, the remains of the RISING SUN can be seen from the beach at Pyramid Point.

There is no opportunity for penetration diving.

| | |
|---|---|
| **Location:** | North off Pyramid Point. |
| **Loran:** | 31799.6/48386.8 |
| **Depth:** | 7 - 12 feet. |
| **Visibility:** | 10 - 20 feet. |
| **Tips:** | The top of the boiler is about 7 feet below the water's surface. This is a good site for skin diving but access is best by boat. It is also a place for underwater photography. |
| **Level:** | Basic. |

# WALTER L. FROST

The WALTER L. FROST was a 235-foot steamer built in Detroit in 1883.

The wooden-hulled ship stranded on the south end of South Manitou Island in a dense fog on Nov. 4, 1903. It was headed north with a load of package freight.

The U.S. Life Saving Service saved the crew of 19 and attempted emergency salvage efforts but high seas turned all boats back. The WALTER L. FROST began to break up on Nov. 7 and was given up as a total loss.

The wreckage of the ship is scattered because in 1960, the FRANCISCO MORAZAN crushed the WALTER L. FROST when it ran aground a few hundred yards north. Today, the hull of the WALTER L. FROST is intact to the knees. There are many small spikes and pieces of metal on the bottom at the site.

There are no boilers, engines or heaving machinery. Some speculate that these items were salvaged since the ship lies in only 30 feet of water. There is no opportunity for penetration diving.

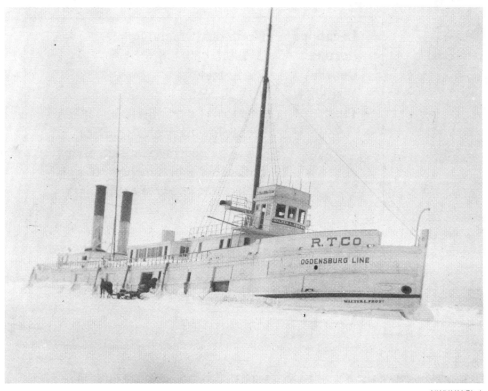

NWMMM Photo

The WALTER L. FROST aground during the winter of 1903-04. The steamer broke up and was later crushed when the FRANCISCO MORAZAN ran aground in 1960 at the same site.

| | |
|---|---|
| **Location:** | About 200 yards directly south of the FRANCISCO MORAZAN at the south end of South Manitou Island. Visible from the surface. |
| **Loran:** | 31859.1/48339.4 |
| **Depth:** | 25 - 30 feet. |
| **Visibility:** | 10 25 feet. |
| **Tips:** | A slight current from the west should be noted by divers. The wreck of the FRANCISCO MO-RAZAN attracts boaters. Watch for boat traffic. |
| **Level:** | Basic. |

# FRANCISCO MORAZAN

The 246-foot steel freighter FRANCISCO MORAZAN was built in Norway in 1922.

It had several owners and saw considerable service in the Atlantic Ocean. The FRANCISCO MORAZAN was bound for Rotterdam from Chicago when it wrecked in shallow water on the south end of South Manitou Island on Nov. 29, 1960.

The ship was carrying a cargo of shampoo, hides and canned chicken when it ran into an early blizzard. The U.S. Coast Guard saved the crew of 14 before the ship sustained heavy damage in the storm.

Some accounts say the captain was ordered to "plant" the FRANCISCO MORAZAN because it was too late to make it through the ice-clogged St. Lawrence Seaway. The owners, some say, did not want to pay the cost of maintaining the ship and crew through the winter.

The FRANCISCO MORAZAN is the most visited wreck of the Manitou Preserve. Many visitors come by boat and simply cruise around it. The ship rests in about 20 feet of water and much of the superstructure is above the water's surface.

Some visitors swim the 300 yards from shore to reach the ship. One death is reported of a teenager who overestimated his ability to swim to the wreck.

Today, the FRANCISCO MORAZAN is covered with guano from ring-billed gulls who find it a perfect perch. The super-structure also hosts several nesting double crested cormorants. Divers should avoid inspecting the superstructure because guano makes surfaces very slippery.

Because there are ragged metal edges and enclosed places, the FRANCISCO MORAZAN is not recommended for skin divers. It is, however, an excellent site for careful scuba divers.

Divers will find the hull broken and partially filled with sand. Much machinery remains available for inspection. The hull can be penetrated with machinery concentrated in the stern.

The FRANCISCO MORAZAN is a shallow but popular dive site on the southwest end of South Maniou Island. It is frequently visited by pleasure boats, gulls and is a nesting site for double crested cormorants.

| | |
|---|---|
| **Location:** | The wreck can be seen from the south end of South Manitou Island. [44 Deg. 59' 07 " ; 86 Deg. 08' 09"]. |
| **Loran:** | 31859.2/48339.3 |
| **Depth:** | 0 - 20 feet. |
| **Visibility:** | 10 - 25 feet. |
| **Tips:** | Watch for sharp metal edges. Not recommended for skin diving. |
| **Level:** | Basic. |

# P.J. RALPH

NWMMM Photo

The P.J. RALPH, after many years of service on the Great Lakes, foundered in South Manitou Harbor in 1924.

The P.J. RALPH was built in 1889 at Marine City, Mich. It was a 211-foot wooden-hulled steamer that hauled a variety of cargoes in the Great Lakes.

The ship sank after it became stranded on a shoal in South Manitou Harbor. No lives were lost in the wreck. The remains were dynamited by the U.S. Coast Guard shortly after its sinking because it was feared to be a hazard to navigation.

Today, the engine, boiler and scattered wreckage are all that is left of the P.J. RALPH. There is no opportunity for penetration diving.

| | |
|---|---|
| **Location:** | In southern end of South Manitou Harbor. [45 Deg. 01' 10''; 86 Deg. 06' 00'']. |
| **Depth:** | 16 - 40 feet. |
| **Visibility:** | 10 - 25 feet. |
| **Tips:** | Wreckage is scattered in a wide area on a drop off. |
| **Level:** | Basic. |

# CONGRESS

NWMMM Photo

The CONGRESS burned at South Manitou Harbor on Oct. 4, 1904. It was set adrift to save the wharf and sank in about 160 feet of water.

The CONGRESS was built in 1867 and at 265 feet, was the longest propeller on the Great Lakes for eight years.

The wooden-hulled ship made many trips between Buffalo, N.Y. and Milwaukee, Wis. and Chicago. In its early years, it was rebuilt several times.

In 1903, the CONGRESS was rebuilt into a coarse freighter and was used in the lumber trade. On Oct. 4, 1904, loaded with lumber, the CONGRESS caught fire at a dock at South Manitou Harbor. The ship was cut loose to save the wharf.

The CONGRESS sank in 165 feet of water -- the deepest part of South Manitou Harbor. Some penetration diving is possible in a   forward cabin that escaped the flames.

The hull is intact with machinery, anchors and boilers still in place. This wreck has been dubbed the "burbot hotel" because of a high concentration of the fish.

| Location: | In South Manitou Harbor on the east side of South Manitou Island. |
| --- | --- |
| Loran: | 31834.3/48330.4 |
| Depth: | 135 - 165 feet. |
| Visibility: | 5 - 15 feet. |
| Tips: | Wreckage from other wrecks may be in the area. South Manitou Harbor is known to host several shipwrecks as a result of fierce storms in the late 1800's. |
| Level: | Intermediate to advanced. |

# H.D. MOORE

The H.D. MOORE was a two-masted schooner built in 1874 in Saugatuck, Mich.

The H.D. MOORE saw many years of service as a freighter until it attempted to make South Manitou Harbor on Sept. 10, 1907. Loaded with lumber, the ship stranded on Gull Point on South Manitou Island in a fierce thunderstorm.

No one was lost in the wreck and 45,000 feet of lumber and some of the gear was saved. The shipwreck lies in about 22 feet of water north of Gull Point and it is sometimes completely covered by sand.

| Location: | North of Gull Point at South Manitou Island. [45 Deg. 02' 01"; 86 Deg. 04' 45"]. |
| --- | --- |
| Depth: | 20 - 25 feet. |
| Visibility: | 10 - 25 feet. |
| Tips: | Wreckage may be completely or partially obscured by sand. The wreck, if not covered by sand, is readily visible from the surface. |
| Level: | Basic. |

# WILLIAM T. GRAVES

The WILLIAM T. GRAVES was the first bulk freighter on the Great Lakes. It was a 1,075-ton steamer that was driven ashore on North Manitou Island in a storm on Oct. 31, 1885.

At the time of her sinking, the WILLIAM T. GRAVES was carrying a cargo of corn. It wrecked on or near North Manitou Shoal. Wreckage of the ship is scattered on the south end of the island on the shoal in shallow water. Some sections are relatively large -- 158 feet -- but there is no opportunity for penetration diving.

| | |
|---|---|
| **Location:** | On North Manitou Shoal on the south end of North Manitou Island about 1/2 mile from shore. Wreck site is buoyed. |
| **Depth:** | 15 - 20 feet. |
| **Visibility:** | 15 - 30 feet. |
| **Tips:** | This wreck can be spotted in calm water from the surface. There are many other large pieces of wreckage in the vicinity but not all is from this ship. Some pieces can be located by climbing "Old Baldy," a sand dune on the island. |
| **Level:** | Basic. |

# SUPPLY

The SUPPLY was a wooden-hulled schooner bound for Leland with a load of bricks when it ran into an October storm in 1862.

The ship was lost off vessel point and was periodically visited by sport divers, but was lost for many years to shifting sand.

Recently, much of the ship has been uncovered. Maritime archeologists have recently conducted research on the ship to gather more information about how it wrecked.

Hundreds of bricks remain on the wreck -- many still stacked in what remains of the broken hull.

| | |
|---|---|
| **Location:** | East of Vessel Point on the east side of North Manitou Island. Wreck site is buoyed. |
| **Depth:** | 12 - 15 feet. |
| **Visibility:** | 10 - 20 feet. |
| **Tips:** | Divers should note a slight current to the north. Wreckage can be found north of this site but may not be associated with this vessel. |
| **Level:** | Basic. |

# MONTAUK

The MONTAUK was carrying a cargo of coal from Buffalo, N.Y. to Chicago when it ran into a northerly gale on Nov. 24, 1882. The schooner, which was built in 1863 in New York, ran aground on the northeast end of North Manitou Island.

The ship was a total wreck as it was battered and broken by heavy seas. No lives were lost.

| | |
|---|---|
| **Location:** | North of Vessel Point on the northeast end of North Manitou Island. [45 Deg. 09' 58"; 85 Deg. 59' 48"]. Wreckage can be seen from surface. |
| **Depth:** | 15 - 35 feet. |
| **Visibility:** | 10 - 25 feet. |
| **Tips:** | Divers should note a slight current to the north. |
| **Level:** | Basic. |

Today, the MONTAUK is little more than a collection of large pieces of wooden hull north of Vessel Point. There is no opportunity for penetration diving. Divers exploring this area may discover one of several wrecks known to have gone down in the area, including a steel landing barge.

# JOSEPHINE DRESDEN

NWMMM Photo

The JOSEPHINE DRESDEN wrecked at Crescent City when a sudden storm arose in 1907.

The JOSEPHINE DRESDEN wrecked at the site of the Crescent City Dock late in 1907.

The two-masted schooner was built in 1852 at Michigan City, Ind. and was operated by Charles Anderson. Anderson used the boat to transport freight from the Manitou islands to various ports in northern Lake Michigan.

The JOSEPHINE DRESDEN gained notoriety as the first ship on the Great Lakes with an auxiliary gasoline engine. That engine was added shortly before the JOSEPHINE DRESDEN was lost.

The ship was at anchor at Crescent City preparing to take on cargo when a storm came up. The JOSEPHINE DRESDEN shifted on her anchors and the gasoline engine could not be started in time to save her.

Divers visiting the Crescent City Dock will find timbers from the ship. Anchor chain and an anchor are known to be in the vicinity. Beachcombers frequently find large timbers that are likely the remains of the JOSEPHINE DRESDEN.

| | |
|---|---|
| **Location:** | Off the Crescent City Dock on the west side of North Manitou Island. Several pilings are visible above the water. [45 Deg. 06' 57"; 86 Deg. 03' 35"]. |
| **Depth:** | 5 - 20 feet. |
| **Visibility:** | 2 - 30 feet (Visibility reduced when waves create turbulent conditions in shallow water. Oc-curs when there is a strong west erly wind.) |
| **Tips:** | Wreckage is covered and uncov-ered periodically by shifting sand. If arriving by boat, watch for large boulders on either side of site. ome to Crescent City Dock straight from west to east to avoid obstructions. |
| **Level:** | Basic. |

# Shoal Wreckage/North Manitou Shoal Light

North Manitou Shoal, located on the south end of North Manitou Island, is littered with wreckage from a variety of ships. Some of the wreckage, like that of the WILLIAM T. GRAVES, has been identified, but much of it remains pieces of unknown ships.

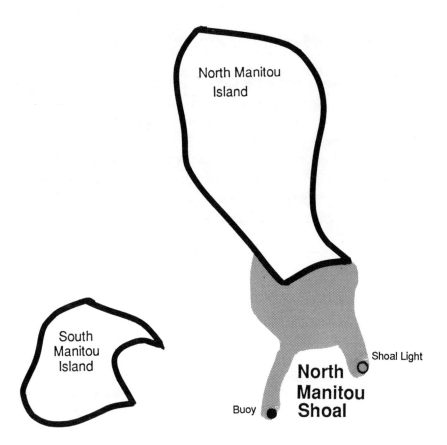

Some of these pieces are large and worth visiting. Most wreckage lies in 20 feet of very clear water. Some pieces of wreckage can be spotted from the top of "Old Baldy," a sand dune on North Manitou Island.

The bottom is generally rocky. It is an excellent area for skin divers. Access may be by boat or from the south shore of the island.

The North Manitou Shoal Light, referred to as the "crib," is also a good exploration site for sport divers. There are many, very large boulders in this area and large schools of fish are attracted to the structure.

# WESTMORELAND

The 200-foot steamer WESTMORELAND is one of the most sought-after ships of the Great Lakes.

Although there is no evidence that the wooden-hulled ship was lost with nothing more than a cargo of oats and whiskey, rumors persist that the ship was carrying a $100,000 gold payroll. That rumor has kept treasure hunters busy combing the Manitou Passage with sophisticated underwater metal detectors and side-scan sonars.

The WESTMORELAND was built in 1853 to carry passengers and freight between Chicago and Buffalo, N.Y. On Dec. 3, 1854, the ship cleared Milwaukee for Port Washington but ran into a blizzard and returned to Milwaukee. A second start was made on Dec. 6 and a snow storm with heavy seas came up from the northeast.

On Dec. 7, the WESTMORELAND sprang a leak and became overburdened with ice about 14 miles south of South Manitou Island. Early in the morning on Dec. 8, lifeboats were launched. There were seven survivors but 17 men -- all lumberjacks -- perished in the wreck.

The survivors landed at the mouth of Otter Creek in Platte Bay and stayed several days. The survivors of the wreck included the first mate of the WESTMORELAND, Paul Pelkey. In 1872, Pelkey is rumored to have salvaged the engines and boilers off the WESTMORELAND. Others say he spent much of his life searching for a gold payroll headed to a northern Michigan lumber camp.

The remains of the WESTMORELAND have never been found. Platte Bay has been searched extensively by treasure hunters but nothing has been found.

# Emergencies

In the event of a diving emergency, call the Leelanau County Sheriff's Department at: (616) 256-9829. If you are away from a telephone but have access to a vhf radio, call the U.S. Coast Guard on channel 16. Describe the nature of the emergency and follow instructions.

The U.S. Coast Guard Air Station at Traverse City has helicopters that can respond to emergencies if commercial medical care is unavailable or insufficient. Because there is a variety of medical help available in the area, it is best to first call the Leelanau County Sheriff's Department. If you are unsuccessful or unable to call, contact the Coast Guard directly.

If you are unable to contact the U.S. Coast Guard, contact the Sleeping Bear Dunes National Lakeshore. Some ranger stations monitor  vhf channel 16. Rangers are trained to provide emergency assistance.

# Accommodations

Lodging is available in Frankfort, Empire, Glen Arbor, Leland, Northport and surrounding communities. There is no shortage of rooms, but in July and August, availability may be limited. It is best to obtain reservations during those months.

Camping is permitted on several mainland campground associated with the Sleeping Bear Dunes National Lakeshore. There are also several private campgrounds near Leland, Empire and Frankfort.

Camping is permitted on most of North Manitou Island but there are virtually no amenities. Limited services are available on South Manitou Island, which has three campgrounds.

Check with the Sleeping Bear Dunes National Lakeshore to determine what campgrounds and facilities are available in the park.

Information about overnight accommodations can be obtained by contacting the West Michigan Tourist Association, 136 E. Fulton, Grand Rapids, MI 49503, (616) 456-8557.

# Important Addresses/Phone Numbers

Sleeping Bear Dunes National Lakeshore
PO Box 277
Empire, MI 49630
(616) 326-5134 (Empire Headquarters)
(616) 334-3976 (South Manitou Island)

Manitou Island Transit
(616) 256-9061 or
(616) 271-4217

Leelanau County Sheriff's Department
112 Chandler
Lake Leelanau, MI 49653
(616) 256-9829

U.S. Coast Guard Air Station
Traverse City, MI 49684
(616) 922-8210

Benzie County Sheriff's Department
7157 Crystal Ave.
Beulah, MI 49617
(616) 941-7940

**Charter Operators:**

Inland Seas Marine
PO Box 389
Frankfort, MI 49635
(616) 352-6106

Scuba North, Inc.
13380 West Bay Shore Dr.
Traverse City, MI 49684
(616) 947-2520

John P. Voss
70 S. Long Lake Road
Traverse City, MI 49684
(616) 943-9158 o9r
(616) 275-6226

Tom Wigton
4298 Bow Road
Maple City, MI 49664

Rick Bailey
PO Box 108
Empire, MI 49630
(616) 326-5445

# Marquette Preserve

The Marquette County Bottomland Preserve consists of two units -- Marquette and Huron Islands. The preserve contains eight major shipwrecks.

This area is important historically because Marquette, the largest city in the Upper Peninsula, played a crucial role in the development of the region. Marquette was a busy port and served as the loading site for tons of iron ore.

Marquette also served as a trans-shipping port, where large ships would unload their cargoes to smaller vessels for delivery to other Lake Superior ports.

Because this was a busy shipping area, there are many unmarked docks that can provide excellent skin and scuba diving experiences. Diving from shore may also yield discoveries of remains from many schooners that were blown ashore during storms. Many of these ships were looted and then left to the elements 100 or more years ago.

Although Marquette was a busy harbor and port, unmarked shoals made navigation difficult and left little room for error. One schooner captain refused to enter the harbor and anchored offshore.

Because there are few harbors in this region, many ships caught in rough seas raced to Marquette for refuge -- a race they sometimes lost.

The Marquette County Bottomland Preserve is one of Michigan's newest. Although Loran coordinates are not readily available for popular dive sites, most such sites are buoyed. Divers should remember that Lake Superior remains very cold even in the hottest summers, so a drysuit is recommended.

The impact of its maritime heritage is not lost on Marquette. The Marquette Maritime Museum offers exhibits displaying the maritime heritage of the region. It is located on Lakeshore Boulevard.

The U.S. Coast Guard Station is located across from the maritime museum. This station features a lighthouse that was erected in 1866. Group tours of the lighthouse can be arranged by contacting the U.S. Coast Guard. McCarty's Cove, a city park and beach adjacent to the station off Lakeshore Boulevard, is a good place to photograph the lighthouse.

Visitors to the Marquette area will also find a variety of cultural activities scheduled for summer months. It is an area that offers many non-diving attractions. More information about those activities is available from the Marquette Area Chamber of Commerce, (906) 226-6591.

# Boating

Like boating anywhere on the Great Lakes, boaters in the Marquette area should watach for sudden storms and fog. A good navigational chart showing reefs and shoals is a good idea because there are many underwater dangers that can arise unexpectedly -- even far from shore.

Marquette is still a busy port so boaters must be aware of shipping channels and keep an eye out for large ships.

There are two main boat launching facilities. One is located a mile north of the city of Marquette at Hot Pond Beach. Marquette also offers a marina with fuel and transient accommodations.

A boat launch is also located at Huron Bay in northeastern Baraga County. The launch can be used to access the Huron Islands Unit of the bottomland preserve. It is off Skanee Road near the intersection of Town Road.

Although the number of dive charters in the area is limited, many sportfishing charter operators are willing to guide divers to the dive sites in this region.

# CHARLES J. KERSHAW

The wooden steamer CHARLES J. KERSHAW was headed west from Sault Ste. Marie with the schooners MOONLIGHT and KENT in tow on Sept. 28, 1895.

That evening, as the ships approached Marquette, a gale blew up and early the next morning, the CHARLES J. KERSHAW was nearly in the Marquette Harbor when its boiler exploded. The two schooners ran aground near shore and the crews were able to leap to the beach.

The 223-foot CHARLES J. KERSHAW, however, struck a reef less than a mile from the mouth of the Chocolay (Carp) River. Through a heroic effort of the U.S. Life Saving Service from Marquette, the entire crew of the CHARLES J. KERSHAW was saved.

The ship took a severe beating in the storm and sank in about 35 feet of water. The schooners were removed from the beach, but the CHARLES J. KERSHAW, which was built in Bangor, Mich. in 1874, was a total loss. It had become wedged in the rocks and a large hole in the bow was discovered after the storm.

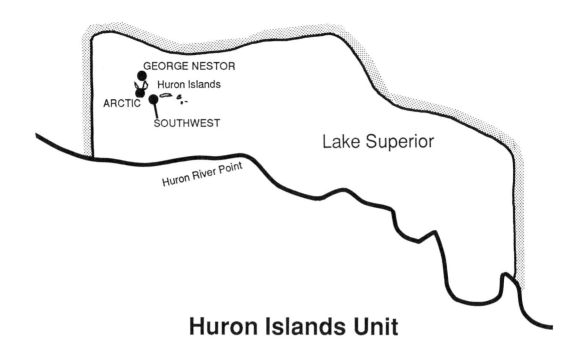

## Huron Islands Unit

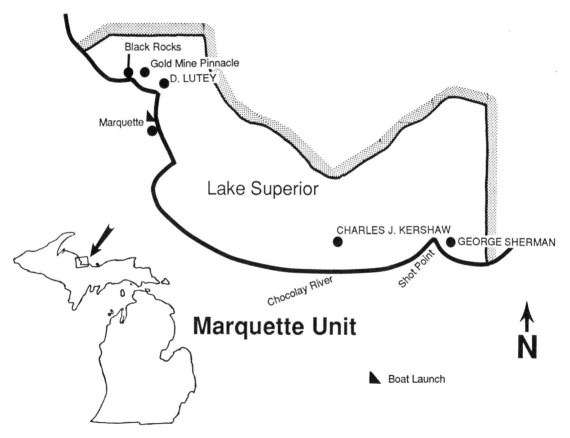

## Marquette Unit

# Marquette Bottomland Preserve
## (144 square miles)

In 1902, a salvage effort was mounted to recover iron from the machinery of the ship. Much dynamite was used in the salvage operation, but little iron was actually brought up. As a result of the operation, however, the remains of the CHARLES J. KERSHAW are scattered widely.

Large pieces of the hull can be seen as well as many small pieces of broken metal. Part of the ill-fated boiler is intact. There is no penetration diving possible at this site.

| | |
|---|---|
| **Location:** | Near the exposed rocks of Chocolay Reef at the mouth of Chocolay River. |
| **Depth:** | 25 - 35 feet. |
| **Visibility:** | 10 - 40 feet. At times, the condition of the Chocolay River will reduce visibility to 10 feet. |
| **Tips:** | Wreckage is scattered over a wide area. Exploring may yield discoveries of interesting artifacts. |
| **Level:** | Basic. |

# GEORGE SHERMAN

The GEORGE SHERMAN was a 140-foot schooner headed for Marquette with a load of coal when it ran into a fierce storm on Oct. 22, 1887. A blinding snowstorm caused the captain to lose his bearings and run aground at Shot Point.

The crew was able to make it to shore in a yawl and eventually made it to Marquette.

The GEORGE SHERMAN was built in Cleveland, Ohio in 1862 and was extensively rebuilt in 1878, 1880 and 1884. Although

| | |
|---|---|
| **Location:** | East of Shot Point. |
| **Depth:** | 15 - 25 feet. |
| **Visibility:** | 20 - 40 feet. |
| **Tips:** | This is a good skin diving site. Many small artifacts may be discovered in this area. |
| **Level:** | Basic. |

minor salvage efforts were made, it was considered a total loss as a result of extensive damage suffered during the storm.

Today, only large sections of the broken hull remain. There is no penetration diving at this site.

# D. LUTEY

The D. LEUTY was a 179-foot steamer built in 1882 in Lorain, Ohio. The ship was bound for Pequaming with a load of lumber when it ran into a snowstorm on Oct. 31, 1911.

Although there were no waves, the captain of the D. LEUTY was blinded by thick snow. The ship ran aground at the Marquette lighthouse. The captain alleged that the lighthouse crew failed to sound its fog whistle.

Attempts were made to pull the D. LEUTY off the rocks but a storm arose from the northeast and made salvage impossible. The ship was abandoned to the elements and sank in about 30 feet of water.

After the storm, most of the ship's machinery, engine, boiler and equipment were recovered. Part of the stern was recovered and converted into a summer cabin on Middle Island Point.

All that remains of the D. LEUTY are pieces of the wooden hull. Some pieces are partially buried in sand.

| | |
|---|---|
| **Location:** | At Lighthouse Point at Marquette's lower harbor. |
| **Depth:** | 25 - 30 feet. |
| **Visibility:** | 20 - 40 feet. |
| **Level:** | Basic. |

# Gold Mine Pinnacle

This dive site is popular because of unusual geologic formations off Presque Isle Park. Many large gamefish, such as trout and salmon, are attracted to the site and can be observed closely by patient divers.

Where there are fish, there are fishermen. This site gets its name from the bounty of fishing tackle tangled in the rocks.

Travel Bureau Photo

The lighthouse at Marquette warned many sailors of the dangers of the area.

| Location: | Northeast of Presque Isle Black Rocks, 1/4 mile off shore. |
|---|---|
| Depth: | 50 - 130 feet. |
| Visibility: | 20 - 40 feet. |
| Tips: | Watch for fishing boats. Take a dive knife in case of entanglement in fishing line. Access by boat. Do not attempt to swim to site. |
| Level: | Intermediate to advanced. |

# Black Rocks

This site is popular among divers interested in unusual geologic formations. Some of the oldest rock formations in Michigan are at this site at the northernmost tip of Presque Isle Park.

Black Rocks is accessible from shore and offers spectacular skin diving. It is also a popular night-diving site.

| Location: | Northernmost tip of Presque Isle Park. |
|---|---|
| Depth: | 10 - 50 feet. |
| Visibility: | 20 - 40 feet. |
| Tips: | Watch for schools of gamefish. Good place for underwater photography. |
| Level: | Basic to intermediate. |

# GEORGE NESTOR

The GEORGE NESTOR was a 207-foot, schooner-barge that broke her tow line in a storm on April 30, 1909. The ship was in the tow of the steamer SCHOOLCRAFT.

The GEORGE NESTOR was driven onto Huron Island where it broke up rapidly. Seven of the ship's crew, including her captain, were lost in the disaster.

The GEORGE NESTOR was constructed in Baraga of Upper

Peninsula lumber and iron.

Sections of the hull are scattered over a 100-yard radius. Because this dive site is relatively remote, many artifacts remain.

| | |
|---|---|
| **Location:** | Near lighthouse on Huron Island. |
| **Depth:** | 30 - 40 feet. |
| **Visibility:** | 20 - 40 feet. |
| **Tips:** | Remember that it is illegal to remove artifacts. |
| **Level:** | Basic. |

# ARCTIC

The steamer ARCTIC was a 237-foot sidewheeler that wrecked at Huron Island in a fog on May 28, 1860.

The ARCTIC struck the rocks with great force and was quickly abandoned. A storm the following day damaged the ship beyond hope of pulling it off. The ship's machinery was recovered.

The remains of the ship are badly broken by wave and ice. But there are many artifacts still at the site but sand covers parts of the wreck in shallow water.

| | |
|---|---|
| **Location:** | West side of Huron Island. |
| **Depth:** | 5 - 150 feet. |
| **Visibility:** | 20 - 40 feet. |
| **Tips:** | This is a good skin diving site. |
| **Level:** | Basic to advanced. |

# SOUTHWEST

The schooner SOUTHWEST was running in heavy fog and smoke on Sept. 18, 1898 when it ran aground 1 1/2 miles southeast of the largest of the Huron Islands. The captain charged that the fog whistle was not sounding at the time of the accident.

The 137-foot SOUTHWEST was returning from a run to the lower lakes with a load of stone. The remains of the wreck have settled in about 100 feet of water. Pieces of hull are scattered but many artifacts can be found. Many fittings are still within a 100-foot radius of the main hull sections.

No penetration diving is possible at this site.

| | |
|---|---|
| **Location:** | 1 1/2 miles southeast of Huron Island. |
| **Depth:** | 90 - 110 feet. |
| **Visibility:** | 20 - 40 feet. |
| **Tips:** | Remember that it is illegal to remove artifacts. |
| **Level:** | Intermediate to advanced. |

# Emergencies

In the event of an injury, it is best to notify the U.S. Coast Guard Station at Marquette by vhf channel 16. The Coast Guard can prepare to meet the incoming injured.

Marquette General Hospital, which has a single-place recompression chamber, is about 1 1/2 miles from the Coast Guard Station. If additional chamber space is required, air transportation to St. Luke's Hospital in Milwaukee, Wis. will be arranged.

Extra patrols are made by the Coast Guard Auxiliary during summer weekends and holidays.

# Accommodations

Marquette is a popular tourist destination because it offers many attractions, including the U.S. Coast Guard Station, lighthouse, Marquette Maritime Museum, Michigan Iron Industry Museum, parks, scenic views and a zoo.

Because of this tourist activity, there are many motels and hotels in the Marquette area. Information about overnight accommodations can be obtained from the Marquette Area Chamber of Commerce, (906) 226-6591 or the Marquette County Tourism Council, (906) 228-7740.

Campgrounds are uncommon in this region. But for those willing to "rough it," there are many miles of beaches and acres of woodland in the Copper County State Forest and the Ottawa National Forest just outside of Marquette where campers can stay overnight undisturbed.

# Important Addresses/Phone Numbers

Marquette County Sheriff's
Department
Marquette, MI 49855
(906) 228-6980

U.S. Coast Guard Station
Marquette, MI 49855
(906) 226-3312

Marquette General Hospital
515 W. College Ave.
Marquette, MI 49855
(906) 228-9440
(800) 562-9753

Marquette Area Chamber
of Commerce
501 South Front St.
Marquette, MI 49855
(906) 226-6591

Marquette County Tourism
Council
501 S. Front St.
Marquette, MI 49855
(906) 228-7740
(800) 544-4321

Upper Peninsula Travel
and Recreation Association
Box 400
Iron Mountain, MI 49801
(906) 774-5480
(800) 562-7134

**Charter Operator:**

Tomasi Tours, Inc.
455 East Ridge St.
Marquette, MI 49855
(906) 225-0410

# Sanilac Shores

The Sanilac Shores Bottomland Preserve includes 163 square miles of Lake Huron bottomland. The site contains a collection of 10 shipwrecks in 15 to 100 feet of water.

Ships went down in this area primarily as a result of accidents or rough weather. The Sanilac Shores Preserve is enjoying increasing popularity among divers because of its proximity to the bulk of the state's population and the discovery of new shipwrecks in the area.

The preserve was established following the discovery of the location of the wreck of the REGINA. Initially, state officials considered designating that single site as a bottomland preserve. But interested sport divers recognized the need to have a much broader area designated so that other valuable dive sites could be protected.

Visibility is variable in this area because the bottom is frequently of fine silt. Wave action and currents sometime disturb these fine sediments and cause reduced visibility. But visibility is rarely less than four feet. Sometimes, visibility is as much as 25 feet.

A group of local sport divers and charter operators are competent amateur maritime archeologists. Much of the information known about the shipwrecks in this area is the result of their careful

research. That group hopes to establish an interpretive center so that divers and non-divers alike will be able to learn about and enjoy the maritime heritage represented by the shipwrecks of this region.

August through October are the best months to dive this area because of increased visibility during that period.

An informative booklet, "Shipwrecks of Sanilac," contains many historical and underwater photos of the wrecks found in this bottomland preserve. The book is available through dive stores or from Lakeshore Charters & Marine Exploration, Inc., 4658 S. Lakeshore, Lexington, MI 48450.

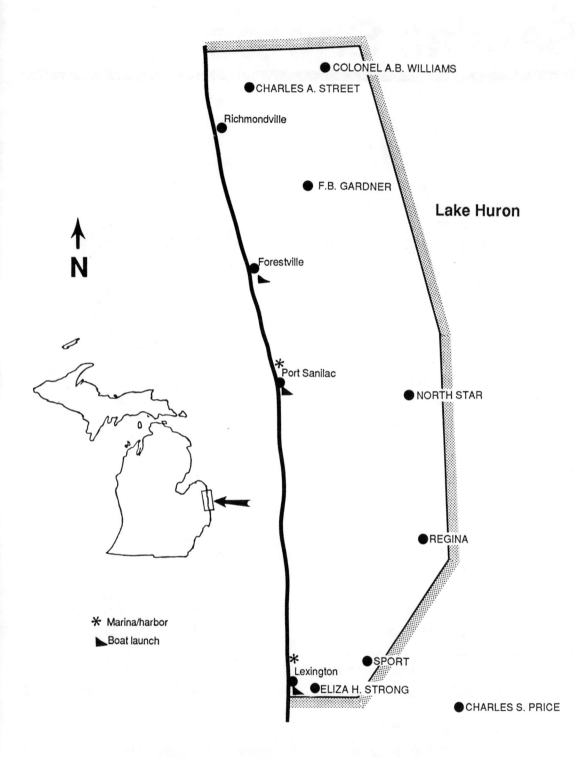

# Sanilac Shores Bottomland Preserve
## (163 square miles)

# Boating

Aside from shipping channel traffic, boaters in this region have no unusual concerns. As always, boaters must be aware of other boat traffic and sudden weather changes.

Marinas with complete services are available in Lexington and Port Sanilac. They offer transient accommodations, gas, water, electricity, restrooms, showers and monitor vhf channel 16.

Boat launching facilities are available at or near both marinas as well as at the Sanilac State Park in Forestville.

# COLONEL A.B. WILLIAMS

The A.B. WILLIAMS was a 110-foot schooner lost in a storm in 1864 while carrying a cargo of coal. It is the oldest shipwreck of the Sanilac Preserve.

The wreck was discovered in 1957 when a diver went down to investigate tangled commercial fishing nets. The A.B. WILLIAMS was found in about 85 feet of water, sitting upright in excellent condition.

Although the stern has fallen away and the masts and cabin are missing, the rest of the wreck is intact with a variety of equipment still on the deck. In the 1960s, divers removed anchors, wheel and steering gear. One of the anchors off the A.B. WILLIAMS is displayed at the Sanilac Historical Museum in Port Sanilac.

Divers can penetrate portions of the cargo hold.

| | |
|---|---|
| **Location:** | About 12.5 miles northeast of Port Sanilac. |
| **Loran:** | 30779.1/49407.2 |
| **Depth:** | 75 - 85 feet. |
| **Visibility:** | 5 - 25 feet. |
| **Tips:** | Because the stern has fallen away, part of the aft cargo area is exposed and provides interesting diving. |
| **Level:** | Intermediate. |

# CHARLES A. STREET

The CHARLES A. STREET was a 165-foot steamer built in Grand Haven in 1888. The ship carried lumber and coal and often towed barges.

The ship was southbound, heading for Toledo, Ohio on July 20, 1908, when the ship suddenly caught fire. The captain was able to bring the CHARLES A. STREET up on a reef about a mile north of Richmondville. No lives were lost in the disaster.

The remains of the ship lie in about 15 feet of water with the top of the engine about four feet from the water's surface. The boiler is missing but some ribs and decking remain. There is no penetration diving at this site.

| | |
|---|---|
| **Location:** | About 11.5 miles north of Port Sanilac. |
| **Loran:** | 30818.2/49413.1 |
| **Depth:** | 4 - 15 feet. |
| **Visibility:** | 5 - 25 feet. |
| **Tips:** | This is a good skin diving site. Be— cause it is shallow and there is ample light, underwater photographers find it appealing. |
| **Level:** | Basic. |

# F.B. GARDNER

The F.B. GARDNER was lost when it suddenly caught fire while in tow on Sept. 15, 1904. But before the F.B. GARDNER was lost, it saw many changes during its nearly five decades as a Great Lakes vessel.

The ship was built in 1855 in Sheboygan, Wis. as a 139-foot brig. Eleven years later, the ship was converted to a bark. Six years later, in 1872, the F.B. GARDNER was converted into a schooner. In 1879, the ship was lengthened to become a 177-foot barge.

The F.B. GARDNER burned and sank in 50 feet of water in the shipping lane. Because there was only 34 feet of water over the wreck, it was considered a hazard to navigation and dynamited.

Today, the F.B. GARDNER is scattered but equipment at the site makes the dive interesting. The equipment includes a large windlass with chain.

There are no opportunities for penetration diving.

| | |
|---|---|
| **Location:** | 6.5 miles northeast of Port Sanilac. |
| **Loran:** | 30802.4/49407.2 |
| **Depth:** | 50 - 55 feet. |
| **Visibility:** | 5 - 25 feet. |
| **Tips:** | Wreckage is scattered. Search the area to find a variety of equipment and artifacts. |
| **Level:** | Intermediate. |

# NORTH STAR

The NORTH STAR was a 300-foot steamer that was built in Cleveland, Ohio in 1888. It had a steel hull and in its first year on the Great Lakes was involved in a collision with CHARLES J. SHEFIELD, which sank without loss of life.

In 1898, the NORTH STAR ran aground to avoid another collision in the St. Mary's River. On Nov. 25, 1908, the NORTH STAR was headed to Buffalo, N.Y. from Duluth, Minn. with a load of grain and shingles when it ran into a thick fog.

| | |
|---|---|
| **Location:** | About 5.5 miles southeast of Port Sanilac, 10 miles northeast of Lexington. |
| **Loran:** | 30787.3/49508.1 |
| **Depth:** | 85 - 100 feet. |
| **Visibility:** | 2 - 20 feet. |
| **Tips:** | Visibility is variable on this wreck, a line reel is advised so that divers can locate ascent line. Divers should be aware of gill netting on certain parts of the wreck. |
| **Level:** | Intermediate to advanced. |

In this fog, the package freighter NORTH STAR struck its sister ship, the NORTHERN QUEEN. The NORTH STAR was struck on her starboard bow and sank quickly, but there was no loss of life.

The ship lies upright, in two pieces, with the pilot house intact on the bow and the engine and boiler on the stern. Divers can explore the pilot house and cargo holds of the NORTH STAR.

# REGINA

Institute for Great Lakes Research Photo

The REGINA was a 250-foot freighter that sank in the "big storm" of 1913.

The REGINA was a 250-foot, steel-hulled package freighter built in Scotland in 1907. Although the REGINA served Great Lakes ports without incident, its demise caused wide speculation that continues today.

The REGINA was caught in the "big storm" of Nov. 9, 1913.

**REGINA**
*Built 1907 - Sank Nov. 9, 1913*
*Discovered by Garry Biniecki*
*July 1, 1986*

Pat Stayer Graphic

The ship was lost with all hands and days later, bodies washed ashore from the REGINA and other ships, including the CHARLES S. PRICE. Speculation began when it was reported that at least one body of a CHARLES S. PRICE sailor washed ashore wearing a REGINA life preserver.

Some theorized that the two ships collided during the storm and sailors from the CHARLES S. PRICE managed to grab REGINA life preservers. But there was no evidence of a collision on the wreck of the CHARLES S. PRICE. The condition of the REGINA was a mystery until it was discovered in 1986.

Although there is no evidence of a collision, there is a hole in the bottom of the ship's hull. Some divers now speculate that the captain of the REGINA tried to run close to shore to find shelter from the raging storm when it ran aground.

When the REGINA sank, it was at anchor with engines and electrical system shut down. This indicates an attempt by the crew to abandon the ship.

The REGINA rests upside down in about 80 feet of water. The keel is about 55 feet from the surface. There is a 56-foot hole in the REGINA'S port side that exposes the cargo holds.

A permit was issued to salvage part of the cargo, but little of value was removed from the ship. Key artifacts, such as the REGINA's bell, were removed for display in area museums. The REGINA is generally considered one of the most attractive dive sites in the Great Lakes because it is a large ship that was conserved for sport divers.

This wreck site offers penetration diving.

| | |
|---|---|
| **Location:** | About 6.5 miles northeast of Lexington, about 7.5 miles southeast of Port Sanilac. |
| **Loran:** | 30801.7/49534.9 |
| **Depth:** | 55 - 80 feet. |
| **Visibility:** | 5 - 25 feet. |
| **Tips:** | Cargo is scattered near the wreck. Remember that collecting is forbidden. |
| **Level:** | Intermediate to advanced. |

# SPORT

The SPORT was built in 1873 in Wyandotte, Mich. It was a 57-foot, steel-hulled tug designed for the lumber industry.

The SPORT started her career towing lumber-laden schooners around the Ludington, Mich. harbor. After two years, a slowdown in the economy forced the sale of the tug and it was significantly rebuilt. In 1913, the SPORT was sold to a Port Huron towing company.

On Dec. 13, 1920, after years of reliable service from Detroit to southern Lake Huron, the SPORT found herself in heavy seas. The boat was abandoned when its boilers went out. The captain and crew managed to row three hours to shore near Lexington.

The SPORT was discovered in 1987 in about 50 feet of water with all but its cabin intact. The port rail is 33 feet from the surface. The boat lies upright with a starboard list. Machinery, engine and boiler are intact within the hull. Many artifacts are on the SPORT's deck on within a few feet on the bottom.

The SPORT is a popular dive site because of its relatively shallow depth. The SPORT can be explored on a single tank. There is limited opportunity for penetration diving.

| | |
|---|---|
| **Location:** | About three miles east of Lexington. |
| **Loran:** | 30824.9/49569.2 |
| **Depth:** | 30 - 50 feet. |
| **Visibility:** | 5 - 25 feet. |
| **Tips:** | The propeller, steering chain and wheel lie a few feet from the wreck. |
| **Level:** | Intermediate. |

# ELIZA H. STRONG

The ELIZA STRONG was a 205-foot steamer built in Marine City, Mich. in 1874. It was a ship that sunk three times.

On May 3, 1895, the ELIZA STRONG ran aground and burned in Lake Erie. The ship was raised and refitted in Buffalo, N.Y. in 1899. Two years later, the ship foundered in rough weather in Lake Superior, but was raised again.

On Oct. 26, 1904, luck ran out for the ELIZA STRONG. The ship had a schooner in tow when it caught fire near Lexington. The crew of 13 was saved.

The ELIZA STRONG burned to the waterline and sank in about 25 feet of water, a little more than 4,000 feet from the Lexington dock. The machinery was salvaged and the U.S. Army Corps of Engineers dynamited the wreck as a navigational hazard.

The ELIZA STRONG lies upright with keel and some decking intact. There is much wreckage scattered throughout the site. There is no opportunity for penetration diving.

| | |
|---|---|
| **Location:** | Less than one mile east of Lexington dock. |
| **Loran:** | 30847.0/49570.4 |
| **Depth:** | 25 - 30 feet. |
| **Tips:** | This is a good dive for beginners but visibility can be reduced depending on weather conditions. |
| **Level:** | Basic. |

# CHARLES S. PRICE

The CHARLES S. PRICE was a 504-foot freighter that was built in 1910. It became one of many victims of the November 1913 storm, one of the worst ever on the Great Lakes.

The ship was caught in the storm that began on Nov. 9 and continued for 76 hours. At this time, steel hulls were relatively new to Great Lakes shipbuilding and many captains placed too much confidence in what they believed were "indestructible" hulls. But for many that autumn, 90 mph winds and 40-foot waves were too much.

After the storm subsided, the hull of a capsized ship was spotted off the Port Huron lighthouse station. For several days, the ship drifted in the shipping lanes unidentified. Finally, a diver was able to determine that the black hull was that of the CHARLES S.ES S. PRICE.

A few days after the ship was identified, the CHARLES S.

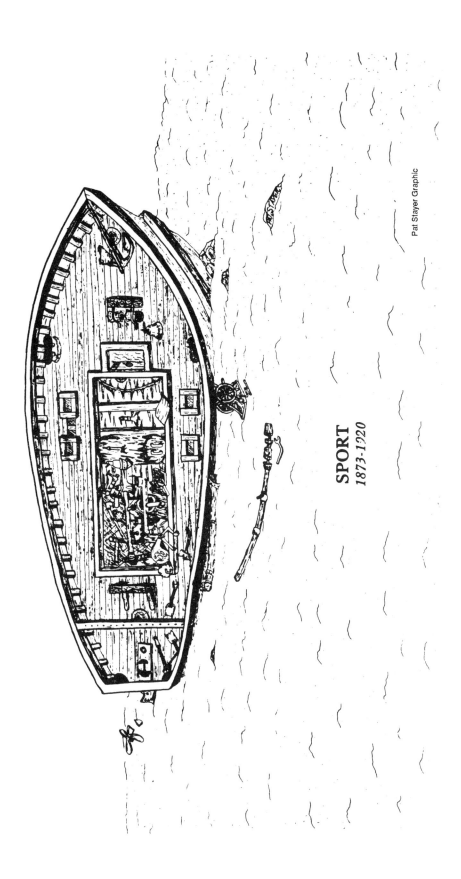

SPORT
1873-1920

Pat Stayer Graphic

PRICE rolled on her side and sunk in about 65 feet of water. Today, the ship lies upside down on the bottom. Twenty-eight crewmen and the captain were lost in the disaster.

The bow of the CHARLES S. PRICE faces south and there are several large holes in the hull, which permit penetration of cargo holds.

| | |
|---|---|
| **Location:** | About 11 miles southeast (141 Deg.) of Lexington Harbor. |
| **Loran:** | 30799.6/49622.5 |
| **Depth:** | 30 - 65 feet. |
| **Visibility:** | 15 - 25 feet. |
| **Tips:** | Use caution penetrating hull. Proper equipment is a must. |
| **Level:** | Intermediate to advanced. |

# CHECOTAH/NEW YORK

Two shipwrecks, the CHECOTAH and NEW YORK have been recently discovered in the Sanilac Preserve. The locations of these ships are being withheld until maritime archeologists have assessed the wrecks.

The CHECOTAH was a scow schooner built in 1870 in Toledo, Ohio. It was a ship that hauled bulk freight and sank, with a loss of three lives, in St. Mary's River in 1882. Six years later, the CHECOTAH was raised and used as a schooner barge to haul lumber.

On Oct. 30, 1906, while being towed, the heavily loaded CHECOTAH began to founder in rough seas. It was separated from other vessels and the crew of seven managed to launch a yawl and save themselves.

The location of the shipwreck was discovered in 1988. The stern of the wreck is broken and scattered. Much of the equipment remains on the bow and there are many small artifacts associated with this site.

Because the stern cabin has fallen off, there is limited penetration diving at this site.

The NEW YORK lies relatively close to the CHECOTAH. The NEW YORK was a steamer that foundered off Harbor Beach in 1876. Maritime archeologists are especially interested in the unusual oscillating steam engines found on the NEW YORK.

The locations of these shipwrecks are expected to be released in mid-1990. For that information, contact Lakeshore Charters & Marine Exploration, Inc., 4658 S. Lakeshore, Lexington, MI 48450.

# Accommodations

Because this area does not attract many tourists, overnight accommodations are somewhat limited.

Campers can find a private campground in Lexington and the Lakeport State Park north of Port Huron offers campsites.

Limited motel and resort accommodations are located in Lexington and Port Sanilac. Some such facilities are found in Croswell and Sandusky.

# Emergencies

Divers with medical emergencies can contact the U.S. Coast Guard Station at Harbor Beach. Another contact is the Sanilac County Sheriff's Department in Sandusky. Both agencies have patrols boats capable of responding to emergencies. The Sanilac County Sheriff's Department dispatches ambulances in Lexington and Port Sanilac.

# Important Addresses/Phone Numbers

U.S. Coast Guard Station Harbor Beach
Harbor Beach, MI 48441
(517) 479-3285

Sanilac County Sheriff's Department
65 N. Elk
Sandusky, MI 48471
(313) 648-2000

Greater Port Sanilac Business Association
PO Box 402
Port Sanilac, MI 48469

Greater Lexington Chamber of Commerce
Lexington, MI 48450

East Michigan Tourist Association
One Wenonah Park
Bay City, MI 48706
(517) 895-8823

**Charter Operators:**

Lakeshore Charters & Marine Exploration, Inc.
4658 S. Lakeshore
Lexington, MI 48450
(313) 359-8660

Blue Water Marine Services, Inc.
11 North Lake St.
PO Box 124
Port Sanilac, MI 48469
(313) 622-9910

William Robinette
28869 Bunert
Warren, MI 48093
(313) 774-0640

# Straits of Mackinac

The Straits of Mackinac Underwater Preserve is one of the most popular of all preserves. This is due, in part, to a reliable dive charter service in St. Ignace.

The Straits Preserve includes an area of 148 square miles. Within its boundaries lie nine major shipwrecks. Another four wrecks are closely associated with the preserve but are outside the boundaries.

Most of the shipwrecks in the Straits Preserve are 80 to 120 feet deep. The depth and unpredictable currents and visibility make this a site primarily for intermediate to advanced divers. Portions of some wrecks can be reached in relatively shallow water, but the temptation to go deeper for further exploration could mean trouble for novice divers.

If there is a current at the dive site, divers must pay close attention to their positions to avoid drifting away from the boat. This can be a dangerous situation because the boat operator will not be able to start the engines to retrieve drifting divers when other divers are still below.

An advantage to the current is increased visibility. Fine silt stirred up by other divers clears quickly with the moving water.

Beginning divers will find old docks, especially in the St. Ignace area, fascinating exploration sites. St. Ignace is one of the oldest communities on the Great Lakes. A wealth of artifacts from Michigan's colonial days are likely waiting to be discovered in shallow water by skin and scuba divers.

The Mackinac County Sheriff's Department has a marine patrol that generally makes at least one patrol through the preserve daily.

Although the Straits of Mackinac appear wide enough to pose little navigation threat to ships, unseen rocky shoals and foul weather combined to send many to the bottom.

This is a popular tourist area and there are many activities for non-divers, or for divers during their spare time. There are many museums and interpretive centers in St. Ignace, Mackinaw City and Cheboygan. Mackinac Island offers a unique environment with many historical exhibits, displays and programs. There are many passenger ferries making hourly trips to the island, much of which is a state park.

# Boating

Boating in the Straits of Mackinac is complicated by the volume of traffic.

The area not only hosts a busy shipping channel, but passenger ferries and pleasure craft are common. Resorts in the region attract many visitors during the summer, so it is best to keep a watchful eye open for passenger ferries and pleasure craft.

The volume of boat traffic is complemented by harbor and launching facilities.

The marina in St. Ignace is sponsored by the Michigan Department of Natural Resources and offers transient accommodations, gas, water, electricity, restrooms, showers and holding tank pumps. Similar facilities, also sponsored by the Department of Natural Resources, can be found at the marina on Mackinac Island.

A marina sponsored by the Village of Mackinaw City and one in Cheboygan offer full services. Basic services are offered by marinas at Bois Blanc Island and at the Cheboygan County Marina.

Boat launching facilities are located in St. Ignace, Mackinaw City and at Wilderness State Park on Sturgeon Bay.

Because the area is so popular, especially in July and August, it is best to make reservations for slip space well in advance. Most marina facilities monitor vhf channel 16.

# CEDARVILLE

The CEDARVILLE was a 588-foot, self-unloading freighter built in 1927. It was carrying a load of limestone bound for Gary, Ind. in a light fog on the morning of May 7, 1965.

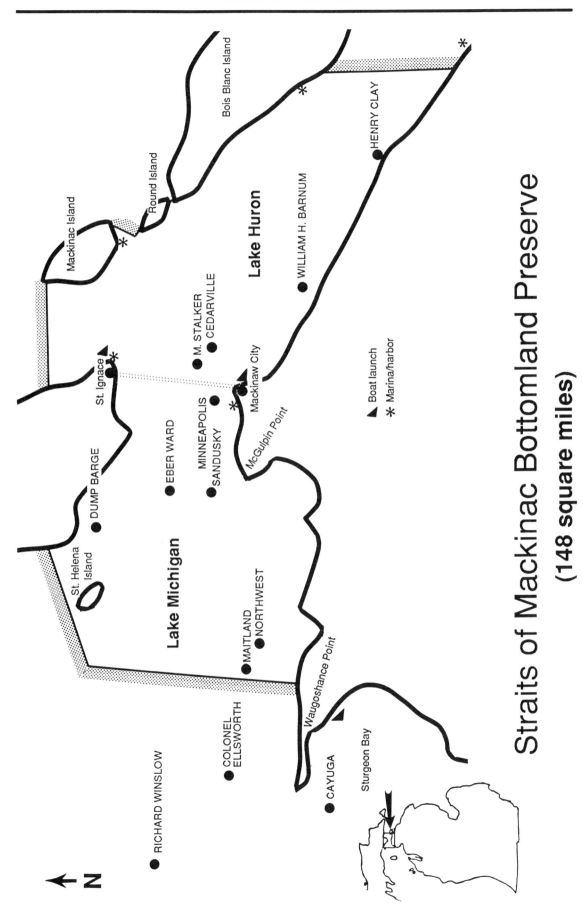

Bois Blanc Island

Round Island

Mackinac Island

St. Helena
Island

DUMP BARGE

EBER WARD

**Lake Michigan**

RICHARD WINSLOW

COLONEL
ELLSWORTH

MAITLAND
NORTHWEST

MINNEAPOLIS

SANDUSKY

CAYUGA

Sturgeon Bay

Waugoshance Point

McGulpin Point

Mackinaw City

St. Ignace

M. STALKER

CEDARVILLE

**Lake Huron**

WILLIAM H. BARNUM

HENRY CLAY

▲ Boat launch

∗ Marina/harbor

← N

Straits of Mackinac Bottomland Preserve
**(148 square miles)**

The CEDARVILLE was proceeding toward the Straits of Mackinac when it was suddenly struck about mid-ship on the port side by the TOPDALSFJORD, a Norwegian freighter. The TOPDALSFJORD suffered only a damaged bow and continued her trip up the St. Mary's River to Sault Ste. Marie. But the CEDARVILLE, suffered a 20-foot gash in her hull.

The captain realized that the ship was about to go down and tried to beach it. The CEDARVILLE capsized in about 110 feet of water and sank about 2.5 miles from Mackinaw City in Lake Huron. Although none of the 35 crew were injured during the collision, many were hurled into the water when it capsized. Ten men were lost.

Although there were conflicting accounts of the disaster, a federal court found that the captain of the CEDARVILLE had overloaded the ship and was proceeding too fast through the fog.

Today, the CEDARVILLE lies in about 110 feet of water with her hull within 35 feet of the surface. The ship's superstructure and cabins are about 75 feet deep and provide penetration diving opportunities.

| | |
|---|---|
| **Location:** | About 2.5 miles east of Mackinaw City. |
| **Loran:** | 31210.7/48130.9 |
| **Depth:** | 35 - 110 feet. |
| **Visibility:** | 2 - 20 feet depending upon current conditions. |
| **Tips:** | If penetrating the superstructure, use caution required for such activity. |
| **Level:** | Intermediate to advanced. |

# EBER WARD

Little information is available about the EBER WARD. It was a steamer that foundered in 1909 in Lake Michigan about 4.5 miles west of the Straits of Mackinac. The ship was cut by ice and sank in five to 10 minutes. Five lives were lost in the wreck.

Because of the shipwrecks' depth, 145 feet, it is one of the least-visited dive sites in the area.

| | |
|---|---|
| **Location:** | About 4.5 miles west of the Straits of Mackinaw. [270 Deg. from south tower of Mackinac Bridge]. |
| **Loran:** | 31253.7/48097.0 |
| **Depth:** | 145 feet. |
| **Visibility:** | 2 - 15 feet. |
| **Tips:** | This wreck is located in the shipping channel. Watch for large ships. |
| **Level:** | Advanced. |

# MAITLAND

The MAITLAND was a bark of 137 feet, built in 1861.

On June 11, 1871, the MAITLAND collided with the schooners GOLDEN HARVEST and MEARS at night. It sank 5 miles west of McGulpin Point in Lake Michigan in about 90 feet of water.

Despite the collisions, the MAITLAND is relatively intact but opportunities for penetration diving are limited.

| | |
|---|---|
| **Location:** | About 5 miles west of McGulpin Point. |
| **Loran:** | 31273.4/48093.03 |
| **Depth:** | 80 - 90 feet. |
| **Visibility:** | 2 - 15 feet. |
| **Tips:** | This wreck is located in the shipping channel. Watch for large ships. |
| **Level:** | Intermediate. |

# MINNEAPOLIS

The MINNEAPOLIS was a combination propeller and three-masted sailing ship. It was loaded with grain and headed through the Straits of Mackinac with two schooners in tow.

The combination of rough weather and hidden shoals in the Straits of Mackinac sent many ships to the bottom.

The MINNEAPOLIS was cut by ice during its early spring trip in 1894. The two schooners were cut loose and the MINNEAPOLIS sank in about 125 feet of water.

| | |
|---|---|
| **Location:** | About 4 miles northeast of McGulpin Point, 400 feet from the Mackinaw Bridge. |
| **Loran:** | 31226.7/48111.5 |
| **Depth:** | 115 - 130 feet. |
| **Visibility:** | 2 - 15 feet. |
| **Tips:** | This wreck is located very near the shipping channel. Watch for large ships. |
| **Level:** | Intermediate. |

# M. STALKER

The schooner M. STALKER was built in 1863. It was struck by a tow barge in 1886 while laying at anchor at night near Cheboygan. This wreck is about 3/4 mile northeast from the wreck of the CEDARVILLE in about 90 feet of water.

The ship sustained major damage in the collision. There are no opportunities for penetration diving.

| | |
|---|---|
| **Location:** | About 1 3/4 mile northwest of Mackinaw City. |
| **Loran:** | 31213.9/48126.0 |
| **Depth:** | 80 - 90 feet. |
| **Visibility:** | 2 - 15 feet. |
| **Tips:** | This wreck is located near the shipping channel. Watch for large ships. |
| **Level:** | Intermediate. |

# NORTHWEST

The schooner NORTHWEST was sunk by ice slightly more than 4 miles west of McGulpin Point on April 6, 1898. The wreck rests in about 75 feet of water in Lake Michigan.

The NORTHWEST is broken up and there is no opportunity for penetration diving.

| | |
|---|---|
| **Location:** | About 4.3 miles west of McGulpin Point in Lake Michigan. |
| **Loran:** | 31270.4/48102.4 |
| **Depth:** | 70 - 75 feet. |
| **Visibility:** | 2 - 15 feet. |
| **Level:** | Intermediate. |

# SANDUSKY

The brig SANDUSKY was built in 1848 in Sandusky, Ohio. The ship was 110 feet long and had two masts, and a square stern.

On Sept. 16, 1856, the ship left Chicago with a load of freight and two days later, found herself in a violent storm at the Straits of Mackinac. The ship was unable to handle heavy seas and sank with a loss of seven men.

One of the most unique features of the SANDUSKY is a figurehead in the shape of a ram's head. It is believed to be one of a few such figureheads lost on Great Lakes shipwrecks.

In 1988, vandals loosened bolts securing the figurehead and concerned divers removed the artifact. The figurehead was taken to the Lake Michigan Maritime Museum in South Haven for conservation. Divers carved a replica of the figurehead and placed it where vandals had nearly stolen the original. The incident testifies to the dedication of Michigan sport divers to preservation of maritime heritage, but it also shows that the commitment is not uniform.

The SANDUSKY rests upright in about 90 feet of water. Divers can explore the interior of the ship. They will find broken masts but most major features remain, including a kedge anchor, pin rail, wheel and tiller.

| | |
|---|---|
| **Location:** | About 5.5 miles northwest of McGulpin Point in Lake Michigan. |
| **Loran:** | 31262.0/48100.8 |
| **Depth:** | 80 - 90 feet. |
| **Visibility:** | 2 - 15 feet. |
| **Tips:** | If exploring interior of ship, use caution. Watch for cables. Note "new" figurehead. Be prepared for daily fluctuations in water temperature. |
| **Level:** | Intermediate to advanced. |

# WILLIAM H. BARNUM

The WILLIAM H. BARNUM was a 218-foot steamer that foundered about 5.5 miles southeast of Mackinaw City in Lake Huron on April 3, 1894.

Details of the sinking are sketchy. Some reports say the WILLIAM H. BARNUM sank in rough weather while others say it was cut by ice. The entire crew was saved in the wreck.

The WILLIAM H. BARNUM lies in about 75 feet of water, upright and mostly intact. The forward portion of the deck is somewhat collapsed. Penetration diving is possible.

| | |
|---|---|
| **Location:** | About one mile northeast of Freedom [village located on M-23 at N. Hebron Mail Road] in Lake Huron. |
| **Loran:** | 31205.4/48158.3 |
| **Depth:** | 70 - 75 feet. |
| **Visibility:** | 2 - 15 feet. |
| **Tips:** | If exploring interior of ship, use caution. |
| **Level:** | Intermediate to advanced. |

# DUMP BARGE

Little is known about an unnamed barge located about one mile southeast of the southernmost tip of St. Helena Island.

The barge lies in about 40 feet of water and offers no opportunity for penetration diving because it is somewhat broken up. There is, however, much machinery associated with the wreck to investigate. Because this wreck was discovered relatively recently and it is located in shallow water, it is experiencing many diver visitations.

| Location: | About one mile southeast of the southernmost tip of St. Helena Island in Lake Michigan. |
|---|---|
| **Loran:** | 31256.1/48074.6 |
| **Depth:** | 40 feet. |
| **Visibility:** | 2 -15 feet. |
| **Tips:** | This is a good "end of the day" dive, a good way to wrap up a full diving experience. |
| **Level:** | Basic. |

# COLONEL ELLSWORTH

The COLONEL ELLSWORTH was a schooner that was lost in a collision in 1896 near Waugoshance Point.

Although the shipwreck is outside the Straits Preserve boundaries, it is generally considered part of that collection of wrecks. It lies in about 85 feet of water in Lake Michigan.

| Location: | About 4 miles north of Waugo– schance Point in Lake Michigan. |
|---|---|
| **Loran:** | 31317.4/48067.7 |
| **Depth:** | 75 - 85 feet. |
| **Visibility:** | 2 - 15 feet. |
| **Level:** | Intermediate. |

# CAYUGA

The CAYUGA was a steamer that sank in Lake Michigan in 1866 about 10 miles northwest of Cross Village. The shipwreck lies in about 125 feet of water.

| Location: | Northwest of Sturgeon Bay. |
|---|---|
| **Loran:** | 31390.5/48090.0 |
| **Depth:** | 125 feet. |
| **Visibility:** | 2 - 15 feet |
| **Tips:** | This shipwreck lies in the shipping channel. Watch for large ships. |
| **Level:** | Intermediate. |

# HENRY CLAY

The HENRY CLAY was a brig that sank near Point Nipigon in 1850. The remains of the ship lie in about 80 feet of water in Lake Huron.

| Location: | 4 miles northwest of Cheboygan in Lake Huron. |
|---|---|
| **Loran:** | 31180.59/48195.32 |
| **Depth:** | 65 - 80 feet. |
| **Visibility:** | 2 - 15 feet. |
| **Level:** | Intermediate. |

# RICHARD WINSLOW

| Location: | About 11 miles northwest of Waugoshance Point north of White Shoal. |
|---|---|
| **Loran:** | 31390.5/48090 |
| **Depth:** | 25 feet. |
| **Visibility:** | 5 - 20 feet. |
| **Tips:** | In addition to this wreck there are others on White Shoal. Look for other wreckage east of the shoal. |
| **Level:** | Basic. |

The RICHARD WINSLOW was a schooner that was lost in 1898 on White Shoals in the Straits of Mackinac.

The wreck has been broken up by wave and ice. There is no opportunity for penetration diving.

# Emergencies

In the event of an emergency, contact the Mackinac County Sheriff's Department or the U.S. Coast Guard station at St. Ignace. Both monitor vhf channel 16. Give details of the nature of the emergency and location. The sheriff's department will coordinate emergency procedures.

# Important Addresses/Phone Numbers

Mackinac County Sheriff's Dept.
Court House
St. Ignace, MI 49781
(906) 643-7324

St. Ignace Ambulance Service
100 S. Marley
St. Ignace, MI 49781
(906 ) 643-8811

Alpena General Hospital
(517) 356-7390

St. Ignace Area Chamber of Commerce
11 S. State St.
St. Ignace, MI 49781
(906) 643-8717

St. Ignace Coast Guard
1075 Huron
St. Ignace, MI 49781
(906) 643-9191

Greater Mackinaw City Chamber
of Commerce

PO Box 856
S. Huron Ave.
Mackinaw City, MI 49701
(616) 436-5574

Mackinaw Area Tourist Bureau
PO Box 658
Mackinaw City, MI 49701
(616) 5664

Michigan's Eastern Upper Peninsula Tourist Association
100 Marley
County Court House
St. Ignace, MI 49781
(906) 643-7343

**Charter Operators:**

Straits Dive Center
587 N. State St.
St. Ignace, MI 49781
(906) 643-7009
(dockside air/equipment sales)

T.B.A., Inc.
3033 N. Glenway Drive
Bay City, MI 48706
(517) 631-0033

# Accommodations

Because the Straits of Mackinac is a popular tourist destination, there are many overnight accommodations available. But it is best to make advance reservations because rooms and campsites fill quickly and stay occupied, especially in July and August.

Contact local chambers of commerce for information and reservations.

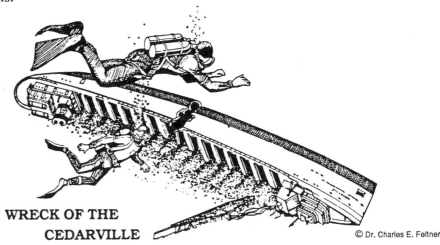

**WRECK OF THE CEDARVILLE**

© Dr. Charles E. Feltner

# Thumb Area

The Thumb Area Bottomland Preserve has 10 major shipwrecks within its 276 square miles. There are also several other areas that provide interesting diving opportunities.

Although there are no major cities now located in this preserve area, the region was once busy with ships traveling between Buffalo, N.Y. and western ports such as Duluth, Minn., Milwaukee, Wis. and Chicago, Ill. Storms, accidents and fires claimed their share of these ships.

Although there are no charter operators in this area specifically serving divers, there are many fishing charters that will accommodate divers' needs.

Divers can expect to find shipwrecks in a variety of conditions -- from intact to scattered pieces. Sites around docks near old port communities offer divers an opportunity to explore and discover artifacts from the past. Visibility in this region is excellent with up to 30 feet of visibility not uncommon.

The Thumb Area Preserve contains many shipwrecks that have yet to be located. When diving in this area, look for debris trails that could lead to important and exciting discoveries of new dive sites. This is especially true in the Grindstone City area.

There are many attractions in this area for after-dive activities. The Lighthouse County Park Interpretive Center focuses on maritime history. It is housed in the Pte. Aux Barques Lighthouse near Grindstone City.

Although this area does not offer substantial support services for divers now, many expect that as bottomland preserves gain national recognition, the Thumb Area Preserve will grow in diver popularity.

# Boating

Boating in the Thumb Area is convenient. Because this is a popular sport fishing region, there are many support facilities.

Boat launches are available at Harbor Beach, Wagener County Park, Port Hope, Stafford County Park, Port Crescent State Park, Lighthouse County Park, Port Austin and Grindstone City.

Marinas are located Harbor Beach, Port Austin and Grindstone City. Those facilities offer transient accommodations, fuel, restrooms and other support services. Most monitor vhf channel 16. Because fishing in late summer is popular in this region, it is best to reserve slips in advance during July and August.

Boaters must be aware that the shipping channel passes through the bottomland preserve and a watchful eye should be posted to keep track of large ships.

# PHILADELPHIA

The ship that collided with the ALBANY, the PHILADELPHIA, rests in about 130 feet of water.

The PHILADELPHIA was a 236-foot steamer that took the ALBANY in tow for a short time after the collision. When the PHILADELPHIA started to founder, it attempted to make it to shore.

The PHILADELPHIA rests on the bottom upright and intact with some penetration diving possible. Divers may be surprised to find a cook stove still upright on the deck of the ship.

| | |
|---|---|
| **Location:** | About 5.5 miles northeast of Pte. Aux Barques Lighthouse. |
| **Loran:** | 30786.2/49183.7 |
| **Depth:** | 120 - 130 feet. |
| **Visibility:** | 10 - 30 feet. |
| **Level:** | Intermediate to advanced. |

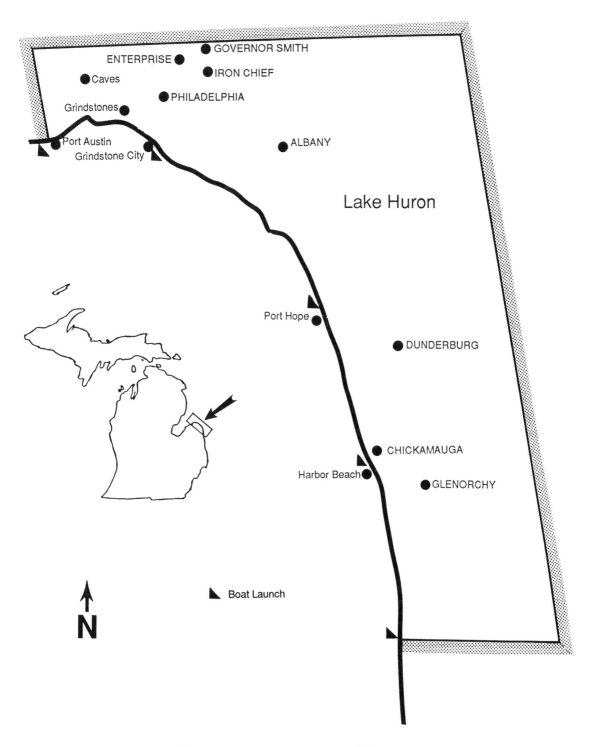

GOVERNOR SMITH

ENTERPRISE

IRON CHIEF

Caves

PHILADELPHIA

Grindstones

Port Austin

Grindstone City

ALBANY

Lake Huron

Port Hope

DUNDERBURG

CHICKAMAUGA

Harbor Beach

GLENORCHY

▲ Boat Launch

N

# Thumb Area Preserve
(276 square miles)

# ENTERPRISE

The ENTERPRISE was a 120-foot steamer that was rated at 303 gross tons. It sank in about 185 feet of water.

| | |
|---|---|
| **Location:** | Northeast of Pte. Aux Barques Lighthouse. |
| **Loran:** | 30779.8/49145.5 |
| **Depth:** | 180 - 185 feet. |
| **Visibility:** | 10 - 30 feet. |
| **Level:** | Advanced. |

# GOVERNOR SMITH

The GOVERNOR SMITH was a steamer that sank after a collision off Pte. Aux Barques in 1906. The shipwreck is scattered in deep water with little opportunity for penetration.

| | |
|---|---|
| **Location:** | About four miles northeast of Grindstone City. |
| **Loran:** | 30763.9/49141.3 |
| **Depth:** | 180 - 190 feet. |
| **Visibility:** | 5 - 20 feet. |
| **Level:** | Advanced. |

# IRON CHIEF

The IRON CHIEF foundered off Pte. Aux Barques in 1904. The shipwreck lies in about 135 feet of water. There is little opportunity for penetration diving on the remains of the 212-foot wooden steamer. Wreckage from this steamer is scattered at this site with machinery still present.

Travel Bureau Photo

The Thumb Area Underwater Preserve offers beautiful scenery in addition to a variety of underwater attractions.

| | |
|---|---|
| **Location:** | About three miles northeast of Grind-stone City. |
| **Loran:** | 30779.0/49172.0 |
| **Depth:** | 125 - 140 feet. |
| **Visibility:** | 10 - 20 feet. |
| **Level:** | Intermediate to advanced. |

# ALBANY

The ALBANY was a steel steamer that collided with the steamer PHILADELPHIA about 12 miles off Pte. Aux Barques in 1893. The ALBANY was taken in tow but sank about eight miles northeast of the Pte. Aux Barques Light in 150 feet of water. The 267-

foot ship was carrying a cargo of grain when it was lost.
Twenty-four lives were lost in the disaster.

| | |
|---|---|
| **Location:** | About eight miles northeast of Pte. Aux Barques Light. |
| **Loran:** | 30775.5/49174.2 |
| **Depth:** | 135 - 140 feet. |
| **Visibility:** | 5 - 15 feet. |
| **Level:** | Advanced. |

# DUNDERBURG

Little is known about the schooner DUNDERBURG, except that it was lost in a collision about four miles off Harbor Beach in 1868. Today, its remains are scattered in about 155 feet of water. There is little opportunity for penetration diving.

| | |
|---|---|
| **Location:** | About four miles northeast of Harbor Beach. |
| **Loran:** | 30740.9/49257.5 |
| **Depth:** | 150 - 160 feet. |
| **Visibility:** | 5 - 15 feet. |
| **Level:** | Advanced. |

# CHICKAMAUGA

The CHICKAMAUGA was a 322-foot vessel that foundered one mile north of Harbor Beach in 1919. The double-deck schooner was later moved to about one-half mile east of the Harbor Beach harbor.

| | |
|---|---|
| **Location:** | About .5 mile east of Harbor Beach. |
| **Loran:** | 30785.1/49292.7 |
| **Depth:** | 35 feet. |
| **Visibility:** | 10 - 30 feet. |
| **Level:** | Basic. |

# GLENORCHY

The GLENORCHY was lost in a collision off Harbor Beach in 1924.

The GLENORCHY was a steel steamer that collided with the LEONARD B. MILLER in 1924. The 365-foot ship was rated at 2,465 gross tons. The collision occurred about 10 miles east-southeast of Harbor Beach.

The GLENORCHY lies in about 120 feet of water and provides penetration diving opportunities.

| | |
|---|---|
| **Location:** | About 10 miles east-southeast of Harbor Beach. |
| **Loran:** | 30750.4/49314.2 |
| **Depth:** | 110 - 120 feet. |
| **Visibility:** | 10 - 20 feet. |
| **Level:** | Intermediate to advanced. |

# HUNTER SAVIDGE

The location of the wreck of the HUNTER SAVIDGE was discovered relatively recently. The discovery was big news locally because many residents lost ancestors on the wreck, which occurred during a squall on Aug. 20, 1899.

The HUNTER SAVIDGE was a 117-foot, 154-ton schooner and capsized with a loss of five lives, including the captain and his wife.

The ship is located 10 miles at 45 Deg. from Port Hope. Although this ship lies within the Thumb Area Preserve, little information regarding its location and condition has been released.

# Other Sites

Other dive sites in the Thumb Area Preserve include caves -- eroded limestone -- and grindstones.

The caves are located near the edge of the reef near Port Austin Lighthouse.

Grindstones -- used in manufacturing -- were once produced in great quantities at Grindstone City. Discarded grindstones can be found off the Grindstone City pier.

# Emergencies

The Huron County Sheriff's Department monitors vhf channel 16 and 69. In the event of a medical emergency, it is best to contact that department. The sheriff's department will coordinate a rescue and it is important to give your location as closely as possible.

If your boat is not equipped with a vhf radio, it is best to flag down a boat that does. Otherwise use signal flares to summon help. A U.S. Coast Guard Station is located at Harbor Beach and the sheriff's department has vessels for search and rescue.

# Accommodations

This area has many state parks and campgrounds. There are about 900 campsites in this region.

There are 18 motels and cottages in Port Austin, which offer more than 300 rooms. Port Hope has 2 motels and Harbor Beach has 3 motels. Information about overnight accommodations can be obtained by contacting the East Michigan Tourist Association.

# Important Addresses/Phone Numbers

Huron County Sheriff's Department
120 S. Heisterman
Bad Axe, MI 48413
(517) 269-6421

U.S. Coast Guard Station
Harbor Beach, MI 48441
(517) 479-3285

Michigan Department of Natural Resources
District Office
501 Hemlock St.
Clare, MI 48617
(517) 386-7991

Harbor Beach Community Hospital
210 S. First St.
Harbor Beach, MI 48441
(517) 479-3201

Port Austin Area Medical Clinic
8731 Independence
Port Austin, MI 48467
(517) 738-5191

Huron Memorial Hospital
1100 S. Van Dyke
Bad Axe, MI 48413

Bay Medical Center
Emergency Department
Bay City, MI 48710
(517) 894-3111

Greater Port Austin Chamber
of Commerce
PO Box 274
Port Austin, MI 48467
(517) 738-7600

Lighthouse County Park
7400 Lakeshore Road
Port Hope, MI 48468
(517) 428-4749

**Charter Operator:**

Thumb Marine Charters
28 Railroad St.
Port Austin, MI 48467
(517) 738-5271

# Thunder Bay

The Thunder Bay Underwater Preserve contains many shipwrecks and unusual natural features that make it a popular dive destination.

The preserve is 288 square miles and contains 14 major wreck sites and several areas to explore unusual limestone walls and reefs. There are many wreck sites that are still being studied and local divers are reluctant to release information about the locations of those sites.

This preserve hosts many shipwrecks because it is an area where shipping traffic must make a turn toward the northwest. If captains overestimated their ships' capabilities during northwestern gales, they sometimes found themselves in trouble. Many hidden reefs and islands contributed to navigation difficulty.

Local divers also guard the locations of certain deep sites. A few fatalities and a rash of near tragedies have prompted some to rethink the wisdom of making it easy for sport divers to go beyond their capabilities. Most dive sites are buoyed throughout the summer.

The Thunder Bay Preserve includes the Lake Huron bottomland around Alpena and east beyond islands protecting the harbor. The eastern bound-

ary of the preserve follows the 150-foot depth.

Although a boat is required to reach dive sites in the Thunder Bay Preserve, there are many sites accessible to skin divers. But skin divers should be aware that although some sites appear close to shore, local charter operators sometimes "rescue" divers who swim out and become too tired to even dive!

Water clarity, probably owing to the concentration of limestone in the area, is one of this preserve's greatest assets. Visibility of 40 feet or more is not uncommon. In shallow areas, however, heavy seas can disturb bottom sediments and reduce visibility to five feet.

The Thunder Bay Preserve offers divers of all skill levels an opportunity to practice their skills. Some shipwrecks, because of condition and depth, are considered ideal for learning wreck diving basics.

For after diving, there are several museums in the Alpena. Some provide information about local shipping ac-

tivity. There are also two lighthouse restoration projects underway at Thunder Bay and Middle islands.

# Boating

Boating in the Thunder Bay area is convenient because of many support services available at Alpena and Presque Isle. Boaters must be aware, however, that the shipping channel veers relatively close to shore in the area so it is a good idea to be watchful of large ships.

A navigation chart showing depths is also a good idea because some areas, especially those around islands, are shallow and must be navigated carefully.

Boaters must use caution when anchoring in this region. The bottom is mostly limestone and secure anchorage can be difficult to obtain. Whenever possible, use mooring buoys provided at dive sites.

A marina offering transient accommodations, including fuel, is located in the Alpena harbor. Another marina is located south of Alpena at Partridge Point. This marina also offers transient accommodations, including fuel.

A marina at Presque Isle, about 25 miles north of Alpena, offers transient accommodations and support services.

Boat launches are located at the municipal marina and Riverfront Park in Alpena. Launches are also located at Partridge Point and at Rockport, about 10 miles north of Alpena.

A boat launch with limited parking is located at athe Ossineke State Forest Campround, about 10 miles south of Alpena.

# MOLLY T. HORNER

The MOLLY T. HORNER was a wooden schooner that stranded on a shoal 1 1/3 miles north-northeast of South Point, between Bird and Scarecrow islands.

The MOLLY T. HORNER was 130 feet long and sank in the 1906. Little remains of this ship except scattered timbers.

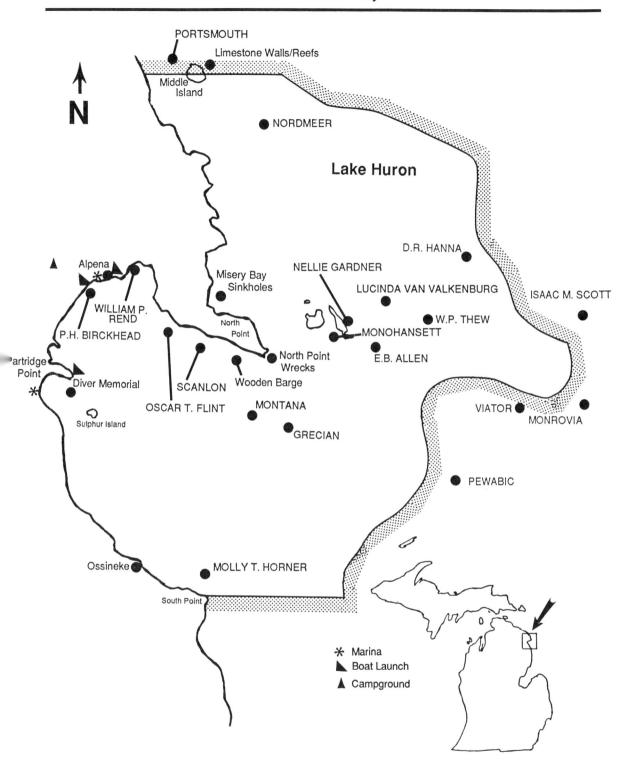

# Thunder Bay Underwater Preserve
## (288 square miles)

| Location: | Between Scarecrow and Bird islands north-northeast of South Point. |
|---|---|
| Loran: | 30893.7/48737.9 |
| Depth: | 18 feet. |
| Visibility: | 20 - 40 feet. |
| Tips: | A good place for skin diving and orientation to the area. |
| Level: | Basic. |

# Diver Memorial Site

Local sport divers have established a memorial site to comemorate divers and sport diving in the Great Lakes. The site contains artifacts, including anchors, from local shipwrecks.

It is located between Partridge Point and Sulphur Island in an area accessible to skin divers.

| Location: | Between Partridge Point and Sulphur Island. Marked by a white buoy. |
|---|---|
| Depth: | 12 feet. |
| Visibility: | 15 - 40 feet. |
| Level: | Basic. |

# E.B. ALLEN

The E.B. ALLEN was a 112-foot wooden schooner that was lost in a collision in Thunder Bay in 1871.

The shipwreck lies intact in about 110 feet of water with much equipment still on the deck, which lies 20 feet from the bottom. A windlass, anchor chains and rudder are still in place.

Cargo holds are penetrable and it is one of the deepest dive sites in the preserve.

| | |
|---|---|
| **Location:** | About 2.5 miles southeast of the south end of Thunder Bay Island. |
| **Loran:** | 30811.6/48693.1 |
| **Depth:** | 90 - 110 feet. |
| **Visibility:** | 20 - 40 feet. |
| **Tips:** | Be sure skill level is adequate. |
| **Level:** | Advanced. |

# GRECIAN

The GRECIAN was a 269-foot, steel-hulled steamer that collided with another ship and foundered south of Thunder Bay Island in 1906. The ship was raised but sank again while being towed to drydock. It was abandoned as a total loss.

Divers can find the GRECIAN upright with excellent visibility of 50 feet or more. Although the ship lies in 105 feet of water, it is only 72 feet to the deck.

This is a good place for novice wreck divers to gain skills. With the proper equipment -- lights and lines -- extensive penetration is possible throughout much of the ship, including the flicker and cargo holds. Because of the structure of the ship and clarity of the water, intermediate divers should find this wreck ideal.

| | |
|---|---|
| **Location:** | About 5 miles south-southeast (176 Deg.) from Thunder Bay Island Light. |
| **Loran:** | 30832.7/48713.3 |
| **Depth:** | 70 - 105 feet. |
| **Visibility:** | 20 - 50 feet. |
| **Tips:** | Be sure to have proper equipment if penetrating wreck. |
| **Level:** | Intermediate to advanced. |

# LUCINDA VAN VALKENBURG

The LUCINDA VAN VALKENBURG, often referred to as "Lucy," was a 128-foot wooden schooner that sank after a collision with another ship north of Thunder Bay Island in 1887.

Many dive charter boats pass this wreck on their way to the NORDMEER from Alpena. There are many broken timbers at the site and the stern of the ship has collapsed. There is limited penetration of cargo holds in the bow.

The anchor, windlass and rudder from this wreck are on display at the Diver Memorial.

| | |
|---|---|
| **Location:** | North-northeast of Thunder Bay Island. |
| **Loran:** | 30807.3/48672.9 |
| **Depth:** | 70 feet. |
| **Visibility:** | 20 - 40 feet. |
| **Level:** | Basic to intermediate. |

# MONOHANSETT

The MONOHANSETT was a 164-foot wooden schooner that sank in 1907. The ship caught fire in Thunder Bay during a storm. The crew thought they had the fire out and the ship got underway again when the fire rekindled. The MONOHANSETT sank in about 20 feet of water.

Today, all that remains are timbers from the hull, boiler, engine and propeller. The 14-foot propeller is a popular attraction at this site.

| | |
|---|---|
| **Location:** | About 500 feet west of Thunder Bay Light. |
| **Loran:** | 30822.6/48681.4 |
| **Depth:** | 20 feet. |
| **Visibility:** | 20 - 40 feet. |
| **Tips:** | This is a good beginner dive. |
| **Level:** | Basic. |

# MONTANA

The MONTANA was a sidewheel steamer that burned and sank in 1914. The ship was 235 feet long.

The engine rises 30 feet from the bottom in 70 feet of water. The sides of the ship are upright and intact so some penetration is possible. There are many artifacts, including machinery, associated with this site. The site usually hosts many fish and it is a good place for underwater photography.

| | |
|---|---|
| **Location:** | Five miles from Thunder Bay Island Light at a bearing of 226 Deg. |
| **Loran:** | 30855.9/48699.9 |
| **Depth:** | 70 feet. |
| **Visibility:** | 20 - 40 feet. |
| **Tips:** | Divers with basic skills can access this site at 40 feet and inspect the engine. |
| **Level:** | Basic to intermediate. |

# NORDMEER

The NORDMEER was a German steel steamer that stranded on the rocks of Thunder Bay Shoal in November, 1966. Soon after the ship struck the shoal, a storm blew up and after nine days, the captain and crew of seven were forced to abandon the ship.

The NORDMEER is described by one charter operator as "550 feet of pure delight." The hull of the ship is intact with much of the superstructure above water. It is considered a good place for divers interested in learning about wreck diving.

There are usually no mooring buoys associated with this dive site because boats can be fendered alongside the wreck. Some boaters prefer to anchor by sending a grappling hook into the hold.

Next to the NORDMEER, is a wooden barge that may provide exploration opportunities.

| Location: | 7 miles northeast of Thunder Bay Island. Can be seen from shore on a clear day. |
|---|---|
| Loran: | 30790.7/48634.7 |
| Depth: | 40 feet |
| Visibility: | 20 - 40 feet. |
| Tips: | Watch current in this area, use lights if penetrating wreck. |
| Level: | Basic to intermediate. |

# OSCAR T. FLINT

The OSCAR T. FLINT was a 240-foot wooden steamer that burned to the water line and sank in 1909.

The OSCAR T. FLINT is broken up and there is much machinery scattered at the site. About seven feet of the hull is intact. Divers can expect to find many fish at this site. During some summer days, water temperature can be unusually warm in this area.

| Location: | 4 miles east of the Alpena marina, about 1 mile offshore. |
|---|---|
| Loran: | 30879.8/48671.9 |
| Depth: | 30 - 35 feet. |
| Visibility: | 20 - 40 feet. |
| Level: | Basic. |

# P.H. BIRCKHEAD

The P.H. BIRCKHEAD burned near Alpena in 1905. The 156-foot wooden steamer is located just south of the Alpena marina.

This is a good site for skin and scuba divers, especially if rough weather prohibits visiting other sites in the preserve. Divers can expect to find boiler parts, propeller and shaft.

| | |
|---|---|
| **Location:** | 2/3 mile offshore south of Alpena marina. |
| **Loran:** | 30908.2/48651.4 |
| **Depth:** | 12 feet. |
| **Visibility:** | 20 - 40 feet. |
| **Tips:** | Although the white buoy marking this site appears close to shore, it is a tiring swim. Use a boat. |
| **Level:** | Basic. |

# PORTSMOUTH

The PORTSMOUTH was a package freighter that burned and sank near the old life saving station on Middle Island in 1876.

Today, the machinery and hull of the PORTSMOUTH attract many fish and only a few divers. It is a good site for skin diving and underwater photography.

| | |
|---|---|
| **Location:** | Off Middle Island. |
| **Loran:** | 30847.6/48588.2 |
| **Depth:** | 15 feet. |
| **Visibility:** | 20 - 40 feet. |
| **Tips:** | Wreckage is scattered. |
| **Level:** | Basic. |

# WILLIAM P. REND

| | |
|---|---|
| **Location:** | Off cement plant. |
| **Loran:** | 30891.0/48649.5 |
| **Depth:** | 20 feet. |
| **Visibility:** | 20 - 40 feet. |
| **Tips:** | Visibility at this site tends to decrease late in the diving season. |
| **Level:** | Basic. |

The WILLIAM P. REND was a 287-foot limestone carrier that ran aground east of the cement plant.

The bow of this ship is split and there is limited penetration. There is much chipped limestone and machinery at the site.

# W.P. THEW

The W.P. THEW was a wooden steamer that sank after a collision in 1909. The 132-foot ship rests in about 90 feet of water.

The W.P. THEW is in the shipping channel and extra care must be taken to avoid large ships. Because large ships have destroyed several buoys, this site is likely to be unmarked.

Divers can expect to find the engine and boiler of the W.P. THEW upright. An anchor is also still at the site. The stern of the ship has settled into a hard clay bottom. And although the ship is "open," the location of machinery and obstructions makes this a potentially hazardous dive.

| | |
|---|---|
| **Location:** | Almost 2 miles northeast of Thunder Bay Island Light. |
| **Loran:** | 30802.7/48679.6 |
| **Depth:** | 90 feet. |
| **Visibility:** | 15 - 30 feet. |
| **Tips:** | Watch for large ships in channel. |
| **Level:** | Advanced. |

# NELLIE GARDNER

The NELLIE GARDNER was a wooden schooner that sunk at Thunder Bay Island in 1883.

The ship lies in shallow water near the island. It's remains are very scattered.

| Location: | Thunder Bay Island |
|---|---|
| **Loran:** | 30893.7/48737.9 |
| **Depth:** | 18 feet. |
| **Visibility:** | 20 - 40 feet. |
| **Tips:** | Use caution getting into this area. Shallow water calls for careful navigation. |
| **Level:** | Basic. |

# SCANLON

Little is known about the circumstances surrounding the grounding of the barge SCANLON. Its location was discovered relatively recently in the Thunder Bay Preserve.

The SCANLON is believed to have been a steam-driven dredge. There are many fish and much machinery associated with this site. It is close to shore and makes a good skin diving and underwater photography site.

| Location: | Offshore between North and Whitefish Points. |
|---|---|
| **Loran:** | 30870.2/48669.1 |
| **Depth:** | 5 - 15 feet. |
| **Visibility:** | 20 - 40 feet. |
| **Tips:** | Machinery is scattered over a wide area. |
| **Level:** | Basic. |

# Wooden Barge

The Thunder Bay Preserve has a collection of unidentified wooden vessels. Many of these vessels are schooner-barges, ships that maintained a few masts, but were primarily towed across the lakes by steamers.

When these barges were in tow and they rounded Middle

Island in rough weather, they ran the risk of losing control.

When heavy seas were too much, barges often broke free and were left to drift. Often, they grounded and broke up in shallow water in Thunder Bay.

One of the most popular of the wooden barge sites is located between Whitefish and North Points.

| | |
|---|---|
| **Location:** | South of the mainland between Whitefish and North Points in Thunder Bay. |
| **Loran:** | 30865.0/48680.8 |
| **Depth:** | 50 feet. |
| **Visibility:** | 20 - 40 feet. |
| **Level:** | Basic. |

# North Point Wrecks

There are many shipwrecks in shallow water off North Point. Some of these wrecks are accessible from shore.

Divers can expect to find a collection of large pieces of wrecks in 12 to 14 feet of water. This debris field contains a huge anchor and windlass.

| | |
|---|---|
| **Location:** | Off North Point. |
| **Depth:** | 10 - 15 feet. |
| **Visibility:** | 20 - 40 feet. |
| **Tips:** | If using a boat, be sure anchorage is secure. In this area, it is difficult to get a good anchor hold. |
| **Level:** | Basic. |

# Limestone Walls/Reefs

Two areas in the Thunder Bay Preserve provide interesting diving along limestone walls and reefs.

The Thunder Bay Island area, including nearby islands, offer divers a variety of terrain. South of the islands are reefs that support large schools of fish. The wreckage of a variety of unidentified wooden ships can also be found in these areas.

These are good places for skin divers to explore. Boats are required to access these areas and good navigation charts are recommended because shallow water extends far into the bay.

On the southeast side of Thunder Bay Island and on the north side of South Point are limestone walls that provide divers with an interesting wall diving experience.

A limestone wall can be found off Middle Island. That wall descends to 70 feet and empties into a large bowl and is a popular area for exploration by scuba divers.

| | |
|---|---|
| **Location:** | Off Thunder Bay Island and South Point. |
| **Depth:** | 5 - 70 feet. |
| **Visibility:** | 20 - 40 feet (less if sediments are disturbed by heavy seas). |
| **Tips:** | Use caution navigating around reefs. |
| **Level:** | Basic to intermediate. |

# Misery Bay Sinkholes

The Misery Bay Sinkholes are fissures in limestone formations. The sinkholes are found in relatively shallow water, five feet or less, and penetrate the limestone for 80 feet or more. Diving these sinkholes is much like cave diving and requires proper equipment, skill and training.

Recent testing of water samples showed a concentration of hydrogen disulfide gas -- a corrosive chemical that occurs naturally. Because of the concentration of this gas, most divers are avoiding this site. It is unknown what effect this chemical may have on expensive diving equipment.

| Location:   | In Misery Bay off Olson's Landing on Echon Beach Road northwest of Alpena. |
|-------------|---------------------------------------------------------------------------|
| Depth:      | 40 - 80 feet.                                                             |
| Visibility: | 2 - 10 feet.                                                             |
| Tips:       | Could be dangerous because of corrosion to scuba equipment. Cave diving environment. |
| Level:      | Advanced only.                                                           |

# D.R. HANNA

The D.R. HANNA, was a large, steel Great Lakes freighter that sank off Thunder Bay on May 16, 1919. The ship was built in 1906 and was loaded with a cargo of wheat when it collided with the QUINCY A. SHAW.

The 552-foot D.R. HANNA was southbound and the captain saw the other ship in the afternoon fog. The QUINCY A. SHAW unexpectedly cut across the bow of the D.R. HANNA and struck

| Location:   | 6 miles 56 Deg. off Thunder Bay Island light. |
|-------------|-----------------------------------------------|
| Loran:      | 30771.3/48666.4                               |
| Depth:      | 90 - 140 feet.                                |
| Visibility: | 25 - 40 feet.                                 |
| Level:      | Intermediate to advanced.                     |

The D.R. HANNA sank in Thunder Bay after a collision with another ship in 1919.

the ship. All 32 hands were rescued by the QUINCY A. SHAW as the seas were relatively calm.

The D.R. HANNA lies upside down in 140 feet of water and rises within 90 feet of the surface. The wreck is penetrable and no serious salvage attempt was ever made.

# Nearby Dives

Although local dive charter operators prefer not to divulge the exact locations of certain shipwrecks in or near the preserve, sport divers may find small buoys on historically important shipwrecks. Local divers contend that the wrecks are too dangerous to be publicized, but that lack of information has not significantly affected popularity among scuba divers.

The NEW ORLEANS was a 231-foot wooden steamer that collided with the WILLIAM R. LINN and sank in Thunder Bay in on June 30, 1906. It was loaded with a cargo of coal. No lives were lost in the mishap.

| Location: | 9.2 miles at 354 Deg. from Thunder Bay Island. |
|---|---|
| Loran: | 30808.0/48613.7 |
| Depth: | 140 - 150 feet. |
| Visibility: | 25 - 40 feet. |
| Level: | Advanced. |

The ISAAC M. SCOTT was one of many ships lost during the great storm of November 1913. It foundered near Port Elgin with a loss of 28 lives. The ship was built in 1909 and was loaded with coal when it sank.

The steel steamer is upside down and half-buried in clay in about 175 feet of water.

| Location: | 7 miles northeast of Thunder Bay Lighthouse. |
|---|---|
| Depth: | 130 - 175 feet. |
| Visibility: | 25 - 40 feet. |
| Level: | Advanced. |

The MONROVIA was a 430-foot Liberian steel steamer that collided with the Canadian ore carrier ROYALTON off Thunder Bay Island.

The MONROVIA was northbound when it sank on June 26, 1959 with a load of steel. The ship's port side was heavily damaged in the accident. A thick afternoon fog and the MONROVIA's excessive speed were blamed for the mishap.

The MONROVIA sank about 13 miles east of the island. There was no loss of life in the mishap.

| Location: | 13.5 miles at 107 Deg. from Thunder Bay Island Light. |
|---|---|
| Loran: | 30723.5/48728.9 |
| Depth: | 110 - 130 feet. |
| Visibility: | 25 - 40 feet. |
| Level: | Intermediate to advanced. |

The PEWABIC foundered after colliding with the steamer METEOR on Aug. 9, 1865. There were 125 lives lost in the seventh-worst disaster on the Great Lakes.

The reason for the collision is unclear because it occurred on a clear evening in relatively calm seas on Aug. 9. The vessels were sister ships and familiar with each other's routes. The PEWABIC was heading south with a load of passenger and copper ore from Lake Superior. The METEOR was neading north from Detroit with a load of passengers.

By all accounts, the captains of both ships could see each other well in advance. Many aboard the 200-foot PEWABIC were killed at the time of the collision. Many others were thrown into the water and clung to wreckage until they were rescued the next morning.

Artifacts from the PEWABIC are displayed at the Jesse Besser Museum in Alpena.

The ship, which was built in 1863, is intact and upright.

| | |
|---|---|
| **Location:** | 6.7 miles 130 Deg. from Thunder Bay Island Light. |
| **Depth:** | 140 - 165 feet. |
| **Visibility:** | 25 - 40 feet. |
| **Level:** | Advanced. |

The VIATOR was a 231-foot Norwegian steel steamer that collided with the ORMIDALE in a heavy fog on Oct. 31, 1935. The ship was northbound from Detroit with a load of cod liver oil and sardines. No lives were lost in the accident.

Today, the VIATOR lies at an angle with the bow of the ship in 190 feet of water and the stern in 250 feet.

| | |
|---|---|
| **Location:** | 8.9 miles 112 Deg. from Thunder Bay Island Light. |
| **Depth:** | 150 - 150 feet. |
| **Visibility:** | 25 - 40 feet. |
| **Level:** | Advanced. |

# Emergencies

In the event of a medical emergency, it is best to contact the Alpena County Sheriff's Depatment or the U.S. Coast Guard Station at Tawas on vhf channel 16. Those agencies will coordinate on-water emergency procedures.

Generally, an ambulance will will meet the injured at an arranged point and transport them to Alpena General Hospital. If recompression is necessary, arrangements will be made by hospital staff to transport the victim to the nearest chamber.

# Accommodations

There are three private campgrounds and more than 400 public campground sites within an hour of Alpena. There are 32 motels, cottages and resorts in the area that can be reserved through the Alpena Area Chamber of Commerce.

# Important Addresses/Phone Numbers

Alpena County Sheriff's Department
320 Johnson St.
Alpena, MI 49707
(517) 354-4128

U.S. Coast Guard Station
Alpena, MI 49707
(517) 356-1656

U.S. Coast Guard Station
Tawas City, MI 48764
(517) 362-4428

Alpena General Hospital
1501 W. Chisholm St.
Alpena, MI 49707
(517) 356-7390

Alpena Ambulance Service
430 Helen
Alpena, MI 49707
(517) 354-5412

Michigan Dept. of Natural Resources
District Office
(517) 732-3541

Michigan State Police
2160 S. State
Alpena, MI 49707
(517) 354-4101

Alpena Area Chamber of Commerce
PO Box 65
Alpena, MI 49707
(517) 354-4181

East Michigan Tourist Association
One Wenonah Park
Bay City, MI 48706
(517) 895-8823

**Charter Operator:**

Thunder Bay Divers
160 E. Fletcher
Alpena, MI 49707
(517) 356-9336

# Whitefish Point

The Whitefish Point Underwater Preserve offers primarily deep-diving experiences on a variety of shipwrecks in its 376-square mile area.

Many of the shipwrecks in this area, despite their depth, were stripped of important artifacts in the 1970s and early 1980s by unscrupulous divers. Today, many of those artifacts can be seen at the Great Lakes Shipwreck Historical Museum, which is located at the tip of Whitefish Point at the end of Whitefish Road. The museum is open seasonally. There is a small fee for admission to the museum, but it is a popular attraction for many divers because it offers video presentations of local shipwrecks.

Good visibility is a hallmark of this preserve. Divers can expect to find 25 to 30 feet of visibility at 100 feet, with greater visibility at shallower depths. And although the surface water temperature may reach 60 degrees in the warmest months, expect much cooler temperatures at even slight depths.

Drysuits are recommended and are a necessity for extended dives.

Because most of the dive sites in the Whitefish Preserve are deep, divers must be certain of their abilities and equipment. This is not a place for second-guessing recompression tables or pressing the capability of equipment.

The Whitefish Bay area is often referred to as the "graveyard of the Great Lakes." The reason is clear; weather is notoriously unpredictable in this region.

July and early August are the best months to visit the preserve because weather patterns are most predictable. But no matter when divers visit Whitefish Bay, it should be with a boat capable of handling rough weather. For that reason, it is especially wise to use local charter services.

# Boating

Charter operators urge boaters to use extreme caution when visiting the Whitefish Point area. They say storms and/or fog and arise quickly and catch even the most careful boater off guard. For that reason, a vhf radio is required at a minimum so that if trouble arises, help can be summoned.

Boat launches are located at Whitefish Point, Little Lake Harbor, Tahquamenon Bay and Brimley State Park and Bay Mills. The latter two are more than 20 miles from the southern boundary of the preserve and may not be the first choice for divers using their own boats in this area.

Boat launches in this area are administered by the Michigan Department of Natural Resources and generally offer ample free parking and facilities to launch even large, trailerable boats.

The nearest U.S. Coast Guard station is located at Sault Ste. Marie. Boaters should be aware that it may take more than an hour for the U.S. Coast Guard to respond from this station so it is best to play it safe.

# INDIANA

The INDIANA was a steamer was headed down from Marquette with a load of iron ore in June 1858 when it began leaking. The ship foundered off Crisp Point with no loss of life.

The INDIANA was built in 1834 and was powered by one of the earliest steam engines. The engine was raised in 1979 and is now on display at the Smithsonian Institute in Washington, D.C.

Limited penetration diving is possible at this site.

| | |
|---|---|
| **Location:** | North of Crisp Point. |
| **Loran:** | 31215.1/47520.3 |
| **Depth:** | 110 to 120 feet. |
| **Visibility:** | 10 - 20 feet. |
| **Level:** | Intermediate to advanced. |

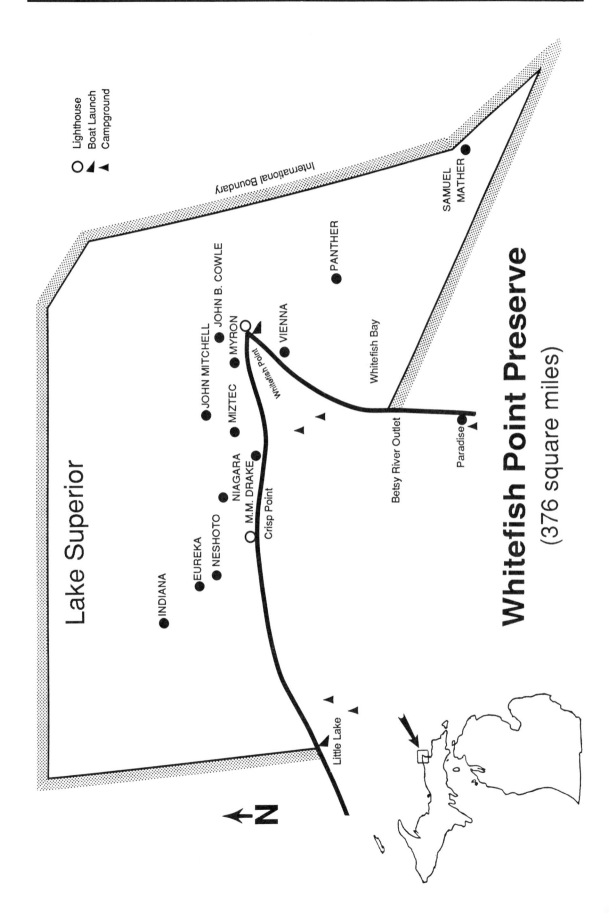

Lake Superior

Lighthouse
Boat Launch
Campground

International Boundary

INDIANA
EUREKA
NESHOTO
JOHN MITCHELL
JOHN B. COWLE
MIZTEC
MYRON
NIAGARA
M.M. DRAKE
Crisp Point
Whitefish Point
VIENNA
PANTHER
SAMUEL MATHER
Whitefish Bay
Betsy River Outlet
Paradise
Little Lake

**Whitefish Point Preserve**
(376 square miles)

# EUREKA

The 330-ton, schooner-barge EUREKA was loaded with iron ore from Marquette when the ship, which was in tow, broke her line and disappeared on Oct. 20, 1886.

The 138-foot schooner sank about six miles north of the Vermilion Life Saving Station. Her entire crew of six was lost in the disaster.

| | |
|---|---|
| **Location:** | About six miles north of Vermilion. |
| **Loran:** | 31181.2/47527.4 |
| **Depth:** | 50 feet. |
| **Visibility:** | 10 - 20 feet. |
| **Level:** | Intermediate. |

# NESHOTO

The true identity of this shipwreck is uncertain, but it is believed to be that of the 284-foot steamer NESHOTO.

The NESHOTO was carrying a cargo of iron ore when it ran aground on a reef about two-and-a-half miles northeast of Crisp Point on Sept. 27, 1908. The accident was caused when the crew was blinded by the smoke of a forest fire raging on the mainland.

The NESHOTO swung broadside to the waves and was broken apart. The crew of 16 was saved by the Crisp Point Lifesaving Station.

Today, there is little left but remnants of machinery and large timbers from the wooden-hulled ship.

| | |
|---|---|
| **Location:** | About 2 1/2 miles northeast of Crisp Point. |
| **Loran:** | 31181.2/47527.4 |
| **Depth:** | 15 feet. |
| **Visibility:** | 10 - 20 feet. |
| **Tips:** | Although this is a shallow dive site, be prepared for cold water. A drysuit is recommended. |
| **Level:** | Basic. |

# NIAGARA

The 205-foot, schooner-barge NIAGARA was in tow by the steamer AUSTRIALASIA when it capsized in heavy seas on Sept. 7, 1887.

The three-masted NIAGARA was hauling a cargo of iron ore. The crew of nine perished in the disaster.

| | |
|---|---|
| **Location:** | About two miles off Vermilion Point. |
| **Loran:** | 31168.3/47543.9 |
| **Depth:** | 100 - 120 feet. |
| **Visibility:** | 10 - 20 feet. |
| **Level:** | Intermediate to advanced. |

# JOHN MITCHELL

The JOHN MITCHELL was headed west off Vermilion Point in a dense fog when it was struck by the freighter MACK on July 10, 1911.

The 420-foot JOHN MITCHELL was carrying a load of coal and a few passengers. Although the ship sank quickly, all but three crew members were able to make it to the MACK.

Some penetration diving is possible at this site, but it is fairly deep and caution must be used.

| | |
|---|---|
| **Location:** | About three miles west-northwest of Whitefish Point. |
| **Loran:** | 31153.7/47545.6 |
| **Depth:** | 140 - 150 feet. |
| **Visibility:** | 10 - 20 feet. |
| **Level:** | Advanced. |

# MYRON

The MYRON was a 186-foot lumber hooker that was claimed by a violent storm on Nov. 22, 1919.

The MYRON was heading east from Munising with a load of lumber and was towing the schooner-barge MIZTEC. Ice began to build and the MYRON made a desperate race for the safety of Whitefish Point but foundered a little more than a mile west-northwest of the point.

The crew of 17 was lost. The captain was rescued by standing on the pilot house, which broke free when the ship sank.

The remains of the MYRON, which was built in Grand Haven in 1888, lie in about 50 feet of water and there is little opportunity for penetration diving. Divers can find the remains of the steamer's machinery, equipment and timbers.

| | |
|---|---|
| **Location:** | About one mile west-northwest of Whitefish Point. |
| **Loran:** | 31142.5/47566.2 |
| **Depth:** | 45 - 50 feet. |
| **Visibility:** | 10 - 20 feet. |
| **Level:** | Intermediate. |

# JOHN B. COWLE

The JOHN B. COWLE was a steel, 420-foot steamer that was headed south near Whitefish Point when it was struck by the steamer ISAAC M. SCOTT on July 12, 1909.

The JOHN B. COWLE, a 4,731-ton iron ore carrier, was nearly cut in two by the force of the collision. It sank rapidly, claiming 14 lives.

The collision occurred during the maiden voyage of the ISAAC M. SCOTT, a ship that later foundered near Thunder Bay in Lake Huron.

Some penetration diving is available on the JOHN B. COWLE, but the depth limits divers.

| | |
|---|---|
| **Location:** | About one mile northwest of Whitefish Point. |
| **Loran:** | 31124.9/47579.0 |
| **Depth:** | 200 - 220 feet. |
| **Visibility:** | 10 - 20 feet. |
| **Tips:** | Use extreme caution on this deep dive site. |
| **Level:** | Advanced. |

# VIENNA

The VIENNA was a wooden steamer that was struck by the steamer NIPIGON on Sept. 17, 1892. The ship sunk rapidly but no lives were lost in the accident.

The VIENNA lies in about 145 feet of water about 1 1/2 miles southeast of Whitefish Point. There is little opportunity for penetration diving.

| | |
|---|---|
| **Location:** | About 1 1/2 miles southeast of Whitefish Point. |
| **Loran:** | 31135.9/47610.4 |
| **Depth:** | 140 - 145 feet. |
| **Visibility:** | 10 - 20 feet. |
| **Level:** | Advanced. |

# PANTHER

The PANTHER was a 249-foot, wooden steamer that collided in a fog with the steamer JAMES J. HILL off Parisienne Island on June 26, 1916.

The 1,643-ton PANTHER was headed north when it was struck amidship. The ship was damaged heavily in the collision and sank rapidly.

The remains of the PANTHER lie in about 100 feet of water. There is little opportunity for penetration diving.

| | |
|---|---|
| **Location:** | About four miles southwest of Whitefish Point off Parisienne Island. |
| **Loran:** | 31105.8/47685.9 |
| **Depth:** | 100 - 110 feet. |
| **Visibility:** | 10 - 20 feet. |
| **Level:** | Intermediate. |

# SAMUEL MATHER

The SAMUEL MATHER was a 246-foot wooden steamer that was loaded with wheat bound for Buffalo, N.Y. from Duluth, Minn. when it was struck on its starboard side by the BRAZIL on

Nov. 22, 1891. The accident occurred in a dense fog and a large gash was torn in the starboard hull of the SAMUEL MATHER.

The SAMUEL MATHER was about eight miles north of Point Iroquois when the accident occurred. The ship did not sink quickly and the crew was able to leave the doomed vessel on lifeboats. The SAMUEL MATHER generally carried coal and was built in 1887.

The remains of this ship are broken up with little opportunity for penetration diving.

| | |
|---|---|
| **Location:** | About eight miles north of Point Iroquois, 15 miles southeast of Whitefish Point. |
| **Loran:** | 31086.7/47734.8 |
| **Depth:** | 170 - 180 feet. |
| **Visibility:** | 10 - 20 feet. |
| **Level:** | Advanced. |

# M.M. DRAKE

The M.M. DRAKE was a steamer towing the schooner-barge MICHIGAN when it began to take on water. The 19-year-old, 201-foot ship sank on Oct. 2, 1901. One crew member, the cook, was lost in the mishap.

| | |
|---|---|
| **Location:** | About a half-mile north of Vermilion Point. |
| **Loran:** | 31167.6/47668.9 |
| **Depth:** | 50 feet. |
| **Visibility:** | 10 - 20 feet. |
| **Level:** | Intermediate. |

# MIZTEC

The 194-foot schooner-barge MIZTEC was a victim of a spring storm that arose suddenly on the night of May 13, 1921.

The MIZTEC was in tow headed north out of Whitefish Bay when it ran into rough seas. The ship was hauling salt bound for Duluth, Minn.

About 10 miles west of Whitefish Point, the tow line broke and the lights of the MIZTEC suddenly disappeared. Two years before, the MIZTEC survived a fierce autumn storm by anchoring in Whitefish Bay.

The ship is broken up with no opportunity for penetration diving.

| | |
|---|---|
| **Location:** | About four miles west-northwest of Whitefish Point. |
| **Loran:** | 31156.9/47561.2 |
| **Depth:** | 50 feet. |
| **Visibility:** | 10 - 20 feet. |
| **Level:** | Intermediate. |

# Emergencies

In the event of an on-water medical emergency in the Whitefish Point Preserve, it is best to contact a nearby boat for assistance on vhf channel 16. Because the U.S. Coast Guard station at Sault Ste. Marie is more than an hour from the Whitefish Point Preserve, the most practical assistance may be from sport fishermen or other dive boats.

The emergency plan for this preserve calls for injured divers to be transported to War Memorial Hospital in Sault Ste. Marie for stabilization. Hospital staff are instructed to contact the Diving Accident Network (DAN) to determine the closest available recompression chamber if that treatment is necessary.

If ground or commercial air ambulances are unavailable, a helicopter from the U.S. Coast Guard Air Rescue Station in Traverse City will be summoned for assistance to transport victims to the nearest recompression chamber.

Ambulances in this region are dispatched by the Chippewa County Sheriff's Department at Sault Ste. Marie. That department does **not** monitor vhf channels.

# Accommodations

Overnight accommodations are available in the Paradise area. There are 10 motels within 12 miles of Paradise. Additional lodging is available in Newberry.

There are more than 400 campsites within 10 miles of Paradise. Some of these campsites are associated with Tahquamenon Falls State Park, a popular tourist attraction.

# Important Addresses/Phone Numbers

U.S. Coast Guard Station
337 Water St.
Sault Ste. Marie, MI 49783
(906) 635-3273

Chippewa County Sheriff's Dept.
331 Court St.
Sault Ste. Marie, MI 49783
(906) 635-6355

Michigan State Police
Newberry, MI 49868
(906) 293-5151

War Memorial Hospital
Sault Ste. Marie, MI 49783
(906) 635-4460

Helen Newberry Joy Hospital
Newberry, MI 49868
(906) 293-5181

Paradise Chamber of Commerce
PO Box 82
Paradise, MI 49768

Upper Peninsula Travel and Recreation Association
PO Box 400
Iron Mountain, MI 49801
(906) 774-5480


**Charter Operator:**

Dennis Dougherty
1931 Riverside Drive
Sault Ste. Marie, MI 49783
(906) 632-6490

# St. Clair River

The St. Clair River offers a challenging dive experience. Divers must be certain they are prepared to handle limited visibility and a strong current.

The St. Clair River is about 40 miles long and connects Lake Huron to Lake St. Clair. Because the current often prevents a buildup of ice, it is "diveable" much of the year. And don't be surprised to see groups of other hearty souls visiting this unique dive site in cold weather. It is popular, especially for those who live in Southeastern Michigan and have a limited amount of recreational time.

There are nine major dive sites -- all near Port Huron where the water is clearer. Although interesting "junk" can be found throughout much of the river, caution must be exercised because the St. Clair is a busy shipping channel. Some divers prefer to hit the water in early morning to avoid boat traffic.

Visibility in the St. Clair River is usually five to 10 feet. A few days of the year, usually in the coldest months, visibility may reach 20 to 30 feet, but such water clarity is uncommon.

Divers can call the Port Huron Waste Water Treatment Plant to determine water clarity on a particular day. Divers should ask for the "turbidity index." Anything less than 1.0 is good. An index of 1.5 or more means less than five feet of visibility.

Another consideration to St. Clair River diving is fishing line. A dive knife is a must because there are many log jams, which attract fish -- and fishermen. Some say they enjoy river diving more than lake diving because fish are more tolerant of divers and permit closer observation.

Diving in the St. Clair River may require an orientation dive. If new to the area, divers should contact local dive stores to find others experienced in the stream. The current is swift and visibility low enough to make a mistake potentially life threatening.

The diving hazards are balanced by the rewards of diving in the St. Clair River. Many divers use the river as a way to maintain diving skills through the winter. And there are plenty of bottles and similar items to find and examine. Unfortunately, wrecks in the river are breaking up as a result of the force of the current.

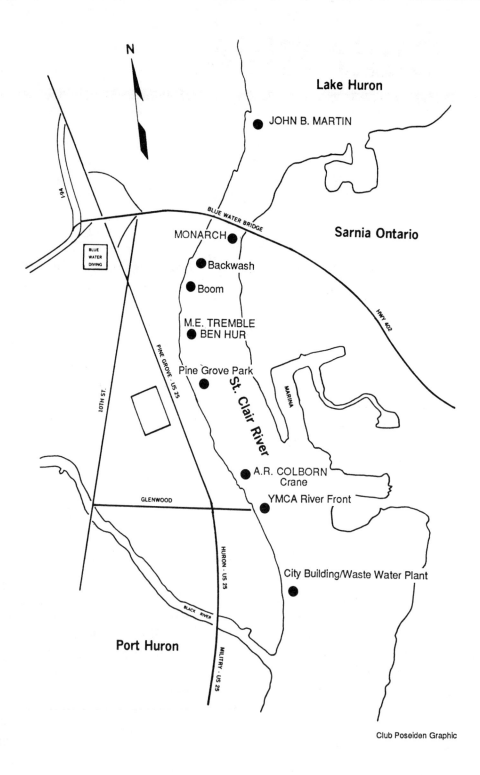

Club Poseiden Graphic

# St. Clair River

Boats are not required to dive the St. Clair River. The common practice is to plan entrance and exit sites and display diver down flags at those places. The current makes it impractical to drag a flag and float while diving.

# JOHN B. MARTIN

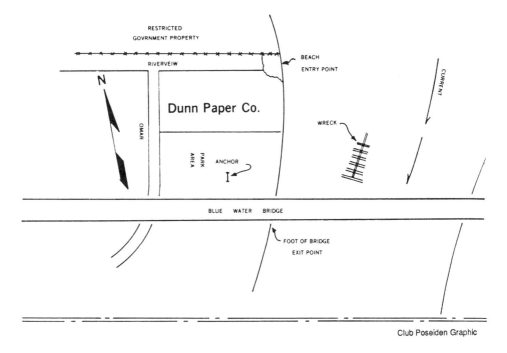

Club Poseiden Graphic

The JOHN B. MARTIN was a 220-foot schooner, built in 1873, that had been trimmed to serve as a barge. In 1900, the ship was being towed south by a steamer and had just entered the St. Clair River when it was struck by the steel steamer YUMA.

The JOHN B. MARTIN sunk rapidly, taking several lives and a cargo of iron ore with her. The incident occurred in about 60 feet of water, about 225 feet from the U.S. side near old Fort Gratiot.

The collision caused extensive damage. The cabin washed ashore the next day. An anchor of the JOHN B. MARTIN was removed and is on display near the Blue Water Bridge.

The wreck is located between the bridge and a public beach at the end of Riverview Street in Port Huron. The beach is the best entrance point and most divers exit at the foot of the bridge. The wreck is broken up but the strong currents in this area make this dive hazardous. Some report that the current holds them against the crumbling hull of the wreck.

| | |
|---|---|
| **Location:** | About 200 yards from the U.S. shore about 100 yards north of the Blue Water Bridge. |
| **Depth:** | 60 feet. |
| **Visibility:** | 2 - 12 feet. |
| **Tips:** | Because of the strong currents, dive first with another diver familiar with this wreck site. |
| **Level:** | Advanced. |

# MONARCH

The 60-foot tugboat MONARCH was towing another ship that swung out of control in the river current and pulled the tugboat over. The incident occurred on July 7, 1934 and although the MONARCH was able to right herself, it had taken on too much water and sank stern first in about 50 feet of water. Four men lost their lives in the disaster.

This wreck is located on the Canadian side of the river just south of the Blue Water Bridge. The MONARCH's hull is intact and hatches have been removed for easy access to the interior. The ship lies on its starboard side with the bow pointing upstream.

There is usually little current associated with this dive site. Access can be gained by parking near a navigational light next to a warehouse. Look for steel stairs and a steel cable that guides divers to the wreck.

Minimal penetration diving is possible at this site.

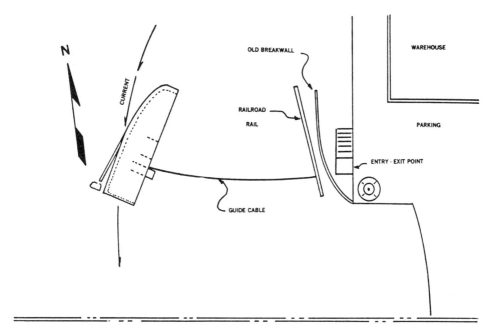

Club Poseiden Graphic

| | |
|---|---|
| **Location:** | South of the Blue Water Bridge on the Canadian side of the river. |
| **Depth:** | 50 feet. |
| **Visibility:** | 5 - 15 feet. |
| **Tips:** | Use heavy gloves to protect hands if following the cable to the wreck. |
| **Level:** | Intermediate. |

# Backwash

This is a popular dive site because it gives divers a comfortable introduction to the St. Clair River and river diving.

At the Backwash, divers can go 30 to 40 feet deep and be gently swept downstream for about 100 yards. The current then shifts to take divers back to the starting point. During this trip, divers may find many artifacts and see schools of large gamefish.

This site is located just south of the Blue Water Bridge on the U.S. side of the river. There is plenty of parking at the site.

| | |
|---|---|
| **Location:** | South of the Blue Water Bridge on the U.S. side of the river. |
| **Depth:** | 30 - 40 feet. |
| **Visibility:** | 5 - 15 feet. |
| **Tips:** | Do not go deeper than 40 feet or the current will not carry divers back upstream. |
| **Level:** | Basic to intermediate. |

# Boom

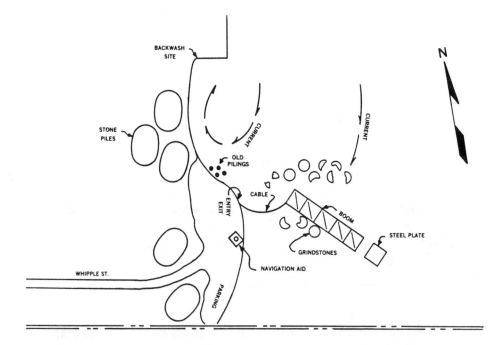

On June 5, 1972, the 356-foot steamer SIDNEY E. SMITH was northbound just south of the Blue Water Bridge when it lost control in the current. The ship swung crosswise in the current and was struck by a southbound freighter.

The collision caused a 20-foot hole in the bow of the SIDNEY E. SMITH and the ship sank quickly. The wreck was removed from the river but a large self-unloading boom remains on the river bottom.

This dive site is interesting not only because divers can explore the boom, but because there are several large grindstones nearby that apparently fell from a ship many years ago.

Access to this site can be gained by going to the parking area near the navigation signal at the end of Whipple Street in Port Huron. The boom lies about 100 feet directly offshore from the signal. The current in this area is usually not strong.

| | |
|---|---|
| **Location:** | South of Blue Water Bridge, at the end of Whipple Street in Port Huron. |
| **Depth:** | 60 - 70 feet. |
| **Visibility:** | 5 - 15 feet. |
| **Tips:** | Look for grindstones north of boom and a steel plate east of the boom. |
| **Level:** | Intermediate. |

# M.E. TREMBLE/BEN HUR

The M.E. TREMBLE was a 693-ton schooner that was loaded with coal and in tow on the St. Clair River on Sept. 7, 1890. The M.E. TREMBLE was unable to steer clear of a southbound steamer and was struck on its port side.

The M.E. TREMBLE sank with the loss of a single life. But the ship was considered a hazard to navigation and ordered removed or dynamited to clear the shipping channel.

To salvage the ship, the schooner BEN HUR was brought to the site. On Nov. 8, 1890, the BEN HUR was moored near shore and was preparing to raise the M.E. TREMBLE in a day or two. But that night, the BEN HUR was struck by a passing ship. The BEN HUR, and all wrecking equipment, were lost.

The next spring, the bow section of the M.E. TREMBLE was dynamited to provide adequate clearance. Today, the wrecks are side-by-side in a confused mass of rubble, equipment and cable.

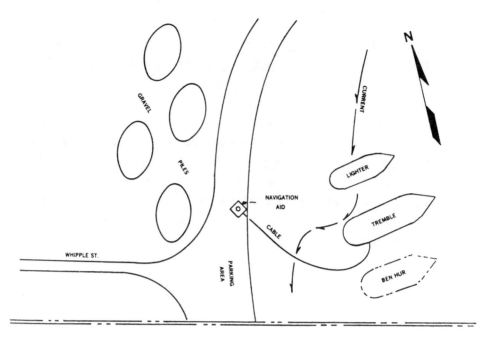

Club Poseiden Graphic

This is considered by many to be one of the most challenging dive sites in the St. Clair River.

Access to this site is at the navigational signal at the end of Whipple Street in Port Huron. A steel cable leads from the signal to the M.E. TREMBLE, which lies in about 70 feet of water. Divers first encounter wreckage, the result of the dynamiting. Then, divers find the M.E. TREMBLE. South of this wreck is the BEN HUR, upside down.

North of the M.E. TREMBLE is another wreck, the LIGHTER, a ship that had tended cables for the BEN HUR during the salvage attempt. These wrecks are mostly broken up.

Because there are many cables associated with this dive site, it is easy to become disoriented and the current can sweep divers into the shipping channel. Plan to return early and keep track of the proper guide cables.

| Location: | At the end of Whipple Street in Port Huron. |
|---|---|
| Depth: | 60-65 feet. |
| Visibility: | 5 - 15 feet. |
| Tips: | Be careful! This can be a dangerous dive in the event of disorientation and panic. Current is swift. |
| Level: | Advanced. |

If divers are swept from the site, it is best to swim west toward the shore. An emergency ascent may cause divers to enter the shipping channel.

# Pine Grove Park

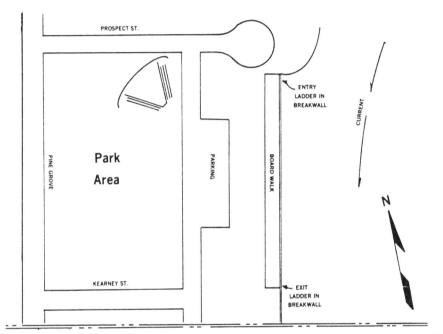

Club Poseiden Graphic

Pine Grove Park, located between Prospect and Kearney streets in Port Huron, is a popular recreation area. It is for good fishing and a good place for new divers.

There is little current at this site but access to the water from the boardwalk can be difficult with scuba gear. Enter the water at the north ladder in the breakwall and exit at the south ladder in the breakwall.

Divers can find a variety of old bottles and other artifacts at this historical site.

| | |
|---|---|
| **Location:** | Between Prospect and Kearney streets in Port Huron. |
| **Depth:** | 25 - 45 feet. |
| **Visibility:** | 5 - 15 feet. |
| **Tips:** | Watch for fishermen. Avoid their lines and be courteous. |
| **Level:** | Basic to intermediate. |

# A.R. COLBORN/Crane

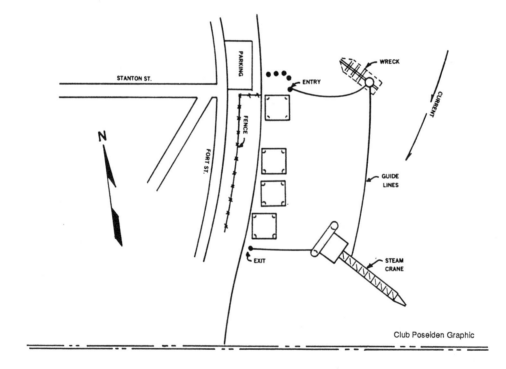

Club Poseiden Graphic

The A.R. COLBURN was a 129-foot wooden-hulled steamer built in 1882 in Saugatuck, Mich. The ship was used in the lumber industry until 1909. The A.R. COLBURN changed owners, underwent major structural changes and was used for hauling salt from St. Clair, Mich. to a railhead at Courtright, Ontario.

In 1920, the ship was purchased for conversion to a tug boat but the owner died and the ship sank at her moorings. It was formally abandoned in 1922.

The engine and boiler of the A.R. COLBURN remain, but the hull is deteriorating with the current. The propeller is displayed on the campus of St. Clair Community College.

The A.R. COLBURN lies east of an old coal dock marked by pilings. Parking is available near the intersection of Fort, Stanton and Merchant streets in Port Huron north of the YMCA building. There is a steep bank leading to the water.

Divers will find a guide cable leading from the A.R. COLBURN to an old steam crane south of the wreck. The origin of the crane is unknown but was probably lost off a barge or dock. The shipwreck and crane lie in about 25 feet of swift water.

Divers can find a steel cable leading from the southwest corner of the crane to the shore.

| | |
|---|---|
| **Location:** | North of the Port Huron YMCA building. |
| **Depth:** | 25 - 35 feet. |
| **Visibility:** | 5 - 15 feet. |
| **Tips:** | Watch for swift water and low visibility. |
| **Level:** | Intermediate. |

# YMCA River Front
# City Building/Waste Water Plant

This dive site is loaded with old bottles and artifacts. A breakwall is found along the shore and divers can enter and exit at several points along the wall. The current in this area is not particularly swift during most of the year.

The northern entry point is at the north YMCA parking lot at the end of Glenwood Street in Port Huron. A convenient exit point is

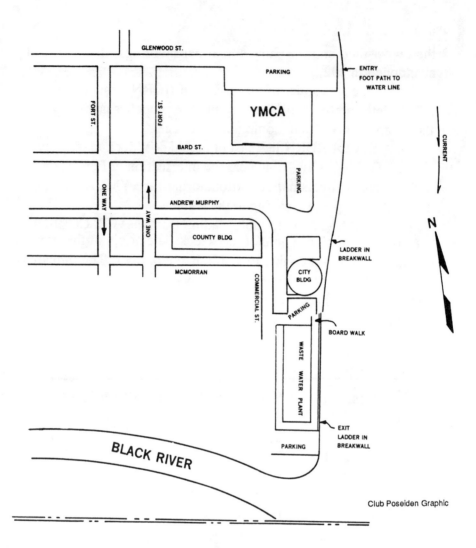

GLENWOOD ST.

PARKING

ENTRY
FOOT PATH TO
WATER LINE

FORT ST.

FORT ST.

YMCA

BARD ST.

CURRENT

ONE WAY

ONE WAY

ANDREW MURPHY

PARKING

COUNTY BLDG

LADDER IN
BREAKWALL

N

MCMORRAN

CITY
BLDG

COMMERCIAL ST.

PARKING

BOARD WALK

WASTE
WATER
PLANT

EXIT
LADDER IN
BREAKWALL

PARKING

BLACK RIVER

Club Poseiden Graphic

at the north end of the city building at a ladder built into the
breakwall. Another exit point can be found at the city's waste
water treatment plant south of the city building.

| Location: | Between the Port Huron YMCA and city buildings east of Fort Street. |
|---|---|
| Depth: | 25 -45 feet. |
| Visibility: | 5 - 15 feet. |
| Tips: | Entries and exits may be difficult due to steep breakwall. |
| Level: | Basic to intermediate. |

# Inland Waters

Diving Michigan's inland waters is exciting. Inland lakes and streams offer their own brand of challenges that make them popular among skin and scuba divers of all skill levels.

One of the greatest advantages of inland diving is accessibility. Michigan has many lakes and streams -- no matter where one stands in the state, water is within six miles.

Inland lakes are generally warmer than the Great Lakes. Although they rarely offer shipwrecks for exploration, inland lakes frequently host abandoned machinery, antique bottles, abandoned fishing boats and a variety of fishing equipment. The most interesting portions of inland waters are usually within 100 feet, so wetsuits are generally adequate during the summer.

But the water is not always warm. Thermoclines form early in the summer and frigid temperatures are common in 50 feet of water in even the hottest summer.

Game fish, such as bluegills, speckled bass, northern pike, perch and bass are commonly seen in inland waters. In the spring, divers may come across large schools of fish in shallow water where they spawn.

Because the ice forms early on inland lakes, they are frequently sites for ice diving. During the winter, sediments are undisturbed by boats and waves and the water is unusually clear. That makes the winter an ideal time for underwater photography. Ice diving is a sport quickly gaining popularity among Michigan sport divers.

Ice diving involves a variety of specialized techniques and novices should seek out the company of experienced ice divers. Drysuits are standard for this type of diving.

The best time to dive in inland waters is the early morning -- before pleasure boat traffic is too heavy. On small lakes and streams, this may not be a problem any time during the day.

Some divers avoid crowds by diving at night. This obviously requires good lights and many divers say fish are less likely to be frightened during the night when approached slowly and quietly.

# Higgins Lake

Higgins Lake in Roscommon and Crawford Counties is popular for night diving and for divers who enjoy observing aquatic life.

There are many sunken logs that attract fish. Because Higgins Lake is popular among boaters and fishermen, divers can also find a variety of items lost overboard.

Besides underwater log jams and aquatic life, Higgins Lake is popular because of water clarity. During summer months, divers can expect visibility of 15 to 55 feet.

Higgins Lake is one of the largest inland lakes in the state. It is also deep -- up to 135 feet in the northwest section of the lake. But there are also many shallow areas where divers can observe fish. In the southern end of the lake is a "sunken island" where a variety of game fish can be found in large schools, especially during the spring spawning season.

There are two state parks with boat ramps and one boat launching facility on the west side of the lake to provide ample access for divers.

Since Higgins Lake is so large, it may be a good idea to contact the Scuba Shack on the northwest shore of the lake for charter services. A charter can take divers quickly and economically to the best sites on this lake.

Higgins Lake accommodates divers of all skill levels.

It is a good idea to make reservations for overnight accommodations well in advance because hotels and motels in this area fill fast because it is a popular tourist destination.

# Getting There

Higgins Lake is located east of US 27 about 10 miles south of Grayling. There are several communities on the lake, including Hillcrest, Sharps Corners and Higgins Lake.

Streets circle the lake and there are two state parks, on the south and north ends, and a boat launch on the west side of the Higgins Lake near Lake City Road.

DNR Graphic

SCALE

Higgins Lake

# Gull Lake

Gull Lake is located in Kalamazoo County and offers skin and scuba divers an opportunity to observe fish life in weed beds and a variety of farm equipment, small boats and fish shanties.

In some areas, it was not unusual for residents to dispose of unwanted items such as obsolete farm equipment and even old cars by taking them out on the ice. When spring came, the disposal was complete.

These days, that practice is uncommon because of environmental concerns, but Gull Lake is one area where farmers' "trash" became divers' "treasure."

The maximum depth of Gull Lake is about 110 feet and most fish and weed beds can be found in 50 feet or less. A popular access site for divers in Prairieville Township Park on the north end of the lake. The beach slopes gently and offers a safe way to enter the lake.

At the southwest end of Gull Lake is another park, Ross Township Park, near the small community of Yorkville. Entry is easy over a grassy slope.

Spring and fall offer the best visibility in this silt-bottom lake. Divers can expect to find a visibility range of 8 to 30 feet. Most divers enjoy aquatic life and discarded farm equipment and cars in 10 to 40 feet of water.

Gull Lake is relatively close to Kalamazoo and Battle Creek. As a result, it can be crowded with boat traffic in July and August. Night or early morning diving may be a good idea, and it is always important to display a diver down flag.

Divers of all skill levels will find Gull Lake worth the trip.

Information about this dive site is available from Sub-Aquatic Sports and Service in Battle Creek, (616) 968-8551. Information about diving and other activities, including wildlife watching at the nearby Kellogg Bird Sanctuary, is available from the Battle Creek Chamber of Commerce, 172 W. Van Buren, Battle Creek, MI 49017.

## Getting There

Gull Lake is 10 miles northwest of Battle Creek off M-89. A system of streets circle the lake and make access easy at many points.

# Brockway Lake

Brockway Lake is a small lake in southern Mecosta County that offers an unusual diving experience.

The lake was created through mining of "marl," which was used to "sweeten" farmers' fields. As a result, there are steep walls that extend to depths of 25 feet.

In addition to steep walls, Brockway lake is thick with vegetation and fish life. Northern pike are abundant and divers can often observe them closely. At times, they are so secure in their weedy hideouts that they must actually be touched to "spook."

Spring in the shallows offers divers tremendous schools of sunfish, bluegills and speckled bass. An occasional smallmouth bass may be seen in the company of these prey fish.

Brockway Lake is a popular fishing lake but because it is relatively small, few fishermen use motors. As a result, visibility of 15 feet is not unusual. Also, there is no danger of being run over by water skiers, but it is still a good idea to display a diver down flag.

The lake supports a variety of uncommon waterfowl spring through fall.

Access to Brockway Lake is by a public fishing site. A gravel path used to launch boats (but not really a ramp) is convenient for diver entry. The maximum depth of Brockway Lake is about 30 feet. This is a good place for beginning divers.

# Getting There

Brockway Lake is in southern Mecosta County. Take US 131 to the Jefferson Road (Morley) Exit and go east about 9 miles to 100th Ave. Turn left (north) and at the first road (Three Mile Road) turn right (west). Follow signs to public access.

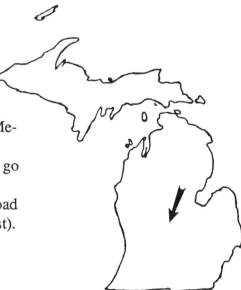

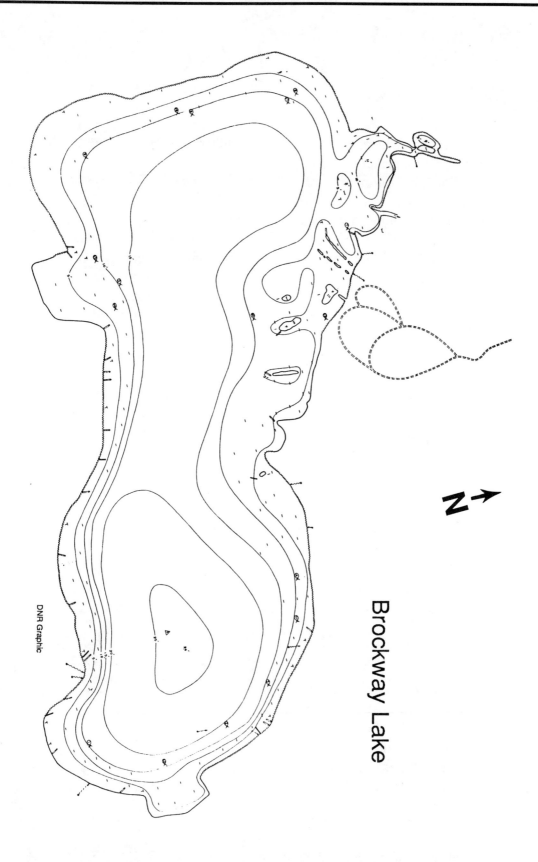

Brockway Lake

DNR Graphic

# Boardman River

The Boardman River is not long, but it offers good diving experiences.

The river drains Boardman Lake and runs through Traverse City before dumping its load in Grand Traverse Bay. Visibility is usually about 15 feet, but can be reduced significantly after rainfall. The maximum depth of the river is about 15 feet.

The Boardman River can be entered at several places in the Traverse City area. One good area for diver entry is west of the dam under Union Street Bridge in Traverse City.

Even casual observers will note the remarkable clarity of the Boardman River water and there are many artifacts to be found by divers.

Occasionally the current will be swift so divers must evaluate their skills carefully depending upon the water conditions on the day of the dive.

Information about this dive site, which is a good alternative in the event of heavy seas on Lake Michigan or Traverse Bay, is available from Scuba North, (616) 947-2520.

## Getting There

The Boardman River drains Boardman Lake and runs 1 1/2 to 2 miles through Traverse City where there are many access sites.

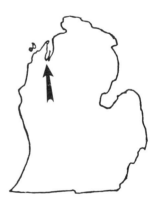

# Murray Lake

When Grand Rapids divers want a convenient, pleasurable dive, they head for Murray Lake in northern Kent County.

Murray Lake is 320 acres of fish and fun. It is an excellent dive site for beginning divers and night diving.

Murray Lake is horseshoe-shaped and there is a public access on each arm. In 20 feet of water and less there is lush vegetation that attracts large schools of small game fish, particularly speckled bass, bluegills, sunfish and small perch. Predatory fish, such as northern pike and bass, are also common.

There is no where to go wrong in Murray Lake if skin and scuba divers are interested in exploration. The shore of the lake is moderately developed, but there is enough adjacent wetland to preserve habitat for an abundant fishery and wildlife.

Murray Lake is a popular ice diving site. Summer brings out water skiers so divers must use caution.

Because Murray Lake is heavily fished, divers can expect to find small wooden boats on the bottom and a variety of fishing equipment. Several outboard motors that have fallen off fishing boats have been discovered by divers.

Visibility ranges from 5 to 15 feet. May and June are the best months for diving this lake because fish are congregated in large schools as they prepare to spawn and boat traffic is minimal.

In addition to two public access sites on each arm of the lake, divers can also enter the lake from the north off Five Mile Road. There is ample parking in lots at the public access sites or along the road at the north end.

Dive shops in Grand Rapids can direct divers to Murray Lake and provide current dive conditions.

## Getting There

Divers can find Murray Lake by taking M 21 (Fulton) to Parnell Avenue (between Ada and Lowell). Go north on Parnell to Four Mile Road and turn right (east) to Murray Lake Avenue and turn left to go to Five Mile Road and the northern access site. Turn right (south) on Murray Lake Avenue and then left (east) on Lally Road and left (north) on Causeway Drive to the public access sites on each arm. Signs guide visitors to these sites.

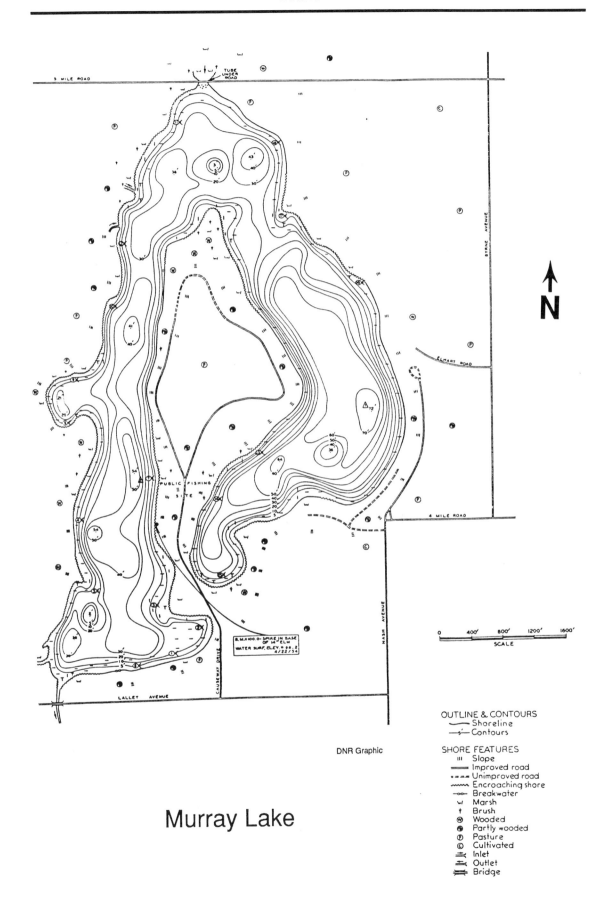

DNR Graphic

OUTLINE & CONTOURS
— Shoreline
—ʳ— Contours

SHORE FEATURES
ııı Slope
═══ Improved road
═ ═ ═ Unimproved road
∿∿∿ Encroaching shore
∘∘ Breakwater
ɯ Marsh
† Brush
Ⓦ Wooded
◉ Partly wooded
Ⓟ Pasture
Ⓒ Cultivated
≋ Inlet
≋ Outlet
ⱷ Bridge

# Murray Lake

# Inland Quarry

The Inland Quarry in Schoolcraft County in the Upper Peninsula combines water clarity, easy access and a variety of underwater attractions to draw sport divers from all over.

This is a good dive site to remember as an alternative when heavy seas on Lake Superior prevent Great Lakes diving. But an excuse is not needed to visit the Inland Quarry. It offers enough worthwhile diving to make it a legitimate dive destination on its own.

The Inland Quarry varies in depth from 5 to 25 feet and visibility is usually 10 to 30 feet. During the winter, visibility can approach 100 feet.

With all that visibility, divers can explore a variety of items discarded, including machinery and old buildings. The quarry was created through the mining of rock.

This is a good site for divers with basic skills.

Information about the site can be obtained at the Dyatomics Scuba Center in Newberry, (906) 293-8060.

## Getting There

Inland Quarry is located off US 2 on Inland Quarry Road, about one mile west of Blaney Park in east end of Schoolcraft County.

# Baw Beese Lake

Baw Beese Lake was created with an impoundment of the St. Joseph River. The lake, southeast of Hillsdale, hosts a variety of small boats, ice shanties and weed beds that attract small game fish.

Baw Beese Lake covers about 300 acres and has a maximum depth of 70 feet. Visibility is generally 15 to 30 feet.

Divers will find a small cabin cruiser at the northeast corner of the lake in about 55 feet of water. Divers will also find bottles and other discarded items on the silty lake bottom.

There are several parks on the lake that provide easy access. Streets encircle the lake making access from other points possible but divers should be sure they are not using private property without permission.

Waterskiing is popular on Baw Beese Lake so use extreme caution and display a diver down flag prominently.

## Getting There

Baw Beese Lake is southeast of the city of Hillsdale. Access can be obtained from many road off M 99, which runs through the city.

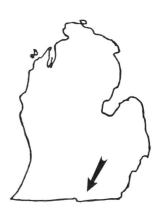

## Heart Lake

Heart Lake in southern Otsego County is known for remarkable clarity, despite heavy water skiing activity.

There was once a sawmill on the south end of Heart Lake and logs were floated across the lake to the mill. Before some logs made it to the saw, however, they became waterlogged and sank. As a result, divers can find massive logs on the silty to sandy bottom.

The logs attract a variety of fish, especially smallmouth bass, trout and small perch.

Heart Lake is divided into two sections with the easternmost section being the largest and deepest. This is where virtually all waterskiing occurs, although the lake is barely large enough. The

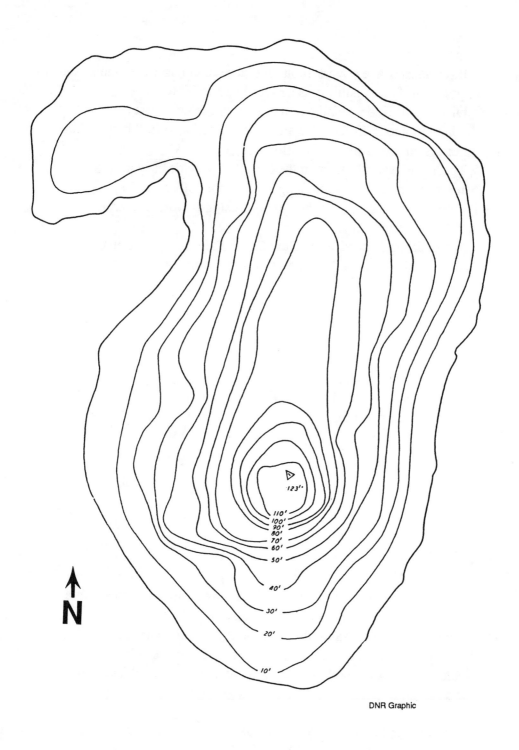

123'

110'
100'
90'
80'
70'
60'

50'

40'

30'

20'

10'

N

DNR Graphic

# Heart Lake

maximum depth of this section is about 125 feet, and a thermocline rarely exceeds 25 feet in the summer. Beyond the thermocline, the water can be extremely cold.

The western section of Heart Lake, however, is shallow and generally very warm in late July and August. This is a good environment for skin diving, although there are few features to interest divers. The bottom is silty and there is little vegetation to attract fish.

The western section, however, often yields curious bottles and fishing equipment. This lake is suitable for divers of all skill levels as long as they do not go too deep for their abilities.

There is a public access site on the south end of Heart Lake that offers plenty of parking and easy diver entry. Divers seeking overnight accommodations in July and August may find hotels and motels booked. There are many campgrounds in the vicinity.

## Getting There

Take US 75 to the Waters Exit, turn right (west) and at the stop sign, turn right (north). About one mile north of Waters there are signs that show the way to a public access site.

# Hardy Pond

The Hardy Pond was created with the impoundment of the Muskegon River in 1932. The 4,000-acre lake created by the dam is a popular West Michigan dive site.

Among the most popular attractions in Hardy Pond is a steel bridge that was submerged with rising water. It rests in 60 feet of water. The maximum depth of Hardy Pond is 110 feet. Visibility is limited because of sediments. Although visibility may be as great as 30 feet in some areas, divers should be prepared for visibility of 10 feet or less.

Hardy Pond is a popular fishing site and log jams can collect masses of monofilament fishing line. Several divers have been thankful they had a good diving knife to remove fishing line that entangled their equipment.

Divers can expect to find a variety of game fish, including walleye, around log jams. Hardy Pond offers good diving for divers of all experience levels.

Campgrounds and an access are available at Newaygo State Park on the east side of the impoundment.

Information about diving Hardy Pond is available from the U.S. Forest Service Ranger Station at White Cloud, (616) 689-6696.

## Getting There

Hardy Pond is located in Newaygo County and can be reached by taking US 131 north to the Jefferson Road - Morley Exit and then heading east.

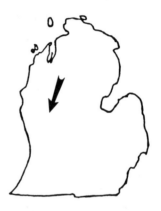

# Diving Law

Laws affect virtually every aspect of our lives and diving is no exception.

Michigan, through the efforts of the sport diving community, has developed a tough set of laws designed to preserve underwater artifacts while ensuring recreation opportunities. These laws are contained in the Aboriginal Records and Antiquities Act.

In 1988, Michigan's laws were amended to provide for stiff criminal penalties for vandals or thieves who tamper with underwater artifacts. As a result, divers of future generations will be able to enjoy our underwater maritime heritage for decades to come.

The law is presented here to answer questions about what may or may not be legal activities in Michigan. Readers will note that there are specific regulations that apply to Michigan's bottomland preserves. These regulations apply to all bottomland preserves, but because the National Park Service has jurisdiction over a larger area around Isle Royale, these laws do not necessarily apply there. Isle Royale regulations are outlined in the chapter covering that area.

There is remarkably little case law to interpret these statutes. But challenges to the constitutionality of the laws have been unsuccessful and it appears as though state courts will take a firm stand to protect the interests of sport divers.

The comment is not part of the law but is provided to help readers understand the implications of the law for sport diving.

Divers who discover what they believe may be historically significant artifacts should contact the Michigan Department of Natural Resources or the Michigan Secretary of State, Bureau of History.

Divers who suspect violations of the Aboriginal Records and Antiquities Act by others should gather enough information to identify the suspects (boat registration, license plate numbers, etc.) and contact the Michigan Department of Natural Resources.

The 24-hour, toll-free hotline used to report poachers may also be used to report violations of this law. That number is **1-800-292-7800.**

# Aboriginal Records and Antiquities Act

P.A. 1929, No. 173, Imd. Eff. May 20

AN ACT to protect and preserve, and to regulate the taking of, aboriginal records and antiquities within this state; to preserve abandoned property of historical or recreational value on the bottomlands of the Great Lakes and regulate the salvage of abandoned property of historical or recreational value; to designate and regulate Great Lakes bottomland preserves; to prescribe the powers and duties of certain state agencies; to create a fund; and to prescribe penalties and provide remedies. Amended by P.A. 1988, No. 452, Eff. March 30, 1989.

## MCL 299.51. Aboriginal records and antiquities; exclusive right in state, exceptions

Sec. 1. (1) The state reserves to itself the exclusive right and privilege, except as provided in this act, of exploring, surveying, excavating, and regulating through its authorized officers, agents, and employees, all aboriginal records and other antiquities, including mounds, earthworks, forts, burial and village sites, mines or other relics, and abandoned property of historical or recreational value found upon or within any of the lands owned by or under the control of the state.

(2) The state reserves to itself a possessory right or title superior to that of a finder to abandoned property of historical or recreational value found on the state owned bottomlands of the Great Lakes. This property shall belong to this state with administration and protection jointly vested in the department and the secretary of state.

## Comment:

This section declares abandoned property of historic and recreational value on Great Lakes bottomlands to be state property. In a Michigan Court of Appeals decision, this section was found to be constitutional and did not conflict with admiralty and maritime law.

It is important to note that historically, the state has broad control over property rights as long as it does not exert confiscatory authority. If property is abandoned, then, the state has the power to protect it for historic and recreational purposes.

## MCL 299.51a. Definitions

Sec. 1a. As used in this act:

(a) "Abandoned property" means an aircraft; a watercraft, including a ship, boat, canoe, skiff, raft or barge; the rigging, gear, fittings, trappings, and equipment of an aircraft or watercraft; the personal property of the officers, crew, and passengers of an aircraft or watercraft; and cargo of an aircraft or watercraft which have been deserted, relinquished, cast away, or left behind and for which attempts at reclamation have been abandoned by owners and insurers. Abandoned property also means materials resulting from activities of historic and prehistoric native Americans.

(b) "Bottomlands" means the unpatented lake bottomlands of the Great Lakes.

(c) "Committee" means the underwater salvage and preserve committee created in section 1b.

(d) "Department" means the department of natural resources.

(e) "Great Lakes" means lakes Erie, Huron, Michigan, St. Clair, and Superior.

(f) "Great Lakes bottomlands preserve" means an area located on the bottomlands of the Great Lakes and extending upward to and including the surface of the water, which is delineated and set aside by rule promulgated pursuant to the administrative procedures act of 1969, Act. No. 306 of the Public Acts of 1969, as amended, being sections 24.201 to 24.328 of the Michigan Compiled Laws, for special protection of abandoned property of historical value, or ecological, educational, geological, or scenic features or formations having recreational, educational, or scientific value. A preserve may encompass a single object, feature, or formation, or a collection of several objects, features or formations.

(g) "Historical value" means value relating to, or illustrative of, Michigan history, including the statehood, territorial, colonial, and historic, and prehistoric native American periods.

(h) "Mechanical or other assistance" means all manmade devices, including pry bars, wrenches and other hand or power tools, cutting torches, explosives, winches, flotation bags, lines to surface, extra divers buoyancy devices, and other buoyance devices, used to raise or remove artifacts.

(i) "Recreational value" means value relating to an activity which the public engages in, or may engage in, for recreation or sport, including scuba diving and fishing.

**MCL 299.51b. Underwater salvage and preserve committee; creation, members, terms, duties.**

Sec. 1b. (1) The underwater salvage and preserve committee is created in the department to provide technical and other advice to the director of the department and the secretary of state with respect to their responsibilities under this act.

(2) The underwater salvage and preserve committee shall consist of 9 members appointed as follows:

(a) Two individuals appointed by the director of the department who have primary responsibility in the department for administering this act.
(b) Two individuals appointed by the secretary of state who have primary responsibility in the department of state for administering this act.
(c) One individual appointed by the director of commerce.
(d) Four individuals appointed by the governor with the advice and consent of the senate from the general public. Two of these individuals shall have experience in recreational scuba diving.

(3) An individual appointed to the committee shall serve for a term of 3 years. A vacancy on the committee shall be filled in the same manner as an original appointment and the term of a member appointed to fill a vacancy shall be for 3 years. Members of the committee shall serve without compensation, except for their regular state salary where applicable.

(4) The chairperson of the committee shall alternate between the representatives from the department and the department of state. The chairperson shall be designated by the director of the department or the secretary of state, whichever is applicable from among his or her representatives on the committee. The chairperson's term shall run for 12 months, from October 1 through September 30. The director of the department shall appoint the first chairperson of the committee for a term ending September 30, 1989. The chairperson shall call meetings as necessary but not less than 4 times per year, set the agenda for meetings, ensure the adequate minutes are taken, and file an annual report of committee proceedings with the head of the departments of state, natural resources, and commerce.

(5) The committee is an advisory body and may perform all of the following functions:

(a) Make recommendations with regard to the creation and boundaries of Great Lakes underwater preserves.

(b) Review applications for underwater salvage permits and make recommendations regarding issuance.

(c) Consider and make recommendations regarding the charging of permit fees and the appropriate use of revenue generated by those fees.

(d) Consider the need for and the content of rules intended to implement this act and make recommendations concerning the promulgation of rules.

(e) Consider and make recommendations concerning appropriate legislation.

(f) Consider and make recommendations concerning program operation.

(6) The committee shall not replace or supersede the responsibility or authority of the secretary of state or the director of the department to carry out their responsibilities under this act.

**Comment:**

This section establishes the membership and function of the Underwater Salvage and Preserve Committee.

Although the primary management functions of the Great Lakes bottomlands remains with the Department of Natural Resources and Secretary of State, a representative from the Commerce Department was added by the 1988 amendments to ensure input from those knowledgeable about the tourism industry.

Divers should note that this committee is advisory and has no authority over any state agency.

**MCL 299.54. Aboriginal records and antiquities; consent of landowner to removal**

Sec. 4. Without the consent of the land owner, a person shall not remove any relics or records of antiquity such as human or other bones; shells, stone, bone, or copper implements; pottery or shards of pottery, or similar artifacts and objects from the premises where they have been discovered.

**Comment:**

Divers in inland lakes and streams must have the permission of the landowners (owners of the bottomlands) to remove artifacts.

**MCL 299.54a. Permits; recovery of abandoned property within Great Lakes bottomlands; human remains; violations, fines**

Sec. 4a. (1) Except as provided in section 4b, a person shall not recover, alter or destroy abandoned property which is in, on, under, or over the bottomlands of the Great Lakes, including those within a Great Lakes bottomlands preserve, unless the person has a permit issued jointly by the secretary of state and the department pursuant to section 4c.

(2) A person who recovers abandoned property without a permit when a permit is required by this act shall transmit the property to the secretary of state and the recovered property shall be the property of the secretary of state.

(3) A person shall not remove, convey, mutilate, or deface a human body or the remains of a human body located on the bottomlands of the Great Lakes.

(4) A person who violates section (1) by recovering or destroying abandoned property with a fair market value of $100.00 or more is guilty of a felony, punishable by imprisonment for not more than 2 years, or by a fine of not more than $5,000,00 or both.

**Comment:**

This section prohibits the removal of <u>any</u> artifacts from Great Lakes bottomland preserves without a permit. Violations involving property worth $100 or more is a felony.

**MCL 299.54b. Permits; recovery of abandoned property outside Great Lakes bottomlands preserves**

Sec. 4b. (1) A person may recover abandoned property outside a Great Lakes bottomlands preserve without a permit if the abandoned property is not attached to, nor located on in, or located in the immediate vicinity of and associated with a sunken aircraft or watercraft and if the abandoned property is recoverable by hand without mechanical or other assistance.

(2) A person who recovers abandoned property valued at more than $10.00 without a permit pursuant to subsection (1) shall file a written report within 30 days after removal of the property with the department or the secretary of state if the property has been abandoned for more than 30 years. The written report shall list all recovered property which has been abandoned for more than 30 years and the location of the property at the time of recovery. For a period of 90 days after the report is filed, the person shall make the recovered property available to the department and the secretary of state for inspection at a location in this state. If the secretary of state determines that the recovered property does not have historical value, the secretary of state shall release the property to the person by means of a written instrument.

**Comment:**

This section requires a permit for certain abandoned property removed from Great Lakes bottomlands outside the preserves. It establishes a reporting procedure for artifacts worth more than $10 removed from Great Lakes bottomlands without a permit.

Abandoned property worth less than $10, removed by hand and not associated with a sunken watercraft or aircraft does not require a permit or report.

**MCL 299.54c. Permits; recovery of abandoned property on or in sunken aircraft or watercraft**

Sec. 4c. (1) A permit issued under this section shall authorize a person to recover abandoned property located on, in, or located in the immediate vicinity of and associated with a sunken aircraft or watercraft.

(2) A person shall file an application for a permit with the department on a form prescribed by the department and approved by the secretary of state. The application shall contain all of the following information:

(a) The name and address of the applicant.

(b) The name, if known, of the watercraft or aircraft on or around which recovery operations are to occur and a current photograph or drawing of the watercraft or aircraft, if available.

(c) The location of the abandoned property to be recovered and the depth of water in which it may be found.

(d) A description of each item to be recovered.

(e) The method to be used in recovery operations.

(f) The proposed disposition of the abandoned property recovered, including the location at which it will be available for inspection by the department and the secretary of state.

(g) Other information which the department or the secretary of state considers necessary in evaluating the request for a permit.

(3) An application for a permit shall not be considered complete until all information requested on the application form and any other information requested by the department or the secretary of state has been received by the department. After receipt of an otherwise complete application, the department may request additional information or documents as are determined to be necessary to make a decision to grant or deny a permit. The department, or the secretary of state, shall notify the applicant in writing when the application is deficient.

(4) An applicant notified that an application for a permit may be deficient and returned due to insufficient information under subsection (3) shall, within 20 days after the date the notice is mailed, provide the information. If the applicant fails to respond within the 20-day period, the application shall be denied unless the applicant requests additional time and provides reasonable justification for an extension of time.

(5) The department and the secretary of state shall, with the advice of the committee, approve or disapprove an application for a permit within 30 days after the date a complete application is filed with the department. The department and the secretary of state may approve an application conditionally or unconditionally. A condition to the approval of an application shall be in writing on the face of the permit. The department and the secretary of state may impose such conditions as are considered reasonable and necessary to protect the public trust and general interests, including conditions that accomplish 1 or more of the following:

(a) Protect and preserve the abandoned property to be recovered, and the recreational value of the area in which recovery is being accomplished.

(b) Assure reasonable public access to the abandoned property after recovery.

(c) Are in conformity with rules applying to activities within a Great Lakes bottomlands preserve.

(d) Prohibit injury, harm, and damage to a bottomlands site or abandoned property not authorized for removal during and after salvage operations by the permit holder.

(e) Prohibit or limit the amount of discharge of possible pollutants, such as floating timbers, planking, and other debris, which may emanate from the shipwreck, plane wreck or salvage equipment.

(f) Require the permit holder to submit a specific removal plan prior to commencing any salvaging activities. Among other matters considered appropriate by either the department or the secretary of state, or both, the removal plan may be required to ensure the safety of those removing or assisting in the removal of the abandoned property and to address how the permit holder proposes to prevent, minimize, or mitigate potential adverse effects upon the abandoned property to be removed, that portion of the abandoned property which is not to be removed, and the surrounding geographic features.

(6) The department shall approve an application for a permit unless the secretary of state determines that the abandoned property to be recovered has substantial historical value in itself or in conjunction with other abandoned property in its vicinity underwater, or the recovery of abandoned property would not comply with rules applying to a Great Lakes bottomlands preserve.

(7) If the property has substantial historical value, the secretary of state, pursuant to subsection (5), may impose a condition to the approval of the application requiring the applicant to turn over recovered property to the secretary of state for the purpose of preserving the property or permitting public access to the property. The secretary of state may authorize the display of the property in a public or private museum or by a local unit of government. In addition to the conditions authorized by subsection (5), the secretary of state may provide for payment of salvage costs in connection with the recovery of the abandoned property.

(8) A person who discovers an abandoned watercraft which is located outside of a Great Lakes bottomlands preserve shall be entitled to recover cargo situated on, in, or associated with the watercraft, if the person applies for a permit pursuant to this section within 90 days after discovering the watercraft. If an application for a permit to recover cargo is not filed within 90 days after a watercraft discovery, subject to subsections (4) and (5) an exclusive cargo recovery permit shall be issued to the first person applying for such a permit. Only 1 permit to recover the same cargo shall be issued and operative at a time. When a watercraft containing cargo is simultaneously discovered by more than 1 person, a permit shall be approved with respect to the first person or persons jointly applying for a permit.

(9) A person aggrieved by a condition contained on a permit or by the denial of an application for a permit may request an administrative review of the condition or the denial by the director of the department or the secretary of state, whichever disapproves the application or imposes the condition. A person shall file the request for review with the department or the secretary of state, whichever is applicable, within 90 days after the permit application is submitted to the department. An administrative hearing conducted pursuant to this subsection shall be conducted under the procedures set forth in chapter 4 of the administrative procedures act of 1969, Act No. 306 of the Public Acts of 1969, as amended, being sections 24.271 to 24.287 of the Michigan Compiled Laws. If neither the department or the secretary of state approves the application and an administrative review is requested from both the department and the secretary of state, the appeals shall be combined upon request of the appellant or either the department or the secretary of state and a single administrative

hearing shall be conducted. The director of the department and the secretary of state shall issue jointly the final decision and order in the case.

(10) A permit issued under this section shall be valid until December 31 of the year in which the application for the permit was filed and is not renewable. If an item designated in a permit for recovery is not recovered, a permit holder may, upon request following the expiration of the permit, be issued a new permit to remove the same abandoned property if the permit holder demonstrates that diligence in attempting recovery was exercised under the previously issued permit.

(11) A permit issued under this section shall not be transferred to assigned unless the assignment is approved in writing by both the department and the secretary of state.

## Comment:

This section requires a permit to be issued for the removal of abandoned property that is associated with a sunken watercraft or aircraft. The requirements of the permit application are established and all information must be submitted before an application will be considered complete.

Generally, this section provides rights of salvage to be balanced against the state's interest in preserving historic and/or recreational diving sites.

### MCL 299.54d. Reports; recovery of abandoned property; examination; removal from state

Sec. 4d. (1) Within 10 days after recovery of abandoned property, a person with a permit issued pursuant to section 4c shall report the recovery in writing to the department. The person recovering the abandoned property shall give authorized representatives of the department and the secretary of state an opportunity to examine the abandoned property for a period of 90 days after recovery. Recovered abandoned property shall not be removed from this state without written approval of the department and the secretary of state. If the recovered abandoned property is removed from the state without written approval, the attorney general, upon request from the department or the secretary of state, shall bring an action for the recovery of the property.

(2) If the secretary of state determines that the recovered abandoned property does not have historical value, the secretary of state shall release the property to the person holding the permit by means of a written instrument.

### MCL 299.54e. Great Lakes bottomlands preserves; establishment, factors; permits to recover abandoned artifacts; area; sinking vessels

Sec. 4e. (1) The department shall establish Great Lakes bottomlands preserves by rule promulgated pursuant to the administrative procedures act of 1969, Act No. 306 of the Public Acts of 1969, being sections 24.201 to 24.328 of the Michigan Compiled laws. A Great Lakes bottomlands preserve shall be established by emergency rule if it is determined by the director of the department that this action is necessary to immediately protect an object or area of historical or recreational value.

(2) A Great Lakes bottomlands preserve may be established whenever a bottomlands area includes a single watercraft of significant historical value, includes 2 or more abandoned watercraft, or contains other features of archeological, historical, recreational, geological, or environmental significance. Bottomlands areas containing few or no watercraft or other features directly related to the character of a preserve may be excluded from preserves.

(3) In establishing a Great Lakes bottomlands preserve, the department shall consider all of the following factors:

(a) Whether creating the preserve is necessary to protect either abandoned property possessing historical or recreational value, or significant underwater geological or environmental features.

(b) The extent of local public and private support for creation of the preserve.

(c) Whether a preserve development plan has been prepared by a state or local agency.

(d) The extent to which preserve support facilities such as roads, marinas, character services, hotels, medical hyperbaric facilities, and rescue agencies have been developed in or are planned for the area.

(4) The department and the secretary of state shall not grant a permit to recover abandoned artifacts within a Great Lakes bottomlands preserve except for historical or scientific purposes or when the recovery will not adversely affect the historical, cultural, or recreational integrity of the preserve area as a whole.

(5) An individual Great Lakes bottomlands preserve shall not exceed 400 square miles in area. Great Lakes bottomlands preserves shall be limited in total area to not more than 10% of the Great Lakes bottomlands within this state.

(6) Upon the approval of the committee, not more than 1 vessel associated with Great Lakes maritime history may be sunk intentionally within a Great Lakes bottomlands preserve. However, no state money shall be expended to purchase, transport, or sink the vessel.

## Comment:

This section details the factors used to determine whether an area may be considered for bottomland preserve designation.

Under this section, the Underwater Salvage and Preserve Committee may approve the intentional sinking of a vessel in a bottomland preserve. No state money may be spent to place such a vessel on the Great Lakes bottomlands.

### MCL 299.54f. Rules

Sec. 4f. (1) The department and the secretary of state, jointly or separately, may promulgate rules pursuant to the administrative procedures act of 1969, Act No. 306 of the Public Acts of 1969, as amended, being sections 24.201 to 24.328 of the Michigan Compiled Laws, as are necessary to implement this act.

(2) Within each Great Lakes bottomlands preserve, the department and the secretary of state may jointly promulgate rules, pursuant to the administrative procedures act of 1969, Act No. 306 of the Public Acts of 1969, which govern access to and use of a Great Lakes bottomlands preserve. These

rules may regulate or prohibit the alteration, destruction, or removal of abandoned property, features, or formations within a preserve.

## MCL 299.54g. Recovery of abandoned property; rights not limited

Sec. 4g. Sections 4a to 4d shall not be considered to impose the following limitations:

(a) A limitation on the right of a person to engage in diving for recreational purposes in and upon the Great Lakes or the bottomlands of the Great Lakes.
(b) A limitation on the right of the department or the secretary of state to recover, or to contract for the recovery of, abandoned property in and upon the bottomlands of the Great Lakes.

(c) A limitation on the right of a person to own either abandoned property recovered before July 2, 1980 or abandoned property released to a person after inspection.

## Comment:

This section specifically states that the above sections are not intended to limit sport diving activity.

## MCL 299.54h. Suspension or revocation of permit; hearing; civil actions

Sec. 4h. (1) If the department or the secretary of state finds that the holder of a permit issued pursuant to section 3 or 4c is not in compliance with this act, a rule promulgated under this act, or a provision of or condition in the permit, or has damaged abandoned property or failed to use diligence in attempting to recover property for which a permit was issued, the department or the secretary of state, individually or jointly, may summarily suspend or revoke the permit. If the permit holder requests a hearing within 15 days following the effective date of the suspension or revocation, the department or the secretary of state shall conduct an administrative hearing pursuant to chapter 4 of the administrative procedures act of 1969, Act No. 306 of the Public Acts of 1969, being sections 24.271 to 24.287 of the Michigan Compiled Laws, to consider whether the permit should be reinstated.

(2) The attorney general, on behalf of the department or the secretary of state, individually or jointly, may commence a civil action in circuit court to enforce compliance with this act, to restrain a violation of this act or any action contrary to a decision denying a permit, to enjoin the further removal of artifacts, geological material, or abandoned property, or to order the restoration of an affected area to its prior condition.

## MCL 299.54i. Scuba diving; acceptance of dangers

Sec. 4i. Each person who participates in the sport of scuba diving on the Great Lakes bottomlands accepts the dangers which adhere in that sport insofar as the dangers are obvious and necessary. Those dangers include, but are not limited to, injuries which can result from entanglements in sunken watercraft or aircraft; the failure of the state to fund staff or programs at bottomlands preserves; and the depth of the objects and bottomlands within preserves.

## Comment:

This section puts scuba divers on notice that they accept certain dangers when diving in the Great Lakes. This section is intended to limit lawsuits against the state and charter operators for death and injuries over which they have no control.

### MCL 299.55. Penalty

Sec. 5. (1) A person who violates section 3 or 4 of this act is guilty of a misdemeanor, and shall be punished by a fine of not more than $100.00 or by imprisonment for not more than 30 days, or both.

(2) A person who violates sections 4a to 4e or a rule promulgated under this act is guilty of a misdemeanor. Unless another penalty is provided in this act, a person convicted of a misdemeanor under this subsection shall be punished by a fine of not more than $500.00 or by imprisonment of not more than 6 months, or both.

### MCL 299.56. Violations; attachment and confiscation of property; complaint, order to show cause, notice; hearing; proceeds

Sec. 6. (1) If a person who violates this act or a rule promulgated under this act uses a watercraft, mechanical or other assistance, scuba gear, sonar equipment, a motor vehicle, or any other equipment or apparatus during the course of committing the violation, the items so used may be attached, proceeded against, and confiscated as prescribed in this act.

(2) To effect confiscation, the law enforcement or conservation officer seizing the property shall file a verified complaint in the circuit court for the county in which the seizure was made or in the circuit court for Ingham county. The complaint shall set forth the kind of property seized, the time and place of the seizure, the reasons for the seizure, and a demand for the property's condemnation and confiscation. Upon the filing of the complaint, an order shall be issued requiring the owner to show cause why the property should not be confiscated. The substance of the complaint shall be stated in the order. The order to show cause shall fix the time for service of the order and for the hearing on the proposed condemnation and confiscation.

(3) The order to show cause shall be served on the owner of the property as soon as possible but not less than 7 days before the complaint is to be heard. The court, for cause shown, may hear the complaint on shorter notice. If the owner is not known or cannot be found, notice may be served in 1 or more of the following ways:

(a) By posting a copy of the order in 3 public places for 3 consecutive weeks in the county in which the seizure was made and by sending a copy of the order by certified mail to the last known business or residential address of the owner. If the last addresses of the owner are not known, mailing a copy of the order is not required.
(b) By publishing a copy of the order in a newspaper once each week for 3 consecutive weeks in the country where the seizure was made and by sending a copy of the order by registered mail to the last known residential address of the owner. If the last residential address of the owner is not known, mailing a copy of the order is not required.
(c) In such a manner as the court directs.

(4) Upon hearing of the complaint, if the court determines that the property mentioned in the petition was possessed, shipped, or used contrary to law, either by the owner or by a person lawfully in possession of the property under an agreement with the owner, an order shall be made condemning and confiscating the property and directing its sale or other disposal by the director of the department. If the owners signs a property release, a court proceeding shall not be necessary. At the hearing, if the court determines that the property was not possessed, shipped, or used contrary to law, the court shall order the director of the department to immediately return the property to its owner.

(5) The department shall deposit the proceeds it receives under this section into the state treasury to the credit of the underwater preserve fund created in section 7.

## Comment:

This section provides for confiscation of diving equipment, including boats, motors and motor vehicles, used to violate this act. Money from the sale of this confiscated property is to be set aside in a special fund.

### MCL 299.57. Underwater preserve fund, creation; appropriation of funds

Sec. 7. (1) The underwater preserve fund is created as a separate fund in the state treasury, and it may receive revenue as provided in this act, or revenue from any other source.

(2) Money in the underwater preserve fund shall be appropriated for only the following purposes:

(a) To the secretary of state for the development of maritime archeology in this state.
(b) To the department of commerce for the promotion of Great Lakes bottomlands preserves.
(c) To the department for the enforcement of this act.

## Comment:

Money from the sale of confiscated property is to be used for the maritime archeology, promotion of the bottomland preserves and/or for law enforcement of this act.

# Glossary

Nautical terms represent a language that may be unfamiliar to most sport divers. But to share information about the underwater world and to learn about maritime archeology, it is useful to have an understanding of basic terminology. These definitions are provided for that purpose.

**a** -- A prefix for "on" or "in." It is used commonly, aback, aboard, astern, etc.

**about** -- A turning around.

**adrift** -- Anything that floats unfastened.

**aft** -- Behind; toward the after or stern part of a vessel.

**afterbody** -- That portion of a ship's body aft of the midship section.

**aground** -- Wholly or partially resting on the bottom.

**air port** -- An opening in the side of the deckhouse of a vessel for light and ventilation.

**alongside** -- By the side of.

**amidships** -- Generally speaking, the middle portion of a vessel.

**anchor** -- A metal hook specially designed to take hold of the bottom in relatively shallow water. Anchors are of many shapes and sizes and may weigh a few pounds to tons.

**apron** -- Knee joining or bridging stem and keel.

**arch** -- A structure running from bow to stern to provide support; common on early, wooden-hulled Great Lakes steamers.

**astern** -- Behind.

**athwart, athwartships** -- Across.

**avast** -- The order to stop or pause in any exercise.

**aweather** -- Toward the weather side; the side upon which the wind blows.

**aweigh** -- Spoken of an anchor when it has been lifted from the bottom.

**backstays** -- Ropes stretched from a mast to the sides of a vessel, some way aft of the mast, to give extra support to the masts against falling forward.

**backstay lever** -- A device for slackening or tightening running backstays.

**bail** -- To remove water from the bilge.

**ballast** -- Weight deposited in a ship's hold when she has no cargo, or too little to bring her sufficiently low in the water for proper navigation.

**bar** -- An ridge of sand.

**barge** -- A general name given to most flat-bottomed craft.

**barkentine (bark or barque)** -- A three-masted sailing vessel, square rigged on the fore- and mainmasts, and fore and aft rigged on the mizzen.

**batten** -- A long strip of wood.

**beacon** -- A navigation light.

**beam** -- The width of a vessel at her widest part.

**bearing** -- The direction or angular distance from a meridian, in which an object lies.

**beat** -- To "beat to windward" is to make progress in a sailing vessel in the direction from which the wind is blowing.

**becket** -- Loop or eye for attachment.

**belay** -- To make fast; as, to belay a rope.

**belaying pin** -- A moveable pin or bolt of wood or metal to which lines are belayed.

**below** -- To "go below" is equivalent, on shipboard, to going downstairs.

**bends** -- Also called decompression sickness, the appearance of tiny nitrogen gas "bubbles" in sport divers' blood from a too rapid ascent.

**bent** -- The condition resulting from the bends; a diver is "bent" when experiencing the bends.

**berth** -- A bed or bunk on board ship; a place for a ship to tie up or anchor is sometimes called a berth.

**between decks or 'tween decks** -- Any place below the main deck on a ship of more than one deck.

**bilge** -- That part of the hull of a ship inside and adjacent to the keel.

**bilge keel** -- Fins of wood or steel approximately paralleling the keel but built into and projecting from the ship at about where the bottom and the sides might be said to join. They are intended to minimize the rolling of the ship.

**bilge water** -- Water that collects in the bottom of the ship. As this is always at the lowest part of the hull, oil and other impurities are always a part of the bilge water, with the result that its odor is generally offensive and it is very dirty.

**billet head** -- A wooden scroll used in place of a figurehead.

**billy** -- Light, portable rope and pulley system that can be used anywhere.

**binnacle** -- The fixed case and stand in which the steering compass of a vessel is mounted.

**bitts** -- Posts of metal or timber projecting from the deck to which lines may be made fast.

**block** -- A pulley used on board ship.

**bob stay** -- A stay or rope made fast to the stempost of a ship at the cutwater and leading to the end of the bowsprit.

**boiler casing** -- Walls forming a trunk leading from the boiler room to the boiler hatch to protect deck spaces from heat.

**bollard** -- A short thick post on a pier for tying up ships.

**booby hatch** -- An access hatch from the weather deck protected by a hood from sea and weather.

**boom** -- The spar at the foot of a fore and aft sail.

**boomkin** -- Extension over the stern of a sailboat to take backstays and/or sheets.

**bottomlands** -- Land below Great Lakes water.

**bottomland preserve** -- An area designated by the state of Michigan to recognize unusual natural features or collection of historical artifacts such as shipwrecks. Special rules apply regarding the removal of artifacts from bottomland preserves.

**bow** -- The front end of a vessel.

**bowsprit** -- The spar projecting from the bow of a ship and to which the fore stays are led from the foremast. It is generally decorative on power boats.

**bowsprit shrouds** -- Horizontal wires supporting the bowsprit against thwartship motion.

**brace** -- Ropes on a square-rigged ship leading to the ends of the yards and used for the purpose of setting the yard at the proper angle to the mast.

**brail** -- A rope leading in from the leech of a fore-and-aft sail to the mast, used to gather in the sail.

**breadth (molded)** -- The greatest breadth of the vessel measured from the heel of the frame on one side to the heel of a the frame on the other side.

**breaker** -- A small water barrel.

**breakers** -- Waves that curl over and break because of shallow water.

**breakwater** -- An artificial bank or wall of any material built to break the violence of the sea and create a sheltered spot.

**breasthooks** -- Knees attaching stringers at the bow.

**bridge** -- A high platform extending from side to side of the ship, which usually supports a pilothouse.

**bridles** -- Several lines leading from a larger line to distribute the stain on an object to which they are attached.

**brig** -- A vessel with two masts (fore and main) both of them square rigged.

**brigantine** -- Same as a brig except that it has a fore and aft mainsail.

**brightwork** -- Varnished wood.

**broach** -- An involuntary swing to parallel with the waves.

**bulkhead** -- A partition of almost any material.

**bulk freighter** -- A freighter designed to carry a variety of bulk cargos, such as grain, fruit, lumber, etc.

**bulwarks** -- A parapet around the deck of a vessel, serving to guard passengers, crew and cargo from the possibility of being swept overboard.

**bumboat** -- A small harbor boat allowed to visit ships in port and supply sailors with various articles.

**buoy** -- A floating marker intended to serve as a guide or warning.

**burbot** -- A harmless but interesting fresh water fish of the cod family. It frequents shipwrecks and can be distinguished by a single barbel below its lower lip. Burbots, also called lawyerfish, have been known to grow in excess of 30 inches but most are about half that size.

**butt** -- End-to-end joints, sometimes against a special piece of material employed just at such joints and called a butt block.

**buttock** -- The rounding part of a vessel's stern.

**cabin** -- A habitable apartment on shipboard.

**cable** -- The rope or chain by which a ship's anchor is held.

**calking** -- Stuffing the seams of wooden ships with oakum.

**camber** -- The athwartship curvature of a deck.

**can buoy** -- A buoy which shows above water the form of a cylinder.

**canaler** -- A vessel built to pass through the Welland and St. Lawrence River canals. These dimensions were roughly 133 to 140 feet long with a beam of 26 feet.

**capsize** -- To turn over.

**capstan** -- A kind of windlass sometimes found on ships and used principally for raising the anchor.

**cargo hatch** -- A large opening in the deck to permit loading of cargo.

**carling** -- short support between beams.

**carvel-built** -- Built with the external planks edge to edge, meeting flush at the seams, flush sided.

**casings** -- The walls or partitions forming trunks above the engine and boiler spaces to provide air and ventilation and enclosing the uptakes.

**catboat** -- A small sailing boat with one mast and a single sail which is generally similar in shape to the mainsail of a sloop.

**cat ketch** -- Two-masted boat carrying only one sail on each mast and having mast sizes and locations proportioned to a ketch.

**cat schooner** -- A boat carrying only one sail on each mast and having mast sizes and locations proportioned to a schooner.

**cat yawl** -- A boat carrying only one sail on each mast and having mast sizes and locations proportioned to a yawl.

**ceiling** -- Inside planking of the hull of a vessel.

**centerboard** -- A moveable sheet of metal or wood sometimes used by small sailboats. It extends through the keel and presents a large surface to the water and tends to eliminate lateral motion while the boat is under sail. A kind of folding keel.

**centerboard pennant** -- Line for centerboard raising or lowering.

**centerboard pin** -- Pivot for a centerboard.

**centerboard trunk or well** -- Watertight enclosure of the centerboard.

**chain plate** -- A fitting at the sides of a hull to which shrouds are attached.

**channel** -- A ledge or narrow platform bolted to and projecting from the outside of a vessel's hull to spread the rigging.

**chart** -- A map of the sea and coast projections for use by navigators.

**cheek knee** -- Strips along the top and bottom of the trail boards.

**chess tree** -- A timber in which a sheave is set, bolted to the topsides of a square-rigged vessel at a point convenient for hauling down the main tack, the tack leading to the inside of the bulwark.

**chine** -- The line at which sides and bottom of a hull meet.

**chock** -- A fitting for guiding rope to a cleat or bitt.

**clamp** -- A longitudinal support member for deck beams.

**cleat** -- A prolonged fitting to which ropes are fastened.

**clinker** -- A method of small boat building in which the covering planks overlap.

**clipper** -- A fast sailing ship developed in the first half of the 19th Century. Generally, clippers were full-rigged ships and were popular for about 50 years.

**coaming** -- A water-stopping strip around a deck opening.

**companionway** -- The entrance to a ladder to flight of stairs leading from one deck to the one below.

**compass** -- A magnetized instrument that points approximately in the direction of the magnetic pole.

**cotter pin** -- Small retaining pin through a larger pin or bolt at right angles.

**counter** -- The under part of the overhang of the stern.

**cradle** -- Framework for hauling or storing a boat.

**crosstrees** -- The arms extending laterally near the head of a mast at right angles to the length of the vessel and to the extremities of which the topmast shrouds are stretched for the purpose of giving support to the topmast.

**cuddy** -- A small cabin usually on a sailboat.

**cutter** -- A sailing boat with one mast carrying staysail, jib, fore and aft mainsail and sometimes a topsail; a large U.S. Coast Guard vessel.

**cutwater** -- That portion of the stem of a vessel that cleaves the water as she moves ahead.

**davit** -- a light crane mounted on a ship's side and used for hoisting and lowering boats.

**deadeye** -- A round block of lignum-vitae in which there are three holes, through which is rove the lanyard.

**deadlight** -- A porthole that does not open (fixed glass).

**deadhead** -- A piece of floating wood.

**deadwood** -- Solid area of a vessel below and aft of garboard and stern rabbet.

**deck** -- The covering of the interior of a ship, either carried completely over her or only over a portion. Decks correspond to the floors and roof of a flat-topped building.

**deckhouse** -- A cabin above the deck.

**decompression sickness** -- See "bends."

**derelict** -- A ship adrift at sea without her crew.

**dinghy** -- A small open boat used as a tender for a yacht.

**dock** -- An artificially constructed basin for the reception of vessels. It may be a wet dock, which ships lie while loading and unloading, or a dry dock, in which they are repaired after the water is pumped out.

**down Lake Michigan** -- In the 1800's, Chicago was considered the head of Lake Michigan so travel was "down" to the Straits of Mackinac.

**draft** -- The depth beneath the surface of the water of the lowest point of a ship's keel.

**draft marks** -- The numbers on each side of a vessel near the bow and stern to indicate the distance from the number to the bottom of the keel.

**drag** -- A vessel's resistance to motion because of shape and friction. Also, slipping of anchor.

**driver** -- The fore-and-aft sail on the mizzenmast of a squire-rigged ship. It is sometimes called the "spanker."

**drouge** -- A sea anchor.

**drysuit** -- A diving suit that permits sport divers to remain dry while underwater. Insulation is provided by clothing worn beneath the suit.

**electrolysis** -- Natural decomposition of metal by an electrical current.

**engine bed** -- Vertical members supporting dead weight, thrust and torque of the engine.

**ensign** -- The flag carried by a ship as the insignia of her nationality.

**entrance** -- That part of the bow that cuts the water.

**eye** -- A fixed, closed loop at the end of a rope.

**fathom** -- A nautical measure equal to six feet.

**fid** -- A bolt of wood or metal which holds the heel of a topmast.

**fife rail** -- A plank or rail in which a group of belaying pins is kept.

**figurehead** -- A decorative carving below the bowsprit.

**flam** -- Cross-sectional curvature of a hull above the water, always convex on outside of topsides.

**flare** -- A concave bulge spreading outward at the bow of a ship.

**Flemish horse** -- A short footrope at the end of a yard.

**floor** -- The inside bottom of a hull.

**fluke** -- The point area of an anchor.

**footrope** -- A rope slung underneath the yard, bowsprit, or jib boom on which the crew stands when furling a sail.

**fore and aft** -- An expressing signifying those sails which, when at rest, lie in a line running from bow to stern of a vessel.

**forecastle** -- Forward cabin.

**foredeck** -- Deck at the bow of a vessel.

**forefoot** -- The point at which the stem joins the keel.

**foremast** -- The mast nearest the bow of a vessel having more than one mast, except on yawls, ketches and other sailboats where the mast nearest the bow is larger than the mast farther astern.

**forepeak** -- Below-deck area at the bow of a boat.

**foresail** -- On a square-rigged ship, the lowest square sail on the foremast. On a schooner, the sail stretched between the boom and the gaff on the foremast.

**forestay** -- Stay running from lowest forward position on mast to forward deck.

**forward** -- The forward part or the forepart; the vicinity of the bow of a vessel.

**founder** -- To sink.

**frames** -- Athwartship structural members that give shape to the hull.

**freeboard** -- That portion of a vessel's side which is free of the water.

**freighter** -- A ship engaged in carrying freight.

**full-rigged ship** -- A ship carrying three masts, each mounting square sails.

**funnel** -- The smokestack or chimney connected with the boilers of a ship.

**gaff** -- The spar at the top of some fore and aft sails, such as the mainsail or foresail of a schooner.

**galley** -- The kitchen of a ship.

**gangway** -- A narrow platform or bridge passing over from one deck of a vessel to another.

**garboard strake** -- The plank just above the keel.

**gear** -- Any part of the working apparatus of a vessel, as the gear of the helm, which consists of the tiller, the chains, the blocks and all other necessary parts.

**gig** -- A small boat carried on shipboard and meant for use when in port.

**gimbals** -- The brass rings in which a compass is mounted, and which permit it to remain horizontal despite the motions of the ship.

**gollwobbler** -- Over-sized sail on a schooner going forward from the top of the mainmast. Also called maintopmast queen staysail.

**gooseneck** -- The ring at the mast end of a boom.

**ground** -- To run a ship into water so shallow that she rests on the bottom.

**ground tackle** -- The gear connected with and including the anchors of a ship.

**gudgeons** -- Fittings on the transom that accept the pintles of a rudder.

**gunkholing** -- Exploring in shallow water.

**gunwale** -- The top of any solid rail along the outside of a vessel.

**gusset** -- Knee or bridge reinforcing two members attached to one another by end-to-end joint.

**guy** -- A steadying rope, as the "guy" of a spinnaker, which serves to keep that sail forward.

**gybe** -- The swinging over of a fore and aft sail when the wind, accidentally or intentionally, has been brought from one side of it to the other around its free edge. This is sometimes a foolish and dangerous maneuver.

**gyro compass** -- A direction indicator not dependent on the earth's magnetic field, works on inertial stability.

**hail** -- To call.

**hair rail** -- The top member of two or three curved timbers, extending from either side of the figurehead to the bow or cathead, to brace the head or projecting stem.

**halyard** -- A rope (sometimes a chain) by which a sail, flag or yard is hoisted.

**hatchway** -- An opening in the deck of a vessel through which persons or cargo may descend or ascend.

**hawsepipes (hawsehole)** -- Short tubes through which the anchor cable passes from the forward deck to the outside of the bow.

**hawser** -- A cable or heavy rope used for towing and for making fast to moorings.

**head** -- Toilet.

**head sails** -- All the sails set between the foremast and the bow and bowsprit of a sailing ship. These are the fore staysail and the inner, outer and flying jibs.

**heave to** -- To stop dead in the water.

**heel** -- To lean to one side.

**helm** -- Used interchangeably with the word "tiller." Theoretically, every rudder is equipped with a helm or tiller, although actually tillers are seldom used except on small boats.

**Hermaphrodite brig** -- A two-masted sailing ship with square sails on the foremast and fore-and-aft sails only on the main. This type is often incorrectly called a brigantine.

**highfield lever** -- A lever used to take up slack quickly in a wire such as a backstay.

**hog** -- A hull bottom distorted by being lower at the ends than at the middle.

**hold** -- The inner space in a vessel in which the cargo is stowed.

**hounds** -- An area of a mast at which a gaff rides.

**horses** -- Footropes.

**hull** -- The hull is the body of a vessel, exclusive of rigging or equipment.

**hull speed** -- The maximum practical speed of a displacement hull of a given length.

**hypothermia** -- The cooling of the core body temperature.

**inboard** -- A boat with engines inside the hull (opposite of outboard).

**jackstaff** -- A short flagstaff at the bow.

**jaws** -- The horns at the end of a boom or gaff, which keep it in its position against the mast.

**jib** -- One of several triangular headsails of a sailing vessel.

**jib-boom** -- A spar running out beyond the bowsprit for the purpose of carrying other jibs.

**jigger** -- The fourth mast from the bow in a ship carrying four or more masts. The second from the bow in a yawl or ketch.

**jolly boat** -- A boat corresponding to a dinghy.

**jumper** -- Wire stays passing over a short strut and having both ends attached to the same spar.

**kedge** -- A small anchor carried by large vessels for use in shallow water or for use in keeping the main anchor clear.

**keel** -- The backbone of a ship. It is a strong member extending the entire length of the center of the bottom, and from it the ribs are built at right angles.

**keel cooler** -- A heat exchange system of pipes inside or along the keel to cool fresh water for the engine.

**keelson** -- An addition to the keel inside the boat. It rests upon the keel and strengthens it.

**ketch** -- A sailing vessel with two masts and with fore-and-aft sails.

**king plank** -- The center plank of a deck, notched to receive ends of curving deck planks.

**knee** -- A right-angled timber acting as a bracket between horizontal and vertical members.

**knightheads** -- Upright timbers inside of and on either side of the stem; the bowsprit sets between them.

**knot** -- A nautical mile per hour, about 1.1 miles per hour (a nautical mile is about 6,075 feet).

**lanyard** -- A short piece of rope used as a handle or to secure an object.

**lapstrake** -- Same as clinker built.

**lashing** -- Binding with light line.

**launch** -- A small vessel propelled by some kind of motor and generally used for pleasure; or to put a new vessel in the water.

**lawyer fish** -- See "burbot."

**lazarette** -- The enclosed storage space at the stern in the hull.

**lazy jacks** -- Ropes leading down vertically from the topping lift to the boom to hold the sail when taking it in.

**lead** -- A leaden weight attached to the end of a line to measure the depth of the water.

**lee** -- The lee side of a vessel is the side opposite that against which the wind blows. A lee shore is a shore on the lee side of a ship, and is therefore to be feared for the force of the wind tends to blow the ship ashore. "Under the lee of the shore," however, is an expression meaning in the shelter of a shoreline from which the wind is blowing.

**leeway** -- Sideward travel of a ship off her course.

**leg-of-mutton** -- A triangular sail sometimes used on small sailboats.

**leeward** -- On the lee side.

**length between perpendiculars** -- The length of a ship measured from the forward side of the stem to the aft side of the stern post at the height of the designed water line.

**lifeboat** -- A boat carried for the purpose of saving lives in case the ship which carried it is wrecked.

**lifeline** -- Rope or wire fence around a vessel; short portable rope for crew member's individual safeguard.

**lift** -- A line running diagonally from the masthead to the end of a yard, which takes the weight of the yard.

**light board** -- A board used to support and shield running lights.

**lighthouse** -- A structure erected ashore or in shallow water and equipped with a powerful light to act as a warning and navigational aid.

**line** -- A small rope.

**list** -- To lean to one side.

**LOA** -- Length overall. The distance from the foremost part of the stem to the aftermost part of the stern.

**log** -- A record of events.

**lunch hook** -- A small anchor used for shot stops in good weather.

**LWL** -- Length at the waterline.

**martingale** -- The rope extending downward from the jib-boom to the "dolphin striker." Its duties are those of a stay or brace.

**mast** -- A long piece or system of pieces of timber or metal placed nearly perpendicularly to the keel of a vessel to support rigging, antennas, halyards, etc.

**masthead** -- Top of a mast.

**maststep** -- Socket or support for the bottom of a mast.

**mayday** -- Prefix to a radio call for help.

**messenger** -- A weight sent down an anchor rode to improve anchor holding ability.

**Michigan Underwater Preserve Council, Inc. (MUPC)** -- A consortium of individuals and representatives from Michigan's bottomland preserves organized to promote visitation of those areas and to solve mutual problems.

**mizzen** -- Generally the third mast from the bow of a ship carrying three or more masts is called the "mizzenmast." The sails set from this mast have the world "mizzen" prefixed to their names.

**moor** -- To moor is to make a ship fast to a mooring which is a kind of permanent anchor to which a buoy is attached.

**moulded depth** -- The vertical distance from the top of the keel to the top of the upper deck beams at the side of a vessel (taken at the middle of the length).

**muck out** -- An instance of no or reduced visibility resulting from the disturbance of fine silt underwater.

**mushroom** -- An anchor shaped like a mushroom.

**narced** -- Feeling the effects of nitrogen narcosis.

**navigation** -- The science which enables seamen to determine their positions at sea and lay down courses to be followed.

**nitrogen narcosis** -- "Rapture of the deep," a feeling of euphoria or drunkenness resulting from excess nitrogen absorbed into divers' blood. Usually occurs at depths of 100 feet or more.

**nun buoy** -- A buoy which shows above water in the shape of a cone.

**NWMMM** -- Northwest Michigan Maritime Museum, located in Frankfort.

**oakum** -- A substance to which old ropes are reduced when picked to pieces. It is used in calking the seams of boats and in stopping leaks.

**outboard** -- A boat with an engine(s) outside the hull (opposite of inboard).

**packet** -- A small passenger or mail boat.

**paddlewheel** -- A large wheel sometimes used by steamboats and on which flat boards are so arranged that when the wheel turns the boards come in contact with the water, thus propelling the boat.

**painter** -- A rope attached to the bow of an open boat by which the boat may be tied.

**pan** -- Prefix to a message concerning safety of ship but not an actual distress; a radio emergency call less urgent than a mayday.

**parcel** -- To protect a line from wear by covering it with another material.

**parrels** -- Rollers on lashings about mast or boom that allow lashings to be raised or lowered without jamming.

**partners** -- Short structural members to support the mast where it goes through the deck.

**peak** -- The upper end of a gaff. Also, the uppermost corner of a sail carried by a gaff.

**peak halyards** -- The halyards or ropes by which the peak is elevated.

**pier** -- A long, narrow structure of wood, steel or concrete built from the shore out into the water and generally used for the transfer of passengers and goods to and from ships.

**pile (spile)** -- A vertical post driven into the bottom as a mooring for ships.

**pilot** -- One qualified and licensed to direct ships in or out of a harbor or channel.

**pilothouse** -- A house designed for navigational purposes.

**pintle** -- The fitting on a detachable rudder that fits into the gudgeon.

**pitch** -- The up and down movement of a ship in response to seas.

**poop** -- An extra deck on the after part of a vessel.

**pooped** -- Inundated by a wave coming over the transom.

**port** -- The left-hand side of a vessel when one is facing the bow.

**porthole** -- An opening in the side of a vessel. The term generally refers to the round windows common on most ships.

**pram** -- A small boat with a square bow.

**prevailing wind** -- The normal wind for a particular place.

**propeller** -- A device that, when mounted on the end of a shaft outside the stern of a vessel and below the water line, moves the ship through the water when turned. Also used to refer to a boat so equipped.

**prow** -- The cutwater of a ship.

**punt** -- A small flat-bottomed boat, generally square ended.

**purchase** -- The use of mechanical power.

**quadrant** -- a quarter-circular fitting at the top of a rudder post.

**quarter** -- That section of a ship's side slightly forward of the stern.

**quartering** -- Running at an angle to the sea.

**quay** -- An artificial landing place, generally of greater area than a pier.

**rabbet** -- A groove in a structural member into which another fits and is fastened.

**rabbit boat** -- A steamer with a covered hold and exposed freight deck with machinery, crew quarters and pilot house located at the stern.

**reef** -- A low ridge of rock usually just below the surface of the water.

**reeve** -- To pass a wire, chain or rope through a hole or pulley.

**ribs** -- The members which, with the keel, form the skeleton of a vessel.

**riding lights** -- The lights a ship is required by law to carry at night while under way.

**rig** -- The manner in which the masts and sails of a vessel are fitted and arranged in connection with the hull.

**rigging** -- The system of ropes on a vessel by which her masts and sails are held up and operated.

**roadstead** -- A place of anchorage at a distance from the shore.

**rode** -- Anchor line and chain.

**ROV** -- Remote-operated vehicle; "robot" controlled from the surface to explore underwater with the use of video.

**rub rail** -- A molding, usually metal, around the hull that acts as a bumper.

**rudder** -- A flat, hinged apparatus hung at the stern of a ship, by the movement of which the ship is steered.

**run** -- The after part of a vessel at the water line where her lines converge toward the sternpost.

**running lights** -- The lights a ship is required by law to carry at night while under way.

**sag** -- distortion in a hull.

**sail** -- A sheet of canvas or other material which, when spread to the wind, makes possible he movement of a vessel.

**saloon (salon)** -- The main cabin of a vessel.

**Samson post** -- A bitt at the bow used for making fast.

**scantling** -- A piece of timber used in ship construction.

**scarf** -- A joint made between two members by tapering and overlapping.

**schooner** -- A fore-and-aft rigged vessel with two or more masts, the foremost of which is the foremast.

**scow** -- A large flat-bottomed boat without power and of many uses.

**scuba** -- Self-contained breathing apparatus. The tank, regulator and accompanying equipment that permits divers to remain submerged for extended periods.

**scuppers** -- Openings in the bulwarks of a ship to carry off any water that may get on the deck.

**scuttle** -- To intentionally sink a vessel.

**seam** -- The space between two planks in the covering of a vessel. It is in the seam that the calking is placed.

**seamanship** -- The art of handling ships.

**seiche** -- Extreme fluctuations in depth in the Great Lakes.

**shaft (shafting)** -- The cylindrical forging used for transmission of rotary motion from the engine to the propellers.

**sheer** -- The straight or curved line that the deck line of a vessel makes when viewed from the side.

**sheer strake** -- The topmost plank in a hull.

**sheet** -- The rope attached to a sail so that it may be let out or hauled in as required.

**shoal** -- A shallow place in the water.

**shrouds** -- Strong ropes forming the lateral supports of a mast, often wire rope.

**sister frame** -- A partial frame fastened to the side of a broken or weak frame.

**skeg** -- A member running out from the keel to support the rudder post.

**skiff** -- A small open boat.

**skin diving** -- Diving with mask, fins and snorkel but without scuba.

**sleepers** -- Bracket-like members connecting the transom to structural members.

**sloop** -- Sailing vessel with one mast, like a cutter but having a jib stay, which a cutter has not. A jib stay is a support leading from the mast to the end of the bowsprit on which a jib is set.

**smokestack** -- A metal chimney or passage through which the smoke and gasses are led from the uptakes to the open air.

**sole** -- The bottom or floor of a cabin.

**sounding** -- Determining the depth of water and the kind of bottom with the lead and line.

**spanker** -- The fore-and-aft sail set on the mizzenmast of a square-rigged ship, sometimes called the driver.

**spar** -- A spar is any one of the timber members of a vessel's gear.

**spinnaker** -- A racing sail of immense spread reaching from the topmast head to the end of a spinnaker boom which is a spar set out to take it.

**spreaders** -- Compression struts from masts used to increase effective support from rigging by holding rigging wires further away from the mast than they would otherwise be.

**spring line** -- A docking line running aft from the bow or forward from the quarter.

**squall** -- A sudden and very strenuous gust of wind or a sudden increase in its force.

**square-rigged** -- That method of disposing of sails in which they hang across the ship and in which they are approximately rectangular in shape.

**stanchion** -- A post supporting a rail.

**standing rigging** -- Ropes or wire ropes that permanently support the spars, such as shrouds and other stays, and are not moved when working the sails.

**starboard** -- The right-hand side of a vessel to a person facing the bow.

**statute mile** -- The unit of land distance (5,280 feet).

**stays** -- Supports made of hemp or wire rope supporting spars, or, more especially, masts.

**staysails** -- Sails set on the stays between the masts of a ship or as headsails.

**steamers** -- Vessels powered by steam engines.

**steering gear** -- Mechanism used to transfer torque to rudder.

**steeve** -- The angle the bowsprit makes with the horizontal.

**stem** -- The foremost timber of a vessel's hull.

**stern** -- The rear end of a vessel.

**sternpost** -- An upright timber joined to and erected above the after end of the keel to which the rudder is hung.

**stock** -- The crossbar in the shank of an anchor.

**stoke hold** -- That compartment in a steamship from which the fires under the boilers are stoked or tended.

**stopwater** -- A dowel in the center of a joint to prevent leakage.

**stove** -- Smashed in by a collision.

**stow** -- To stow a cargo is to pack it into a ship so that it will not shift as the vessel pitches and rolls.

**strake** -- A length of hull planking.

**stringer** -- A sturdy fore and aft structural member in the bilge.

**strut** -- A fitting for supporting the extended propeller shaft.

**studding sails** -- On square-rigged ships, narrow supplementary sails are sometimes set on small booms at the sides of the principal square sails.

**superstructure** -- A structure built above the uppermost complete deck; a pilothouse, bridge, galley house, etc.

**swell** -- An undulating motion of the water, always felt at sea after a gale.

**tack** -- To change the course of a vessel from one direction or tack to another by bringing her head to the wind and letting the wind fill her sails on the other side, the object being to progress against the wind.

**taffrail** -- The sternmost rail of a vessel, that is, the rail around the stern.

**tail shaft** -- The aft section of the shaft which receives the propeller.

**tender** -- A small vessel employed to attend a larger one.

**thermocline** -- That point between two layers of water that differ significantly in temperature.

**throat** -- That part of a gaff that is next to the mast, and the adjoining corner of the sail.

**throat halyard** -- The rope that elevates the throat.

**thwart** -- Athwart means across, and in a boat the seats are called the thwarts because they are placed athwart or across the boat.

**tiller** -- The handle or beam at the top of the shaft to which the rudder is attached, and by which the rudder is turned. It is in use only on comparatively small vessels.

**tonnage** -- The measure of a ship's internal dimensions as the basis for a standard for dues, etc.

**top** -- In square-rigged ships, the platform built on the masts just below the topsails, and to which the sailor climb.

**topgallant mast** -- In a mast built up in sections, the topgallant mast is the third section above the deck.

**topmast** -- In a mast built up of two or more parts the topmast is the second from the deck.

**topping lift** -- A line from boom end to mast head.

**topsail** -- The second sail from the deck on any mast a of a square-rigged ship.

**topgallant sail** -- The third sail from the deck on any mast of a square-rigged ship, except when the ship is equipped with lower and upper topsails, in which case the topgallant sail is the fourth.

**topsail schooner** -- A schooner which, on the foremast, spreads a square topsail.

**trail board** -- A curved board extending from the figurehead to the bow, often carved or embellished.

**tramp** -- The name usually given to merchant freighters that have no regular routes.

**transom** -- The outside stern of a hull.

**transverse** -- At right angles to the ship's fore-and-aft center line.

**trawler** -- A vessel usually driven by power and used in fishing, it tows a heavy net called a trawl.

**trestle trees** -- Short timbers running fore and aft on either side of a mast that rest on the "hounds." They support the "top platform" and cross trees.

**trick** -- The time allotted to a man to be at the wheel or on any other duty.

**trim** -- The attitude of a vessel with respect to the water surface.

**trip(ping) line** -- Light line used to release snaps on spinnaker pole; light line used to raise an anchor from fluke end.

**truck** -- The very top of the mast.

**trunk** -- The upper part of a cabin rising through the deck.

**trysails** -- Small sails used in bad weather when no others can be carried, or occasionally, for rough work.

**tug** -- A small, powerful vessel used to assist larger ships about protected waterways. Tugs are also used to tow or push barges or almost anything that can float. The term is also used to refer to certain fishing vessels.

**twin screw** -- A ship equipped with two propellers.

**up Lake Michigan** -- In the 1800s, Chicago was considered to be at the head of Lake Michigan, thus sailors went "up" the lake to Chicago.

**Underwater Salvage and Preserve Committee** -- An advisory group of state officials and citizens that offers guidance on the development of bottomland preserves and the issuance of salvage permits.

**underway** -- A ship afloat that is not tied or anchored.

**unship** -- To take away or remove from a secure position.

**vail (vale or bale)** -- Strap around boom to which sheet attaches and allows a pulley block to swing in the direction of the load.

**vang** -- Tackle used for controlling a boom.

**vessel** -- A general term for all craft larger than a rowboat.

**vhf** -- Very high frequency.

**waist** -- That part of a vessel between the beam and the quarter.

**wake** -- The track a vessel leaves behind her on the surface of the water. The surface turbulence left by a ship in motion.

**wale** -- A stake of planking running fore and aft on the outside of the hull, heavier than the regular planking.

**watch** -- Tour of duty.

**weather** -- A nautical expression applied to any object to windward of any given spot; the "weather" side of a vessel is the side upon which the wind blows. A vessel is said to have "weathered" a gale when she has lived safely through it.

**weather helm** -- The tendency of a ship to head into the wind.

**wedges** -- Tapered pieces under the stern of a powerboat to keep it from squatting.

**weigh** -- To lift the anchor from the bottom.

**well** -- A depression sometimes built in the decks of yachts or sailboats which is not covered by a deck. It is also called a cockpit and is for the convenience and protection of passengers and crew. Also, an opening leading to the lowest part of the bilge in which the depth of bilge water may be measured.

**well found** -- A fully equipped ship.

**wetsuit** -- A suit of neoprene foam or other material designed to permit a layer of water to remain between the suit and a diver. The suit offers insulation and prevents water from circulating.

**whaleback** -- A Great Lakes steamer with a rounded, steel hull.

**wharf** -- A loading place for vessels.

**wheel** -- The wheel by which a ship is steered.

**winch** -- A hoisting or pulling machine fitted with a horizontal single or double drum.

**windjammer** -- A slang expression for a person who prefers sails to engines.

**windlass** -- An apparatus in which horizontal or vertical drums or gypsies and wildcats are operated by means of a steam engine or motor for the purpose of handling heavy anchor chains, hawsers, etc.

**windward** -- That side of a vessel or any other object upon which the wind is blowing is the windward side.

**wind sail** -- A tube of canvas with wings of canvas at the top so arranged as to direct fresh air below decks; a temporary ventilator.

**wing and wing** -- Running before the wind with jib on one side and the main on the other.

**work** -- Structural parts that have loosened sufficiently to move against each other.

**worm** -- To wind a rope in a spiral.

**wreck** -- The destruction of a ship; the ship itself or the remnants of it after the catastrophe.

**wreckage** -- Goods or parts of a ship cast up by the sea after a shipwreck.

**wreck raper** -- One who illegally removes historical artifacts from shipwrecks. Also called "scurvy dogs."

**yacht** -- A pleasure boat, usually large and elaborate.

**yard** -- A spar suspended from a mast for the purpose of spreading a sail.

**yardarm** -- The crosspiece near the top of a mast.

**yaw** -- To deviate from the true course.

**yawl** -- A sailing vessel equipped with two masts, the main and the jigger.

**zebra mussel** -- A clam-like organism introduced into the Great Lakes from discharged ships' ballast.

# Dive Shops

There are plenty of dive shops in Michigan that offer air, instruction and equipment. Some dive charter operators also have boats equipped with compressors.

But before scuba divers blindly hand their spent tanks to anyone for a fill, they should inspect the facility. There are no state regulations requiring licensing of these facilities and although the vast majority operate in a responsible manner, there are no guarantees.

Look for a professional, clean appearance. If led to a poorly ventilated shed housing an aging compressor, scuba divers may want to think twice before purchasing air. A contaminated fill can be lethal -- hardly a bargain at any price.

There are also no state regulations regarding instruction and certification. Many dive shops will not require a card before filling scuba tanks -- cards are not required by any law and do not absolve the fill station operator of liability.

But formal, qualified instruction is obviously a good idea. Scuba divers are handling highly compressed gases to enter a unique environment. This is one of a few recreational activities where ignorance can be fatal.

Most dive shops offer a variety of courses and certification through one or more private organizations. These courses start with the basics and give divers a chance to determine whether they want to continue the sport -- nearly all do. Most students find scuba courses fun and exhilarating.

Dive shops often offer several lines of quality equipment. Trained salespersons can be valuable in providing information about particular brands and models. But before purchasing, divers should be sure they will have confidence with their equipment. Remember that the salesperson is not going to be using the equipment -- **you** are.

The following list is not an endorsement of any dive shop but is offered to provide information about where air, instruction and equipment may be obtained.

**1. A & C Diving Academy**
918 E. Fulton
Grand Rapids, MI 49503
(616) 458-1062

**2. Advanced Aquatic Diving, Inc.**
25020 Jefferson Ave.
St. Clair Shores, MI 48080
(313) 779-8777

**3. Adventure Dive Travel**
25650 Cherry Hill
Dearborn Heights, MI 48127
(313) 562-3036

**4. Adventures in Diving**
1411 Nassau
Kalamazoo, MI 49001
(616) 381-9220

**5. Anchorage Marine Hardware**
265 Kollen Park
Holland, MI 49423
(616) 396-0607

**6. Aqua Hut**
5030 N. Bennett
Toledo, OH 43612
(419) 476-4168

**Call ahead to determine products and services available.**

7. **Beaver Island Marine, Inc.**
   St. James, MI 49782
   (616) 448-2300

8. **Bob's World of Blue**
   27180 James
   Warren, MI 48092
   (313) 574-0849

9. **Bruno's Dive Shop**
   34740 Gratiot
   Mt. Clemens, MI 48043
   (313) 792-2040

10. **Cheboygan Skin Diving Center**
    9576 M-33
    Cheboygan, MI 49721
    (616) 627-6673

11. **Chippewa Landing Marina**
    Bay Mills Point Road
    Rt. 2
    Box 259
    Brimley, MI 49715
    (906) 248-5278

12. **City Sales**
    809 Lake Antoine Road
    Iron Mountain, MI 49801
    (906) 774-3555

13. **Commercial Diving Service**
    890 Georgia
    Marysville, MI 48040
    (313) 364-8898

14. **Curley's Motel**
    M-123
    PO Box 57
    Paradise, MI 49768
    (906) 492-3445

15. **Deep Six Scuba Schools**
    884 N. Pine Road
    Essexville, MI 48732
    (517) 892-2715

16. **Diver Down Scuba Shop**
    321 S. Lakeshore Blvd.
    Marquette, MI 49855
    (906) 228-7777

17. **Diver's Den**
    604 S. Lapeer Road
    Lake Orion, MI 48035
    (313) 693-9801

18. **Divers Inc.**
    3380 Washtenaw
    Ann Arbor, MI 48104
    (313) 971-7770

19. **The Dive Shop**
    G-4020 Corrunna Road
    Flint, MI 48532
    (313) 732-3900

20. **Dive Shop of Escanaba**
    2260 N. Sixth Ave.
    Escanaba, MI 49829
    (906) 786-3483

**Call ahead to determine products and services available.**

**21. Dive Site**
9125 Portage Road
Portage, MI 49002
(616) 323-3700

**22. Diver's Mast**
2900 Lansing Ave.
Jackson, MI 49202
(517) 784-5862

**23. Don's Dive Shop**
29480 W. 10 Mile
Farmington Hills, MI 48024
(313) 477-7333

**24. Dyatomics Dive Center**
113 1/2 E. Truman
Newberry, MI 49868
(906) 293-8060

**25. Four Fathoms Diving, Inc.**
75 E. Argyle
Sandusky, MI 48471
(313) 648-4893

**26. Grand Island Venture**
410 Mill St.
Munising, MI 49862
(906) 387-4477

**27. Great Lakes Dive Locker**
122 44th St. SE
Kentwood, MI 49508
(616) 531-9440

**28. K & B Scuba**
2670 US 23 South
Alpena, MI 49070
(517) 354-8394

**29. Lake Shore Sporting Goods**
323 N. Third
Rogers City, MI 49779
(517) 734-4150

**30. Len's Dive Shop**
924 W. Fulton
Grand Rapids, MI 49504
(616) 456-7314

**31. M & M Diving**
US 41
Menominee, MI 49858
(906) 863-7330

**32. Macomb Dive Shop**
28869 Bunert
Warren, MI 48093
(313) 774-0640

**33. Michiana Scuba**
301 E. Main St.
Niles, MI 49120
(616) 683-4502

**34. Michigan Underwater
School of Diving**
3280 Fort St.
Lincoln Park, MI 48146
(313) 388-1322

**Call ahead to determine products and services available.**

**35. Narcosis Corner Dive Shop**
474 Third
Calumet, MI 49913
(906) 337-3156

**36. Ocean Sands Scuba**
659 Douglas Ave.
Holland, MI 49423
(616) 396-0068

**37. Ocean Technology Group**
818 Phoenix
Ann Arbor, MI 48104
(313) 971-3333

**38. Off-Shore Diving, Inc.**
1820 N. Lapeer Road
Suite 3
Lapeer, MI 48446
(313) 667-2911

**39. Port Huron Marine Service**
1426 Stanton
Port Huron, MI 48060
(313) 984-8313

**40. Pro Scuba Center**
4130 Dixie Highway
Drayton Plains, MI 48020
(313) 674-3483

**41. Recreational Diving, Inc.**
4424 N. Woodward
Royal Oak, MI 48072
(313) 549-0303

**42. Rod's Reef**
3134 W. Johnson Road
Ludington, MI 49431
(616) 843-8688

**43. Scuba North**
13380 W. Bay Shore Drive
Traverse City, Michigan 49684
(616) 947-2520

**44. The Scuba Shack, Inc.**
9982 W. Higgins Lake Road
Higgins Lake, MI 48627
(517) 821-6477

**45. Seaquatics**
979 S. Saginaw
Midland, MI 48640
(517) 835-6391

**46. Seaside Dive Shop, Inc.**
28612 Harper
St. Clair Shores, MI 48081
(313) 772-7676

**47. Skamt Sport Shop**
5055 Plainfield
Grand Rapids, MI 49505
(616) 364-8418

**48. Spring Lake Divers Den, Inc.**
915 W. Savidge
Spring Lake, MI 49456
(616) 842-4300

**Call ahead to determine products and services available.**

**49. Spud's Underwater Outfitters**
2579 Union Lake Road
Union Lake, MI 48085
(313) 363-2224

**50. Straits Diving Center**
587 N. State St.
St. Ignace, MI 49781
(906) 643-7009

**51. Sub-Aquatic Sports & Service**
347 N. Helmer
Battle Creek, MI 49017
(616) 968-8551

**52. Summit Sports**
224 E. Chisholm
Alpena, MI 49707
(517) 356-1182

**53. Thumb Explorer Dive Shop**
147 Grindstone Road
Port Austin, MI 48467
(517) 738-5256

**54. Thunder Bay Divers**
160 E. Fletcher
Alpena, MI 49707
(517) 356-9336

**55. Tom & Jerry's Scuba Shop**
8655 Dixie
Fairhaven, MI 48023
(313) 224-1991

**56. Tom & Jerry's Scuba & Sport**
20318 Van Born
Dearborn Heights, MI 48127
(313) 278-1124

**57. Underwater Diving Technology**
800 Lakes Side Drive
Box 117
Mackinaw City, MI 49781
(616) 436-7241

**58. Underwater Specialties**
579 Lake Ave.
Quinnesec, MI 49876
(906) 774-5512

**59. U.S. Scuba Center**
3260 S. Rochester Road
Rochester, MI 48063
(313) 853-2800

**60. West Michigan Dive Center**
2367 W. Sherman
Muskegon, MI 49441
(616) 755-3771

**61. Wolf Divers Supply**
250 W. Main St.
Benton Harbor, MI 49022
(616) 926-1068

**62. ZZ Underwater World**
1806 E. Michigan
Lansing, MI 48912
(517) 485-3894

# Information Sources

Michigan Travel Bureau
PO Box 30226
Lansing, MI 48909
(800) 543-2937
[Brochures on bottomland preserves,
campgrounds, boat landings, lodging,
charters, etc.]

East Michigan Tourist Association
One Wenonah Park
Bay City, MI 48708
(517) 895-8823 or
(800) 292-6154
[General tourist information]

Southeast Michigan Travel & Tourist
Association
PO Box 1590
Troy, MI 48099
(313) 524-3200
[General tourist information]

West Michigan Tourist Association
136 E. Fulton St.
Grand Rapids, MI 49503
(616) 456-8557
[General tourist information]

Upper Peninsula Travel and Recreation Association
PO Box 400
Iron Mountain, MI 49801
(906) 774-5480
(800) 562-7134
[General tourist information]

Michigan Sea Grant College Program
Michigan State University
334 Natural Resources Building
East Lansing, MI 48824
(517) 353-9568
[Great Lakes research, diving surveys,
general information, etc.]

Michigan -- MAPCO
PO Box 68
Williamsburg, MI 49690
[Public and private campgrounds]

Michigan Charterboat Association
2738 N. Grand River
Lansing, MI 48906
(517) 321-2255
[Charter services]

Michigan Department of Transportation
Public Information Office
PO Box 30050
Lansing, MI 48909
[Highway maps, lighthouse brochure]

Great Lakes Submerged Lands Management Unit
Land and Water Management Division
Department of Natural Resources
PO Box 30028
Lansing, MI 48909
(517) 373-1950
[Salvage permits/applications]

Archaeology Section
Bureau of History
Michigan Department of State
717 W. Allegan St.
Lansing, MI 48918
(517) 373-6358
[Salvage permits/applications]

## Maritime Museums

**Beaver Island Marine Museum**
PO Box 263
St. James, MI 49782
(616) 448-2479 or
(616) 448-2486

**Dossin Great Lakes Museum**
100 Strand
Belle Isle Park
Detroit, MI 48207
(313) 267-6440

**Empire Historical Museum**
Empire, MI 49630

**Grand Marais Maritime Museum**
Grand Marais, MI

**Great Lakes Shipwreck Historical Museum** (Whitefish Point)
111 Ashmun
Sault Ste. Marie, MI 49783
(906) 635-1742

**Great Lakes Shipwreck Museum and Mall**
Star Lines Main Dock
St. Ignace, MI 49781

**Lake Michigan Maritime Museum**
PO Box 534
South Haven, MI 49090
(616) 637-8078


**Leelanau County Historical Museum**
PO Box 246
Leland, MI 49654
(616) 256-7475


**Lighthouse County Museum**
Port Hope, MI
(517) 428-4749


**Mackinac Maritime Museum**
PO Box 873
Mackinaw City, MI 49701


**MADELINE**
Maritime Heritage Alliance
PO Box 1108
Traverse City, MI 49685
(616) 941-0850


**Marquette Maritime Museum**
Lakeshore Boulevard
Marquette, MI 49855
(906) 226-2006


**Northwest Michigan Maritime Museum**
PO Box 389
Frankfort, MI 49635
(616) 352-7251


**Old Presque Isle Lighthouse and Museum**
5295 Grand Lake Road
Presque Isle, MI 49777
(517) 595-2787


**Sanilac Historical Museum**
228 South Ridge
Port Sanilac, MI 48469


**Sleeping Bear Dunes National Lakeshore**
PO Box 277
Empire, MI 49630
(616) 326-5134
[Facilities at Empire, Glen Arbor, South Manitou Island]


**S.S. VALLEY CAMP and Marine Museum**
PO Box 1668
Sault Ste. Marie, MI 49783
(906) 632-3658


**WELCOME**
PO Box 873
Mackinaw City, MI 49701
(616) 436-5563


**Grand Traverse Lighthouse**
PO Box 43
Northport, MI 49670
(616) 386-7553

# Charters

Dive charter operators are usually available in the most popular dive sites in the Great Lakes. A few charters are also available in inland lakes.

Charters are an ideal way to become acquainted with an area. Even divers with their own boats frequently use charters to learn about new dive sites and to meet other divers. Finding some dive sites can be tricky and charter operators can provide tips that can make a trip especially enjoyable.

Charter operators generally use boats large enough to accommodate a minimum of six divers. They usually provide ample room for donning equipment and ladders for climbing back aboard. Some may provide specialized equipment to accommodate diving in a particular area, such as air compressors, lights, ROVs, etc.

All charter services in Michigan are required to be licensed. This means an extensive inspection and a qualified captain. Some services also provide dive masters.

When shopping for a dive charter compare prices with services offered. Some "bare bones" operators offer cut-rate prices and their services often reflect an economical price. Other operators may cost a bit more, but they may also offer special services that will make a dive experience more enjoyable.

The best charter service is one that offers divers confidence. It can be difficult to enjoy a dive if divers are worried about what is happening topside. There is no substitute for competent captains, proper equipment and seaworthy boats.

Local dive shops can often refer divers to competent charter services. Many dive shops also offer these services as part of their business.

When calling charter operators, don't be afraid to ask questions. Remember that **you** are paying for a service and you can avoid dissatisfaction -- and even danger -- by being selective. Here are some questions you may want to ask charter operators:

**How many <u>dive</u> charters do you generally run in a year?** Some operators offer the service as an adjunct to sport fishing or cruise charters. That does not necessarily mean those operators are incompetent, but it may be an indication of how well they know dive sites.

**What services are offered and for what prices?** Remember that you generally get what you pay for. A cut-rate price often means a cut-rate diving experience. Don't blame the operator for unpromised services.

**What certification requirements are required?** Most operators expect all participants to be certified by a nationally recognized agency. Unfortunately, there are many such agencies. Be sure they will accept the certification of everyone in your group.

**Is special equipment required and if so, is that equipment provided or can it be rented?** Some dive sites require special equipment, such as dry suits in the Isle Royale area. Knowing this ahead of time can prevent disappointments.

**How long is the charter?** Generally, the longer the charter, the more expensive it is. You may also want to know if lunch or refreshments are provided.

**Is alcohol permitted?** Most know that when it comes to diving, water and alcohol don't mix. Even if you don't drink it is an important question to ask because others in the party can create a dangerous situation if alcohol consumption is permitted by the operator.

**Is a dive master provided?** More and more operators are providing such services. Some even provide discounts to instructors or dive masters.

**How deep are the dives?**

**What can be seen?**
**How is the visibility?**
Perhaps the best measure of a charter service's performance is a recommendation by another diver. Asking a charter service for several references is not a bad idea, but be aware that you may get the names of that operator's friends who may be somewhat biased.

Once you have decided to use a particular charter service, be sure you understand the price and what services are offered for that price. Misunderstandings can lead to disappointments.

Ideally, you will find an operator who knows the area and spends no time searching for dive sites and can provide historical and/or geologic information about the site. Most important, the charter operator should be one that fosters confidence and is worthy of repeat business and recommendation to other divers.

Just as divers are entitled to certain expectations, so are charter operators. Divers who make life miserable for the operator may find themselves "black-listed" among the operators and have difficulty finding a competent charter in the region. Here are some guidelines that make divers valued customers.

**Respect the boat.** Charter operators have substantial investments in their boats and they appreciate it when divers are careful not to damage that investment.

**Respect the captain.** Captains are not getting rich by offering dive charter services. For many, it is little more

Great Lakes dive charter operators use boats large enough to accommodate divers' needs.

than a break-even business, one that they started because they enjoy sharing special diving experiences. Captains should be considered part of the "team" and their knowledge of an area should be respected.

**Follow orders.** Remember that the captain and crew have probably spent many hours on the water and if they ask divers to do or not do something, it is for a good reason. Don't question orders -- hesitating to grab a line or move from one area of the boat to another could mean trouble.

**Be safety conscious.** It is always better to be extra safe, it is an attitude that will be appreciated by the charter operator, too. Don't push your diving skills. If a dive is too deep or demanding, say so. There is shame only when you let others dictate your behavior.

**Make reservations.** Don't expect to be able to walk out to a dock unex-

pected and get a charter. Most services book well in advance, especially in the peak diving months of July and August.

**Be punctual.** If you are expected to be at the dock at 9 a.m., be there at 8:30. Have your equipment packed and ready. Don't inconvenience others with unpreparedness. When it is time to leave an area, be sure you are ready for that, too. "Extending" a charter by using all the air you brought will earn you a special place in the operator's memory.

**Be polite.** Manners are appreciated everywhere.

**Tip if appropriate.** If an operator provided an especially good service, a small tip for the captain and/or crew will be appreciated. No more than $5 or $10 is suitable. Divers can also share their appreciation by offering dinner at a local restaurant.

**Recommend the charter.** If service is good, let it be known to other divers. Your word will help others locate good charter services. Some operators offer discounts to divers who refer business. And there is nothing more appreciated than a valued repeat customer.

The following is a list of charter services, but the list is undoubtedly incomplete. Some fishing charter services also offer dive charter services. And each year, there are new services while others go out of business. Call ahead to determine services offered.

## Lake Michigan

Alan Start
Lot 59
17990 N. Shore Road
Spring Lake, MI 49456
(616) 846-6077
[Ferrysburg, Grand Haven]

Rick Bailey
PO Box 108
Empire, MI 49630
(616) 326-5445
[Glen Arbor, Empire, Frankfort, Leland]

Dana Bonney
Danel Charters
PO Box 286
Grand Haven, MI 49417
(616) 842-9045 or
(616) 842-1359
[Grand Haven]

Albert Krzyston
552 August Drive
Monroe, MI 48161
(313) 243-6787
[Ludington]

Jack Kirby
3104 Coit NE
Grand Rapids, MI 49505
(616) 364-8828
[Muskegon, Grand Haven]

Frank English
7378 Chief Road
Kaleva, MI 49645
(616) 889-3461
[Onekema, Arcadia]

Steve Freeman
1391 100 St. SE
Byron Center, MI 49315
(616) 698-8579
[Saugatuck]

Can't Miss Charters
PO Box 531
Saugatuck, MI 49453
(616) 857-4481
[Saugatuck]

Shelley Lee Charters
5651 Dowling Road
Montague, MI 49437
(616) 894-2101
[White Lake, Muskegon]

Inland Seas Marine, Inc.
PO Box 389
Frankfort, MI 49635
(616) 352-6106
[Frankfort, Leland, Glen Arbor]

Jack Spencer
Scuba North, Inc.
13380 West Bay Shore Dr.
Traverse City, MI 49684
(616) 947-2520
[Leland, Glen Arbor, Traverse Bay]

John P. Voss
70 S. Long Lake Road
Traverse City, MI 49684
(616) 943-9158 or
(616) 275-6226
[Frankfort, Leland]

Tom Wigton
4298 Bow Road
Maple City, MI 49664
[Glen Arbor]

Jon Bonadeo
St. James, MI 49782
(616) 448-2489
[St. James - Beaver Island]

Ernie Piotrowski
52737 E. Cyprus Circle
South Bend, IN 46637
(219) 271-0192
[South Bend]

Spring Lake Divers Den, Inc.
Ross Lieffers
915 W. Savidge
Spring Lake, MI 49456
(616) 842-4300
[Spring Lake]

Straits Diving Center
587 N. State St.
St. Ignace, MI 49781
(906) 643-7009
[St. Ignace]

Kent Huber
T.B.A., Inc.
3033 North Glenway Dr.
Bay City, MI 48706
(517) 631-0033
[Cheboygan, Mackinaw City,
Mackinac Island]

## Lake Huron

Dave Harbin
Alma-D Charter
Box 1466
Caseville, MI 48725
(517) 856-4749
[Port Austin, Caseville]

Carl M. Lukaszewski
38267 Mast
Mt. Clemens, MI 48045
(313) 465-7495
[Port Sanilac, Port Austin
Lexington]

James Dinsmore
730 Lake St.
PO Box 268
Tawas City, MI 48764
(517) 362-5052
[Tawas, Rockport, Bay City]

Randy Lanski
428 Matthews St.
PO Box 332
Tawas City, MI 48764
(517) 362-8048
[Tawas, Oscoda, Harrisville,
Alpena, AuGres]

William Robinette
28869 Bunert
Warren, MI 48093
(313) 774-0640
[Lexington]

Blue Water Marine Services, Inc.
11 North Lake St.
PO Box 124
Port Sanilac, MI 48469
(313) 622-9910
[Port Sanilac]

**Lake Superior**

Pete Lindquist
Grand Island Ventures
410 Mill St.
Munising, MI 49862
(906) 387-4477
[Munising]

Jim Stayer
Lakeshore Charters
4658 South Lakeshore
Lexington, MI 48450
(313) 359-8660

Thumb Charters
28 Railroad St.
Port Austin, MI 48467
(517) 738-5271
[Port Austin]

Thunder Bay Divers
1105 Partridge Pt. Marina
Alpena, MI 49707
(517) 356-9336
[Alpena]

Straits Diving Center
587 N. State St.
St. Ignace, MI 49781
(906) 643-7009
[St. Ignace]

Three Devils Dive Charters
PO Box 617
Munising, MI 49862
(906) 387-3165
[Munising]

Superior Diver, Inc.
PO Box 388
Grand Portage, MN 55605
[Grand Portage]

Bill Gardner
Scuba Adventures, Inc.
1080 Roseland Ave.
Roseville, MN 55113

Tomasi Tours, Inc.
455 East Ridge St.
Marquette, MI 49855
(906) 225-0410
[Munising]

Dennis Dougherty
1931 Riverside Dr.
Sault Ste. Marie, MI 49783
(906) 632--6490
[Sault Ste. Marie]

Thunder Bay Marine Services
PO Box 2565
Thunder Bay, Ontario P7B 5G1
Canada
[Thunder Bay]

Superior Trips
2540 Buchanan St. NE
Minneapolis, MN 55418
[Duluth]

Northland Divers, Inc.
3000 White Bear Ave.
Maplewood, MN 55109

## Lake Erie

Albert Krzyston
552 Augusta Dr.
Monroe, MI 48161
(313) 243-6787
[Bolles Harbor]

Dennis Hansen
35710 Erie Dr.
Rockwood, MI 48173
(313) 379-9005
[Rockwood, Monroe, Detroit, Port Huron]

## Lake St. Clair

Pete McInnes
8655 Dixie
Fair Haven, MI 48023
(313) 725-1991
[Fair Haven]

Anchor Bay Charters
7778 Swan River Dr.
Fair Haven, MI 48023
(313) 725-6766
[Fair Haven, Mt. Clemens, New Baltimore, Algonac]

Carl M. Lukaszewski
38267 Mast
Mt. Clemens, MI 48045
(313) 465-7495
[Mt. Clemens]

Have Boat - Will Cruise
47876 Jefferson
New Baltimore, MI 48047
(313) 949-5388
[New Baltimore, Algonac,
Fair Haven, Mt. Clemens,
St. Clair Shores]

**Inland Lakes**

The Scuba Shack, Inc.
9982 W. Higgins Lake Road
Higgins Lake, MI 48627
(517) 821-6477
[Higgins Lake]

# Recompression Chambers

Recompression (hyperbaric) chambers are divers' best friends when decompression sickness arises. These chambers are becoming more common, especially with the development of bottomlands preserves.

Fortunately, decompression sickness is uncommon. But when divers attempt especially deep or repeated dives, it should be a primary concern. Strict adherence to decompression tables can avoid problems, but even with these tables or diving computers that calculate decompression stops, there are no guarantees.

Perhaps the best advice is to avoid problems by knowing limitations and planning dives carefully. It is always better to err on the side of safety than to take chances.

Play it safe by knowing the symptoms of decompression sickness and treating what may appear to be even minor cases. In a U.S. Navy diving manual, the most frequent decompression errors were listed as: failure to report symptoms early, failure to treat doubtful cases, failure to treat promptly, failure to recognize serious symptoms and failure to treat adequately.

In general, it is best to transport ill divers to the nearest hospital emergency room.

The Divers Alert Network (DAN), which is based at Duke University in Durham, North Carolina, can provide information about treating such injuries to emergency room personnel. DAN can also assist in arranging transportation to the nearest recompression chamber.

Each Michigan bottomland preserve and Isle Royale have an emergency procedure to handle diving accidents. Those procedures are outlined in the chapters covering those areas. If an accident occurs outside of those areas, contact the local county sheriff's department for assistance.

The U.S. Coast Guard Air Station in Traverse City conducts air rescue and emergency evacuation operations throughout the Great Lakes. They can transport divers to recompression chambers if no other emergency transportation is available. But it is best to first contact local officials to determine if such emergency transportation is needed.

For on-water assistance, contact the nearest U.S. Coast Guard Station on vhf channel 16.

**1. Bronson Methodist Hospital**
   Kalamazoo, Michigan
   (616) 341-7654 or
   (616) 341-7778

**2. Marquette General Hospital**
   Marquette, Michigan
   (906) 225-3560

**3. St. Lukes Hospital**
   Milwaukee, Wisconsin
   (414) 649-6577

**4. Hennepin County Hospital**
   Minneapolis, Minnesota
   (612) 347-3131

Emergency Numbers:

**U.S. Coast Guard**
Traverse City Air Station
(616) 922-8214

**Divers Alert Network (DAN)**
Duke University
Durham, North Carolina
(919) 684-8111 or
(919) 684-2948

# Spearfishing

Underwater spearfishing in Michigan waters is regulated by the Michigan Department of Natural Resources (DNR).

A valid Michigan fishing license is required and spearfishing must be exercised with caution to prevent danger to other divers. Fishermen should also be aware of certain fish consumption advisories on the Great Lakes issued by the Michigan Department of Public Health.

The variety of contaminants affecting fish in the Great Lakes includes: polychorinated biphenyls (PCBs), mercury, dioxins, polycyclic aromatic hydrocarborns (PAHs), polybrominated biphenyls (PBBs) and chlordane. Tumors on some fish are of unknown origin.

The health department recommends limited consumption of fish from the Great Lakes to avoid health problems. The risk of problems can be minimized by removing fat when cleaning fish and consuming smaller fish. Consumption should be limited by children and pregnant women.

Restrictions on consumption are recommended for fish taken from certain inland waters.

Information about contaminants can be obtained by contacting the health department at (800) 648-6942. Information about health advisories and proper fish cleaning techniques is available in the "Michigan Fishing Guide," a free booklet available at most sporting goods stores in the state.

According to rules created by the DNR, spearfishing can be divided into two types: hand and spring or rubber propelled. The following rules are subject to change and it is a good idea to contact the DNR for the most current information. The address is: Michigan DNR, Fisheries Division, PO Box 30028, Lansing, MI 48909. Ask for the "Michigan Fishing Guide" and list number DFI-132.

Suckers, carp, freshwater drum, whitefish, ciscoes, catfish, bullheads, bowfin and gar may be taken by hand spears all year on the Great Lakes and connecting waters. Restrictions apply to inland waters.

Rubber and spring-propelled spears may be used at any time for taking carp, bowfin (dogfish), gar and suckers in the Great Lakes and connecting waters provided the person using the spear is submerged in the water and has the spear under control by means of an attached line not exceeding 20 feet in length.

Exceptions to the rule include Portage Ship Canal and Huron Bay in Lake Superior; Potagannissing Bay, Pike Bay, Island Harbor and Les Cheneaux Channels and within a three-mile radius of Fort Gratiot light in the St. Mary's River; part of Little Bay de Noc in Lake Michigan and Northport Harbor in Lake Michigan; Lake Erie; Lake St. Clair and the Detroit River.

The following inland waters are open to rubber and spring-propelled-spearfishing for carp, bowfin, gar and suckers with an attached line:

**Alcona County**
Hubbard Lake

**Alger County**
Grand Sable Lake

**Allegan County**
Gun Lake

**Barry County**
Duncan Lake
Gull Lake
Gun Lake
Leach Lake
Middle Lake
Payne Lake
Pine Lake
Wall Lake

**Berrien County**
Big Paw Paw Lake

**Branch County**
Coldwater Lake

**Calhoun County**
Duck Lake
Goguac Lake

**Cass County**
Diamond Lake

**Chippewa County**
Carp Lake
Frenchman Lake

**Clare County**
Long Lake

**Crawford County**
Jones Lake

**Genesee County**
Ponemah Lake

**Hillsdale County**
Bear Lake

**Iosco County**
Foote Impoundment

**Jackson County**
Michigan Center Chain of Lakes (Michigan Center, Price, Big and Little Olcott, Big and Little Wolf Lakes and connecting waters -- no spearing January - February)
Round Lake
Wamplers Lake

**Kalamazoo County**
    Campbell Lake
    Gull Lake
    Indian Lake
    Sugarloaf Lake

**Kalkaska County**
    Big Twin Lake

**Lake County**
    Idlewild Lake

**Lenawee County**

    Devils Lake
    Evans Lake
    Round Lake (both)
    Wamplers Lake

**Livingston County**
    Portage Lake
    Silver Lake

**Luce County**
    Round Lake

**Mason County**
    Round Lake

**Mecosta County**
    Chippewa Lake

**Missaukee County**
    Lake Missaukee

**Oakland County**
    Cass Lake
    Buckhorn Lake
    Lakeville Lake
    Pine Lake
    Orchard Lake
    Oxbow Lake

    Union Lake
    Walled Lake

**Oceana County**
    Stony Lake
    Pentwater Lake

**Ogemaw County**
    Clear Lake

**St. Joseph County**
    Fishers Lake
    Klinger Lake

**Tuscola County**
    Cat Lake

**Van Buren County**
    Lake of the Woods
    Van Auken Lake

**Washtenaw County**
    Four Mile Lake
    Halfmoon Chain of Lakes
    Horseshoe Lake
    Huron River
    Big and Little Portage Chain
        of Lakes
    Round Lake
    Silver Lake
    Pleasant Lake

# Index

# About the Author

David Kenyon/DNR

Twenty years of diving is only the beginning for Steve Harrington. He says each dive is unique and provides a "tremendous learning experience." He is always ready to share those experiences with others, the main reason he wrote DIVERS GUIDE TO MICHIGAN.

Harrington began diving as a teen in West Michigan lakes and rivers. The last few years have found him prowling the bottom of the Manitou Passage. When he saw shipwrecks disappearing piece by piece, Harrington organized the Manitou Passage Bottomland Preserve Committee, a group that successfully advocated state preserve designation for that area.

When not diving, Harrington is usually writing. He earned a bachelor of science degree from Michigan State University in 1977, majoring in natural resources education. Harrington was a naturalist for a public school district for seven years before turning to writing. He has worked as a reporter for several major newspapers and his freelance articles have appeared in many national publications.

In 1984, Harrington captained a log raft 1,700 miles down the Mississippi River, from Minneapolis to New Orleans. Upon his return, he entered law school and earned a law degree in 1988.

Michigan sport diving remains an important interest for Harrington. He is legal counsel for the Michigan Underwater Preserve Council, Inc. and continues to write articles about sport diving in the Great Lakes region from his Lansing home.

If he is not at his word processor or underwater, Harrington can be found camping on North Manitou Island or cruising the Manitou Passage in his 16-foot inflatable boat dubbed BURBOT.